The *Fabulous* Flotilla

Scotland's Adventure
on the Rivers of Burma

PAUL STRACHAN

Whittles Publishing

Published by
Whittles Publishing Ltd,
Dunbeath,
Caithness, KW6 6EG,
Scotland, UK

www.whittlespublishing.com

© 2023 Paul Strachan

ISBN 978-184995-32-4

Contents

Introduction   IX

PART ONE:

THE IRRAWADDY FLOTILLA COMPANY

1   The Business   3
2   The Wars   17
3   The Steamers   31
4   The Commanders   46
5   A Voyage on an IFC Ship   54
6   The Hazards   67

PART TWO:

A RIVER VOYAGE IN THE 21ST CENTURY

7   Rangoon and the Delta   79
8   Middle Burma   98
9   Royal Burma   117
10   The Upper Irrawaddy   138
11   The Chindwin   163
12   The Salween   176

Bibliography   191

In memory
of two *sayas*:

Alister McCrae

&

U 'Taik Soe' Than Htut

By the old Moulmein Pagoda, lookin' lazy at the sea,
There's a Burma girl a-settin', and I know she thinks o' me;
For the wind is in the palm-trees, and the temple-bells they say:
'Come you back, you British soldier; come you back to Mandalay!'
Come you back to Mandalay,
Where the old Flotilla lay:
Can't you 'ear their paddles chunkin' from Rangoon to Mandalay?
On the road to Mandalay,
Where the flyin'-fishes play,
An' the dawn comes up like thunder outer China 'crost the Bay!

Rudyard Kipling

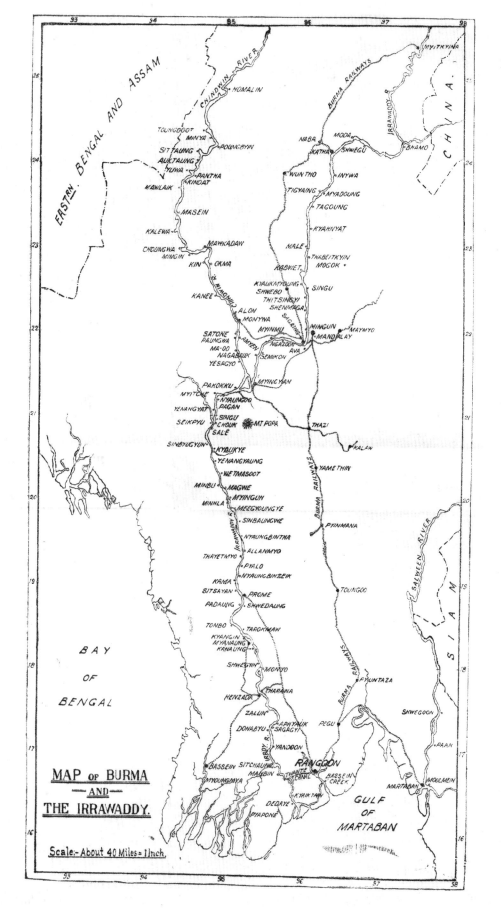

MAP OF BURMA
AND
THE IRRAWADDY.

Scale:- About 40 Miles = 1 Inch.

Author's Note

Nomenclature: in any country when there is a change of regime, place names are changed. Burma is no exception, and while many places, and indeed the name of the country itself, have been renamed by the current and recent administrations, I have chosen to retain the forms that I have over the years become most familiar with. In many places, a footnote linking the Burmese name to the British has been inserted.

Measurements: the units used in connection with the Irrawaddy river ships are imperial, per tradition, whereas for general purposes I have mostly used metric, as it is more easily recognisable by most people on the whole, though in some places I have given the imperial equivalent. This reflects the wonderfully flexible and evocative dual system of measurements used in the UK now, in the 2020s.

Translations, explanations: on the basis that you are unlikely to know many, if any, of the Burmese words I've used to enhance my account, on the first presentation of each I have shown it in italics with its translation following it. Other words or phrases that I feel may require elaboration, but which you may well already be familiar with, have been given footnotes, in order to minimise interruptions to your reading enjoyment.

Burmese personal names: the Burmese employ a rare nomenclature system, in that all the elements of each name are given ones, with no family surname. The older generation tend to have one-word names such as U Thant (U being an honorific), and younger people names made up of two, three or four elements.

Introduction

Standing anywhere along the bank of the Irrawaddy, or Ayeyarwady, river, you will see an average of at least 500,000 cubic feet of water flowing past you every second. In the monsoon it it would be just over 2,000,000 cubic feet per second. Such a flow represents one of the greatest challenges to navigation, and as the channels and sands shift daily the river cannot be charted. It is buoyed – haphazardly – only in the low water season. Officially the river begins at a confluence of streams from the Himalayas near Myitkyina in Kachin state, from where it flows 1,370 miles into the Indian Ocean. It is navigable by larger vessels for just over 1,000 miles. Its main tributary is the Chindwin, which runs for 750 miles, of which 600 are navigable by lighter vessels.

These are not of course the only rivers in Burma. The Irrawaddy has several other tributaries, which extend into a vast area, and altogether the Irrawaddy basin covers over 150,000 square miles. Then there is the Salween which, at 1,749 miles, is the longest river in Burma, though navigable for only its lowest 50 miles or so, such is the strength of its flow. From the south-eastern port of Moulmein[1] there is a whole network of rivers, mainly navigable for some distance, and in the western coastal region of the Arakan there is a river system of dazzling complexity, the main form of communication in a land with few roads. Finally, the several thousand square miles of the Irrawaddy Delta have an uncounted number of creeks and channels. To say that Burma is a land of rivers is an understatement.

In the distant past peoples migrated from deep inland down these river valleys; first came the Pyu, the proto-Burmans, ethnically Tibeto-Burmese, then the Mien, or Myan, the Burmans themselves. They lived in city-states that were like oases in jungles full of wild animals. Upriver came trade from India, bringing Indian religious cults, Hindu and Buddhist – the latter in a mix of what was later to be defined as Mahayana and Theravada, but until the 'purification' by the 11th-century kings of Pagan[2] these two divisions would have been seen as one and the same.

All movement – of goods, cultures, religions, armies – in this country was by river, and this remained so till the late 20th century. Back in the 12th century the King of Ceylon mounted a naval raid and, having crossed the Indian Ocean, sailed upriver to seize valued elephants to take back home. In the 13th century the Mongols under Genghis Khan were to sail down the river and take Pagan. There followed several

---

1   now Mawlamyine
2   pron. p'gahn; now Bagan

centuries of Mon–Burmese[3] conflict in which armies were shipped up and down the Irrawaddy in great barges. Then the British arrived, and in three short, sharp river wars annexed the country in stages. Thereafter the British colonisation and economic development (or exploitation, depending on your viewpoint) all took place along the rivers, assisted by the development of the Irrawaddy Flotilla, which after 1864 became a Scottish concern.

This book is about that flotilla and the rivers it plied. In the 1920s it was at its zenith, as indeed was the country itself in terms of economic prosperity. The Irrawaddy Flotilla Company (IFC), as it became, was almost entirely Scottish owned and managed, and in terms of capitalisation was, I believe, the largest overseas Scottish commercial enterprise ever.

Although this is a story that has been told before – the standard works being McCrae and Prentice's *Irrawaddy Flotilla*, and Captain Chubb's marvellously detailed monograph for the National Maritime Museum, both published in the 1970s – it is, alas, a story much forgotten, and I hope this book will revive interest. It is a story not just of commercial acumen, technical brilliance and management efficiency, but of a beautiful country, abundant in natural resources, booming and blooming at the time, but with tragic consequences from independence in 1948 onwards.

Fortunately, in the 1980s and 1990s, when I first became interested in the flotilla, there were still a number of former Irrawaddy Flotilla people around in both Burma and Scotland, and I was lucky enough to have met and got to know a variety of fascinating characters at both ends of the organisation's reach. In Burma, where I spent a number of years, the memory of the flotilla remained strong, and I was constantly running into people who had served with the flotilla, and later their offspring, who would retell family stories from its glory days. Nearly all older Burmese remembered trips on flotilla ships affectionately, and always remarked on the high levels of maintenance and good timekeeping.

Back in Scotland, Alister McCrae, who had been with the company through the 1930s and 1940s, lived near my parents in Killearn, Stirlingshire, and was a family friend. He became a great friend and mentor to me, as well, and in my publishing days I produced his book *Scots in Burma*. It sold amazingly well in Helensburgh, a sleepy suburb downriver from Glasgow. When I asked the bookshop owner there what was going on, he told me that nearly all the flotilla people had retired to that area and there were literally hundreds of their descendants there, all with a soft spot for Burma. Later, when I started running boats myself on the river, Alister, then in his eighties, would ring up at strange times with bits of advice like 'mind those rocks off Sagaing' or 'never moor off Ava – gusty winds'.

---

3   The Mon, who had originated in China, had spread into Burma from the third century BCE.

My own maternal great-grandfather had been a captain of one of the steamers that from the late 19th century operated a service between Glasgow and Rangoon,[4] which had been started in the late 19th century by Paddy Henderson, a partner in the Irrawaddy Flotilla. Our family house in Glasgow, still occupied by various elderly aunts when I was growing up in the 1960s and 1970s, was full of Burmese bits and bobs, not to mention beautifully carved teak steamer chairs in the garden – my first taste of Burma!

Even so, I had never heard of the flotilla till I arrived in Rangoon at the age of 18 in 1981, and on my first day there Charlie – the manager of John Brown Engineering, my employer – took me to lunch at the Strand Hotel, then a congenial, somewhat down-at-heel muddle, so unlike the sterile international hotel it has now become. Charlie, who had come up through John Brown's Clyde shipyards, talked passionately about the flotilla, the greatest ever of Scottish enterprises, and my interest was kindled. When I went to functions at British embassy houses, all splendid colonial mansions, I would be told that these had once been the homes of the flotilla's managers. On Phayre Street stood the company's magnificent former office building, and everyone would tell you that it had been the office of the Irrawaddy Flotilla. And along the Strand Road itself, the jetties that had been used by the IFC still bustled with activity as ships loaded up and moved off to the delta and beyond, a scene hardly changed from the days of the flotilla. The flotilla had somehow lingered on, and not just in memory – its presence was all around in 1980s Burma, where nothing much ever changed. Or so it seemed back then.

The flotilla, though, gets a bad press in modern-day Burma; every Burmese school-child is taught the story of U Nar Auk, a Mon businessman who in 1910 had attempted to disrupt the flotilla's near-monopoly but was ruined in the attempt by the company's aggressive business practices. In 1948 the flotilla was nationalised, the first foreign company in the newly independent Burma to be so. It was a victim of its own success; to the political leaders of the newly independent Burma, it was of course seen as emblematic of the reviled colonial experience. Having generated an extraordinary prosperity and wealth such as the majority of Burmese had never known before or since, it was thus, ironically, something to be embarrassed about. In a country where everything is about 'face', and the country's colonisation represented the greatest possible loss of face ever, the flotilla was a fitting scapegoat, and the company was painted as a vicious exploiter.

But back in Scotland the flotilla, and indeed the Scotland–Burma connection, are now forgotten. Yet Burma was Scotland's very own colony. Nearly all businesses there, large and small, were Scottish. Some, like the IFC, were blue-chip listed stocks on the Glasgow stock exchange; others, like Steel Brothers, the Bombay Burmah Trading

---

4   now Yangon

Corporation and Burmah Oil, were to develop into multinationals. Small and medium-sized businesses such as sawmills, department stores and rubber and tea plantations were usually Scottish owned and managed. Scots ran everything – they were the down-to-earth policemen and customs officers, lofty 'heaven born' civil servants, gnarled ships' skippers and their sooty engineers, and of course the ubiquitous Scottish doctor in the city hospital or hill station clinic. Genteel Scottish ladies ran boarding houses, tea rooms and bookshops in the Rangoon back streets. If you went into a Rangoon bar you would have heard only the dour murmur of Scots voices as their owners sipped their India pale ales. Some of these men brought their wives out, leaving them in the said boarding houses when they went for tours of duty upcountry; some took mistresses to be discarded when homeward bound; others married the silken beauties of this bewitching land, leaving behind great dynasties of Scottish-Burmese who thrive to this day and are extremely proud of their Scots origins.

Of the 3,000 Europeans in Rangoon in 1930, the largest single ethnicity was the Scottish, and it can be guessed that up country the proportion of Scots would be higher still. There was a Scots Kirk on Signal Pagoda Road, and a St Andrew's Society organising highland balls, and a Burns Society organising annual dinners. Reels and recitals almost unknown to their fellows at home became passionate pursuits amongst homesick Scots afar. According to J.M. Barrie, 'there are few more impressive sights in the world than a Scotsman on the make', and this could have applied to many a Scot in Burma as they amassed their fortunes; the Scots merchants sat at the pinnacle of traders with Chinese and Indians beneath, not to mention Persians, Armenians, Germans and German Jews amongst a great melee of nationals who had come to Burma to seek their fortune.

So in Rangoon the minority race was the Burmese, as indeed Rodway Swinhoe was to write in 1923 in *The Incomplete Guide to Burma*:

> As you walk along the street
> Many curious people you meet,
> Nearly every sort of man
> From the shores of Hindustan;
> Persians, Turks and bland Parsis,
> Moguls, Gurkhas, Siamese
> Placid folk from Cathay –
> Where's the Burman stowed away?

By the 1920s there were just 100,000 Burmans in a Rangoon of 400,000 Indians, and in this story we shall see how the mass immigration of Indians into the country up to and during that decade continues to have a malign effect on the Burmese view of them. Today, it is a similar story in Mandalay, where the Burmese are outnumbered by the Chinese by an equivalent factor under the newer, even less benign, sort of colonialism: Belt and Road.

Just why Burma became Scotland's colony is surprising. India, which had been absorbed into the British interest over 200 years before, was also run by Scots and hard won by Scottish regiments in the 18th-century wars against the French. There too were abundant Scots doctors, engineers and planters, but they were hardly alone. Unlike Canada, Australia and New Zealand, Britain's Asian colonies were not destinations for the mass emigration of Scots looking for a better life or forced to emigrate through enforced clearances. Rather, from the days of the East India Company onwards the Asian colonies offered enterprising young men a chance of economic betterment, and the idea was to get rich quick and home again even quicker. By the mid-19th century the Indian Civil Service offered British university-educated men a stable, well-paid career in India, with a good pension when retired back to the home country. Few stayed on abroad. Those that did were considered eccentric, perhaps having 'gone native' or become social outcasts, having taken an Indian wife.

There were lots of Scots in Singapore and Hong Kong as well, not to mention Malaya, yet in none of those Asian colonies did the Scots make such an impact as in Burma, where they dominated every aspect of life. This was because between the first British annexation, of Burma's coastal provinces in 1825, and the final one, of Upper Burma in 1886, there was an influx of highly energetic, talented Scots trade makers who established businesses that grew into massive concerns. The four pillars of the burgeoning Burmese economy were all Scots concerns: transport, under the IFC; commodities (the bulk of which was rice), under Steel Brothers, founded by William Strang Steel; teak, under William Wallace's Bombay Burmah Trading Corporation; and oil under the Burmah Oil Company, founded by David Sime Cargill. These firms were registered and had their head offices in Scotland, had their shareholders in Scotland, were financed by Scottish banks and insured by Scottish underwriters, and their goods were shipped on Scottish ships. All were part of a close-knit and interlinked mercantile community centred on Glasgow, so had the ability to raise money quickly and seize opportunity as it arose. Likewise, these firms were directed and managed by Scots in the field. That is why there came to be so many Scots in Burma.

And Burma had a very Scottish feel to it. The hill stations where Europeans spent the hot months were architecturally a sort of tropical Scots baronial style. The Candacraig Hotel in Maymyo, once a 'chummery' for the young gentlemen of the Bombay Burmah, was named after the Wallace estate at Candacraig in Royal Deeside (until 2014 the home of Billy Connolly). In E.M. Powell-Brown's wonderful book about life on board an Irrawaddy steamer skippered by her husband (more about this in Chapter 4), the Burmese butler talks in broad Scots, and this might well have been the case with servants throughout the country. The Scots, with their natural openness and reluctance to stand on ceremony, endeared themselves to the Burmese; I remember an elderly Burmese friend describing shopping in a Scots-owned department store in Rangoon and saying how when he was buying shoes the Scottish assistant would quite happily kneel down to put a shoe on his foot, something no Englishman would have done. Up country, away from the snobberies of colonial club life, the Scots mixed freely and easily in Burmese society, and the Burmese welcomed them. In Burma the single greatest asset anyone seeking success can possess is a sense of the ridiculous, and this is something both the Scots and the Burmese excel in.

The Irrawaddy Flotilla had originally belonged to the Bengal Marine, as a naval task force for the prosecution of the Second Anglo-Burmese War in 1852. Following that somewhat arbitrary annexation of lower Burma with its rich teak forests, but without any form of treaty, the British administration, originally based in Moulmein, moved to Rangoon, and with it went a number of merchant houses, including the firm of Todd Findlay.

The firm had been established in Burma since 1839, when as the Burma Steam Tug Company it had run a fleet of coastal steamers between Moulmein and Victoria Point,[5] 450 miles away, the very southernmost tip of Burma. It also acted as agent for the Glasgow shipping firm of P. Henderson & Co., managed from its Glasgow office by the dynamic entrepreneur James Galbraith. (Paddy Henderson's ran ships between Scotland and New Zealand, which on their way back to Scotland would call at Moulmein to load teak.) James Todd was trading out of Moulmein, and James Findlay had come out originally to manage a Glasgow-owned department store in Penang but, realising the opportunities provided by the newly acquired Tenasserim province of Burma, had relocated to Moulmein, opening a general store and trading in teak and other commodities. His brother, Thomas D. Findlay, handled the Glasgow end of the business, and T.D. Findlay & Co. was to develop from teak merchants into a huge colonial trading conglomerate.

In 1863, Colonel Phayre, the British chief commissioner,[6] decided to auction off the government steamers. The flotilla was a key strategic resource in time of war, and privatising it was a crafty way of keeping it on hand in case of trouble, as it could be requisitioned when necessary whilst the government avoided running costs.

T.D. Findlay, backed by James Galbraith and the ship builder William Denny of

---

5   now Kawthaung

6   As Burma was then a province of British India, it was a chief commissioner rather than a governor or lieutenant-governor who headed the British government administration

Dumbarton, successfully acquired the vessels, together with a sweetener of contracts to deliver the mail to the military station at Thayetmyo, on the northern border of British Burma. Thus in 1865 the Irrawaddy Flotilla and Burmese Steam Navigation Company was incorporated in Glasgow, with William Denny as chairman. This would have been the perfect triumvirate – a ship owner, a ship builder and a Burma-based merchant firm – but James Todd was tragically lost in 1864 on his way back to Rangoon from Calcutta, where he had just purchased two further vessels for the flotilla, when his ship, the British India *Persia,* sank in the Bay of Bengal.

Todd Findlay had discovered early on that the conditions of the Irrawaddy were not like those of other rivers. The fast currents, a seasonal rise and fall of anything from 30 to 200 feet, and sands that shifted by the hour, making charting impossible, were but a few of the hazards. The ships they had acquired from Phayre – built in the 1830s by Maudslay, Sons & Field in Lambeth and acquired by Phayre from the Bengal Marine in 1864 – may have been suited to the deep smooth channels of the Hooghly and the Bengali Sundarbans, but were underpowered and too deep-drafted for the wild beast that is the Irrawaddy. So William Denny came out to undertake a survey, and came up with new designs that were technically radical and highly innovative. New ships were built and new investors were found.

The company was reincorporated in 1876, as part of a public share offering, as the Irrawaddy Flotilla Company on the Glasgow stock exchange. This was the era when the rich old ladies of Kelvinside speculatively invested in South American railways and South African mines, when the risks were high and the potential rewards great. There was, unsurprisingly, a volatility to this, so Glasgow banks were forever going bust and bringing down their investors with them; this happened to the Findlays when the City of Glasgow Bank crashed in 1878.

Despite the challenges of navigation, eventually overcome by a new class of powerful ultra-shallow-draft ships, the IFC realised the possibilities of opening Burma to trade using the flotilla. First Mandalay, then the great Chindwin tributary and eventually routes to Bhamo, far up in the north in Kachin state, with China beckoning beyond, were established. The fleet grew, and at the time of its demise in 1942 numbered 633 units; but over its 80 years a total of no less than 1,186 units were acquired, mostly from Clyde shipyards. This has given rise to the boast that the flotilla was the largest privately owned fleet in the world.

In a single year the Fabulous Flotilla would carry a number of passengers equating to half the population of the country and the bulk of its freight, and it did this for year upon year with barely any loss of life. The larger Siam class vessels could carry 3,000 passengers, and had shops and restaurants on board. The IFC owned the first airline; it managed vast dockyards employing several thousand workers; its agents were in every river port, and were consular in their importance and duties. With over 10,000 employees, this entire enterprise was run at any one time by a manager and about ten assistants, mainly originating from the Glasgow area and often quite young. The flotilla truly was one of Scotland's greatest achievements.

PART ONE:

The
Irrawaddy Flotilla
Company

1

The Business

'Ye'll find the furrst thurrty years the wurrst'

Harold Braund

Having struggled over the past 25 years to keep a few boats running on the Irrawaddy, I am at a loss to understand quite how the Irrawaddy Flotilla Company managed to keep several hundred running successfully for many years. To find people with the right skill set to undertake such challenges must in itself have been a challenge. Responsibilities were huge; you could not sit in Scotland and micromanage an operation using Whatsapp (as I do). If there was trouble, you could not hop on a plane. Whether the communication was in the form of a letter from head office or a visit by a director, it took at least a month to get there by steamer, and a month back. The telegraph was prohibitively expensive and only used in emergencies. Managers were thus on their own and had considerable latitude to make on-the-spot decisions without recourse to head office. Perhaps this is why it all worked so well!

Typically, the company's 'assistants', as the managers were called, came from West of Scotland middle-class families and had been well educated in one of Glasgow's celebrated academies. They were rarely university men, though, and few had been public school educated. I am of an age where I am fortunate enough to have met the last generation of Scots who served in the flotilla. In the introduction I mentioned Alister McCrae; he was a typical recruit for the flotilla, in that his father had been a well-established timber merchant and Alister had been educated at the Glasgow High School, joining the shipping line Patrick Henderson & Co. in 1927 and serving in the accounts department at its St Vincent Street offices. Hendersons part-owned the IFC, and its office was the registered office of the IFC.

In 1930, at the age of 21, Alister was transferred to the IFC secretariat in the same Glasgow office. Here a staff of just three managed the affairs of one of the largest companies in Scotland, liaising between head office in Rangoon and the directors in Scotland, who in those days were what we now call non-executive. Henderson watched over its recruits, and if they were of high enough standard invited them to go out to Burma and join the IFC. It is worth noting that these recruits had their basic training in accounting.

In 1933, it was Alister who was selected and sent out to Burma; after a stint in the cash department at head office in Phayre Street he was sent off to manage operations, often in remote areas with little or no contact with the office other than letters and written reports. Living for months on end in the delta, in a fast patrol boat heavily screened against mosquitoes, he raced around the creeks pouncing on lascar-commanded steamers for ticket inspections and cash counts. It was said that while nobody could really know the delta it took a minimum of six months in it just to begin to comprehend its complexity.

The new IFC offices in Phayre Street, 1934.

Reading Alister's memoir of his time in Burma in the 1930s, what comes over is the high calibre of these young men and the fact that they mostly came from distinguished Scottish families: Charles Bruce, son of Sir Robert Bruce, editor of the *Glasgow Herald*; John Roberton, whose father, Sir Hugh Roberton, was founder of the famous Glasgow Orpheus Choir; Christopher Lorimer, son of the distinguished architect Sir Robert Lorimer; Charlie Cowie, whose son became the famous Scottish high court judge Lord Cowie.

These young Scots were steady characters, self-disciplined and nearly all deeply sympathetic to the Burmese and their world. They were required to learn Hindi to

Rangoon office staff, 1914.

be able to talk to the crews, and Burmese to talk with passengers, and on passing exams in these subjects they would receive bonuses. Consequently, they could freely interact with the Burmese and, as I have discovered, when you know the language you get a much better idea of what's going on.

It is customary to talk of dour Scots, but I do not think any of these young men were very dour, not the ones I met. Rather they were outgoing, very social, and keen golfers. They worked five years in the country and then were

The original IFC office on Strand Road, probably dating from the 1880s.

granted passage home for six months' furlough; they were not allowed to get married until their second furlough, after ten years, when they would bring their bride back to Rangoon. No assistant that I know of ever took a Burmese wife, though a number of officers and engineers did, and the assistants were perhaps a little bit 'goody-goody' in resisting the temptations of the East. One assistant who married on his first furlough back in Scotland, on returning to Rangoon with his new bride was dismissed on the spot. The company was equally intolerant of any form of incompetence, and preferred a small close-knit team of sharp, focused men to a bureaucracy of dead wood and time-servers.

Living in the Rangoon chummery,[7] Irrawaddy House, in the company's residential estate at Belmont, the unmarried assistants played rugby, tennis and golf in their spare time. The Scots kirk was just across the road, and in the moral mire that was (and is) the port city of Rangoon these Presbyterian lads lived cleanly, and for that reason earned the respect and admiration of the often prim Burmese.

*IFC executive staff, 1947. Alister McCrae is in the middle row,
fourth from the right.*

There were just 20 assistants, half of whom would at any time have been on leave, or sick or on furlough. So just 10 men ran over 600 vessels with 5,000 crew, 5 dockyards with a further 5,000 workers, and a mostly Scottish expatriate team of 200 officers and engineers. Alister, sent up to Mandalay at the age of 29, managed the main transport infrastructure for an area the size of Scotland. He was allowed to send one telegram a month with one line in it – the monthly takings. There was a telephone, but picking it up and calling head office was regarded as the ultimate sign of failure, so it was rarely used.

Within the country the assistants would go on leave in one of the hill stations. The largest, Maymyo, at 3,000 feet, had a good golf course and apparently the largest man-made network of bridle paths in the world. On the river the young men shot duck on the sand flats and fished for mahseer[8] in the rapids. It was only the superintendent

---

7   For 'chummery' read *commanderie*, as the assistants were the Templars of colonial commerce.
8   giant carp, the ultimate game fish of the region

of pilotage who would go back to Scotland annually – during the three months of the monsoon, when pilotage operations were suspended – to make a report to the directors.

Travelling widely around the country, the flotilla men possessed a knowledge and understanding of Burma that made them very useful in the Second World War, nearly all being commissioned into the 14th Army and a number decorated for distinguished service. After the war they went on to have successful second careers, Alister returning to the Paddy Henderson office in Glasgow, now as a partner, and later becoming chairman of the Clyde Port Authority.

Whilst the great commercial success of the flotilla might be attributed to either market conditions or the clever design of ships, none of this would have been possible without robust management. A succession of highly capable and often visionary managers in late 19th century had created the structure and ethos that was to continue until the flotilla's demise. The motivator behind the rapid early development of the company through the 1870s was James Galbraith, who never visited Burma and from his Glasgow office managed the affairs not just of the Irrawaddy Flotilla but also the shipping lines Paddy Henderson's and the Albion Line, not to mention a variety of other colonial interests such as the Rangoon Oil Company. Galbraith was the epitome of the great Glasgow entrepreneur, managing diverse companies that were all interlinked through their business operations and the investors backing them. This was not untypical of shipping circles in the West of Scotland, where the ship owner, builder, financier, insurer and charterers were all part of a small circle, often intermarried; and in some cases you would find that a member, such as the ship builder Peter Denny of Dumbarton, would be directly involved in all of these activities.

Galbraith, who came from Strathaven, had joined Henderson's as a clerk in 1844 when he was 26 years of age, and was made a partner within four years; he remained with the company until his death 41 years later. In 1876 he effectively took the company public, floating shares on the Glasgow stock exchange; the take-up was, and remained till the company's demise, almost entirely by investors from Glasgow and the

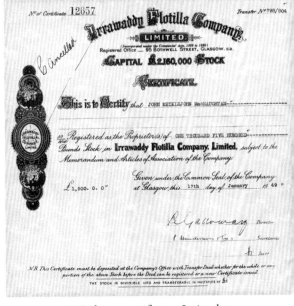

IFC share certificate. In its day IFC had been a good blue chip stock.

West of Scotland. Thus the largest privately-owned fleet in the world and Scotland's greatest ever overseas commercial endeavour was owned, managed and operated from within a relatively confined geographical area.

Whilst Galbraith raised the finance, made the connections and built up the fleet from the Clyde shipyards, particularly Denny's of Dumbarton, the day-to-day running of the company was in the hands of a manager in Rangoon. The company was fortunate in having a succession of highly able men in that position, each of whom nurtured his assistants to ensure a flow of capable successors. Able men tend to promote other able men, whilst incompetent managers tend to appoint managers even less competent than themselves. The success of the flotilla was that the former course was followed.

George Jameson Swan from Perthshire was the first of these great managers, coming out in 1867 at the age of 27 from Henderson's office to manage the flotilla's accounts under the agency of Todd Findlay and Co. Within a couple of years Swan was managing the entire fleet. With the formation of the new company in 1876 he set up his own office, and when Todd Findlay resigned as agent following the collapse of the business on the 1878 City of Glasgow Bank crash, Swan had the freedom to set up a structure that would endure for the next 60 years. Indeed, this structure was still in place in the nationalised IFC (now Inland Water Transport, IWT) after Burma's independence in 1948.

Swan oversaw the terrific expansion of the fleet through the 1870s and 1880s, from 11 paddlers and 32 flats[9] in 1875 to nearly 200 vessels by 1888. He was assisted by Frederick Charles Kennedy, a civil engineer from Leith whom Galbraith recruited in 1877. Fred Kennedy, as with all assistants joining, had been given a sound training in bookkeeping, and his first appointment was as cashier in Rangoon. Given the proclivity for money just to seep away in Burma, financial discipline was essential. By the 1880s Swan was spending only the winter months in Burma, returning to Scotland for the rest of the year, and Kennedy became manager in Burma.

Undertaking several river expeditions across the delta, first up the Irrawaddy to Bhamo, and then up the Chindwin in 1881, Kennedy opened new routes on these rivers and effectively opened up large parts of the country to cultivation and trade during the reign of King Mindon, the king of Royal Burma. Galbraith died in 1886, and Peter Denny became chairman, continuing growth and expansion. Kennedy retired in 1896, returning to Edinburgh where he was to die in 1916 at the age of just 56. During his tenure as manager he had increased the fleet from 200 vessels to 500, so it is not surprising that he was worn out.

---

9   barges

Rangoon office staff with George Swan seated in centre, c.1877.

Management was of course very much about financial discipline in a totally cash-based economy. In my days working with the IFC's successor, the IWT, I used to visit the cash department in the Phayre Street[10] office to make payments. Presided over by a slightly scary Anglo-Burmese lady, the department had an enormous walk-in strong room with a steel door a foot thick where all the money would have been kept. No cash was visible whenever I visited.

The operation of the flotilla was left to three senior superintendents: marine, dockyard and pilotage. The marine super would be in charge of the commanders and officers, and would ensure all vessels were well maintained and safely operated. Usually this position would be filled by a senior captain who had experienced many years, often decades, on the river. Most commanders were experienced men of a seagoing background, recruited through Henderson's office in Glasgow to be sent out to serve a year as a first officer learning the river. The fact that, as mentioned earlier, in any given year the company could carry people representing half the population of the country with barely any loss of life in some of the world's most hazardous waterways speaks volumes.

The superintendent of dockyards took care of the company's four yards at Dalla, Athlone, Moulmein and Mandalay. Under him, engineers – almost entirely from Dumbarton, who had served their time at Denny's – assembled the ships from kits

10   now Pansodan Road

sent out from the Clyde (more about this in Chapter 3). The engineers maintained the fleet to a high level, and mechanical breakdowns were almost unknown, so the ships would have a lifespan of as much as 50 years. Dalla also offered repairs to seagoing vessels, and by the 1930s was beginning to build ships from scratch, a trend that would have continued had the Second World War not interrupted.

Dalla dockyard: Dalla was the company's main dockyard, occupying a large estate across the river from the downtown area. Several thousand workers maintained the fleet and assembled the new ships sent out from Glasgow under the supervision of Scots engineers.

The superintendent of pilots took care of the buoying of the river, and lived on his own pilot launch, patrolling the river and using floating bamboo poles and riverbank markers to guide the commanders. This was a free service to all other users of the river. The Chindwin had its own superintendent of pilots, and in the 1930s Stanley White, 'Chindwin' White, lived on his own little steamer plying the river and poking bamboo poles and flags into the strangest of places.

Each river town in Burma had its Irrawaddy *kozalay*, agent, who was well housed, usually in a roomy *dak* bungalow within the civil lines, whilst his godown[11] and office were on the river's bund.[12] This position was an important and highly respected one, often the prerequisite of senior captains on retirement. In places like Pagan and Bhamo the agents also acted as tourist information officers – and some, like Captain Medd in

11   warehouse
12   embankment

Bhamo, were tourist attractions in themselves, with tales of the Irrawaddy in times of peace and war.

Larger ports like Mandalay or Moulmein would have an assistant assigned as the agent; Alister McCrae was one such, sent to Mandalay. These larger agencies had a dockyard under the ubiquitous Dumbarton engineer, and with a network of routeings converging in these locations, they were essentially regional hubs. Alister would go down to the Mandalay bund early each morning to watch

IFC agent's residence, possibly at Prome, typical of the Anglo-Indian dak bungalow type.

the steamers depart, always a moment of great excitement with the parting cries of well-wishers, the mischievous jokes and repartee between sailors and stevedores, the cackling of the hawkers, the hoot of the horn and in those days the wonderful whoosh as the boilers got up steam; and let's not forget that very Kiplingesque clunk of paddles. Seeing the ships off was my job, too, for many years; the whoosh and clunk were replaced by a diesel throb, but the crowd and its craic would have been much the same.

Married assistants were well housed; in Rangoon this was at the Belwood estate at Kandawgalay, which George Swan had purchased in 1875. Belmont itself was the manager's house, and the first Belwood was a classic timber-built dak house, to be replaced in the 1930s by a sprawling brick one. Senior assistants lived on the estate in Belmont, Belstone and Belfield – large houses too, but not as grand as Belmont. After nationalisation, the estate's lease passed to the British foreign office, and Belwood houses the British ambassador and the other houses the embassy staff.

Moulmein Engineer's bungalow, 1918.

*The original Belwood, dating from 1855,
and the manager's residence.*

Belfield is, I think, now the British Club.

At Dalla, across the water from Rangoon proper, the superintendent and his engineers were housed in bungalows overlooking the Rangoon river, and today the Burmese engineers of IWT occupy them. The company's estate across the country as a whole was considerable, including agents' houses and offices and dockyards – and the grandest building of them all was the head office in Phayre Street. This was rebuilt, as indeed much of Phayre Street was, in the 1930s, superseding the original neo-colonial building of the 1870s. Designed by A.G. Bray in 1933 in the grand corporate style of the period, the Phayre Street office remains one of the main landmarks of downtown Rangoon. Situated on the first floor, up a monumental white marble staircase, was the teak-panelled assistants' meeting room. In the 1990s I often found myself there in interminable meetings about fuel supplies and spare parts. As I would drift off, I could just see the assistants sitting round the same table, except they would have been discussing more exciting things like planning Burma's first airline.

Inside the new Belwood, rebuilt in the 1930s and the residence of the manager. It is now the residence of the British ambassador.

Contrary to what is taught in Burmese schools today, the IFC was not a monopoly. Though it was the largest operator of inland-water ships in Burma there was plenty of competition, and the company had to stay ahead of the game. In addition to numerous local operators of country boats, barges and all manner of craft that carried a considerable volume of passengers and cargo, there were a number of attempts to set up steamer services to compete with the company on key routeings.

The first of these was King Mindon's fleet of river steamers, ordered from Italy in the 1870s. One of these was said to have sailed out loaded up with Venetian furnishings for his new Italian-style palace being built in the new capital he had founded at Mandalay in 1857. These vessels were never operated commercially, but from time to time raced against each other along the Mandalay riverfront, a spectacle much enjoyed by the king. In the Third Anglo-Burmese War of 1885 some were sunk as a result of military action and the survivors were later absorbed into the IFC.

The main challenges to the IFC, however, came from the wealthy Indian business community and the Burma River Transport Company, formed in 1910, which operated 22 steamers and a fleet of oil flats. Its ships were technically ahead of the IFC's and faster, so the IFC built the *Otara* and *Osaka* with the latest water-tube boilers, which achieved speeds of 15.5 knots. These were known as shadow steamers, as they would shadow a competitor and then nip round and get into port first, for first pick of passengers and goods. A situation developed not unlike what was common on the West Coast of Scotland, with competing captains racing to get into port first and taking daring shortcuts at some risk. Needless to say, the Burmese would have loved the excitement and drama of this, but ultimately the winner was the company that could keep lowering its ticket prices and had the deepest pockets. At one point the IFC was not only offering free tickets but also free meals; eventually the Burma River Transport Company went into liquidation and its steamers were bought up by the IFC to be absorbed into the fleet.

Then in 1913 the Delta Navigation Company was acquired by Kennedy, as was in 1916 Gulab Hussein Atcha's fleet, operating out of Bassein. Each had successfully competed on popular IFC routings in the delta areas, and the owners were happy that Kennedy had bought them out.

Flotilla steamers and flats moored at Mandalay, c.1890s.

Earlier, we met U Nar Auk, known to every Burmese schoolchild. He was a former cattle herder who became a millionaire in Mon state by means of his timber and banking interests, and wished to challenge what was perceived as Indian and British exploitation of the Burmese peasantry with a fully Burmese-owned flotilla company. In 1910 he formed the Burmese Steam Navigation and Trading Company, which operated out of Moulmein on the Salween and Ataran river systems. He was, though, a devout Buddhist, so gave free passage to monks and nuns, who tended to take up a lot of deck space, leaving little for fare-paying passengers. His company lost further revenue when the IFC inevitably undercut him and even gave its passengers presents. There were dockside battles over loading and unloading, and subsequent lawsuits. Kennedy won, and U Nar Auk was ruined. In many respects the populist decision by the newly independent government to nationalise the IFC in 1948 was a direct consequence of the U Nar Auk story.

Not all of Kennedy's acquisitions were quite so aggressive as that. For example, a Mr Dawson had operated a fleet of steamers out of Moulmein; on retirement in 1898 he sold the business to the IFC, and with it Dawson's Railway, which he had built to connect Thaton, between Moulmein and Rangoon, with Duyinzeik, its nearest river port. Then in the 1920s IFC bought out the Indian-owned Burma Steam Launch Company, which had been drawing away business from the IFC for decades.

In the 1920s, Burma was booming, and the majority of its abundant produce and busy people were carried on the flotilla's ships. But with the Great Depression of the early 1930s Burma went from boom to bust. The task of the then manager, Thomas Cormack, was to keep the ships running and the flotilla solvent, which he managed to do. Unsurprisingly, in this period not many new ships were ordered. This was a troubled time, with peasant uprisings in the countryside and race riots in Rangoon, the reactions of Burmese impoverished by unscrupulous Indian moneylenders. But business picked up in the late 1930s with the capture of Chinese seaports by the Japanese, and the Burma Road thus becoming the main American military supply conduit to its ally, Chiang Kai-shek, trapped in the Chinese interior. So shipping up to Bhamo became important again, and on one occasion the company shipped an entire aircraft factory to Bhamo, which was then carried over the hills – only to be bombed to smithereens by the Japanese.

By the 1930s an increasing number of Burmese had joined the management of the company. The Burmese, with their natural inclination towards learning, were by this time producing a new generation of highly educated young men and women, who attended the University of Rangoon, founded in 1920. The trend would inevitably have been for the Burmese to have had an increasingly significant role in the running of the flotilla; a glance at the office staff photograph on Cormack's retirement in 1937 gives a good idea of the racial mix, with as many smart young Burmese as Indians. Alister McCrae and his wife, who visited Rangoon on their way to New Zealand in 1954, were treated to a banquet by former Burmese colleagues, and he was touchingly told that his nickname in the office had been Mandalay McCrae.

Rangoon office staff on Thomas Cormack's retirement, 1937. Note the increased number of Burmese staff in this period.

Likewise, in the 1920s and 1930s the Scots engineers on the ships were being replaced by the Anglo-Burmese – the many sons of the Scots engineers who had married and stayed on. It was a similar story on the railways, which became an Anglo-Burmese fiefdom. After the Second World War and nationalisation this Westernised generation took over the running of the flotilla, and there were few changes in working practices; when I worked with the IWT in the 1990s I found that the entire system, right down to timetables and routeings, was identical to that of the old IFC! Virtually nothing had been changed. I have an IFC handbook dated 1941 and an IWT handbook dated 1962, and they are more or less identical. That was perhaps the flotilla's most enduring legacy; but then the malaise and inertia of the Ne Win years, 1962–1988, brought about the IWT fleet's decay.

Dorothy Laird, in her book *The Story of Paddy Henderson and Company*, attributes the great success of the flotilla to the devotion of the commanders and crews in maintaining their ships to such a high standard. The other secret of success was financial probity, and a very Scots concern with good bookkeeping was drummed into every young assistant, whether training in the office of Paddy Henderson & Co. or in the cash department of the Phayre Street office. You have 600 ships, each one with a cash box and ledger, you have 50-odd agents selling tickets and consigning cargoes, and all this is controlled by a manager with a dozen assistants who spend much of their time buzzing around the delta in speedboats to check that every passenger has a ticket. Alister McCrae told me how he made a 600-mile voyage up the Chindwin to check on the agent at Homalin who, it was rumoured, was on the take.

When, however, the investors of the Irrawaddy Flotilla Company attempted to set up a an almost identical operation in Argentina in 1886, without the financial stability of the British imperial economy and the probity of the company's officers, the project was destined to fail; the Rio Platanese Flotilla was plagued with losses, and the money just flowed away. The same would have happened in Burma had it not been for the assistants.

For the investors back home, the dividends paid out were not particularly high, but IFC shares were regarded as a solid, safe blue chip, and the ships would sail on forever. The company weathered the 1930s depression well and was progressively moving forward into new developments like ship building at Dalla – and, well ahead of its time, aviation.

In 1942 the bulk of the fleet was scuppered to deny its use to the invading Japanese, and although that was a tragedy, the company was by no means finished. It was due substantial war reparations, and in 1947 ordered half a dozen M-class ships from Denny's to replace those lost, and in 1948 a similar number of P-class vessels for the Bhamo run. So it was all set to start up again in the newly independent Burma – but such dreams were put paid to by the nationalisation of 1948. So complex were its affairs that it took several years to wind up, with the disposal of so much property, but even so, when in 1957 it was finally struck off the register of companies in Scotland, the investors all received something.

2

The Wars

The Irrawaddy Flotilla may be remembered for opening up a great and rich country to trade and travel, and for providing a prosperity to its citizens that they have never known before or since, but it is not always remembered that it was born out of war and met its demise in war. Whilst never a government monopoly, and most certainly never part of a ship owner's cartel, the flotilla always enjoyed a semi-official status with the colonial government in Rangoon, carrying the proconsuls of empire and, perhaps more profitably, benefiting from mail contracts that subvented services on less profitable routeings, not unlike the mail steamers on the Scottish West Coast routes.

In fact, the flotilla was formally deployed in four wars, and it could be argued that the flotilla had its roots in the earlier First Anglo-Burmese War of 1824. Post-independence, the ships of the new flotilla under the IWT have continued in a martial role in the civil wars that have ravaged the land since. To tell the story of these flotilla wars is to tell the story of Burma, of why and how it was colonised, lost in the Second World War, won back and then abandoned to internal conflicts that continue to this day.

At the outset of the First Anglo-Burmese War in 1824 the paddle-steamer *Diana* crossed over the Bay of Bengal with a task force of 63 ships carrying 8,500 British and Indian troops under the command of Sir Archibald Campbell. The *Diana* was in fact the first steam ship ever to be deployed by the British in battle, as up till then steamers had mainly been used as tugs to tow sailing ships in and out of port. (It would still be decades, however, before the Admiralty woke up to the advantages of having vessels that were not dependent on the vagaries of the wind.) Fitted out with Congreve rockets and commanded by 32-year-old Frederick Marryat,[13] the *Diana* had a funnel as high as its mast, with 'the very sight of her causing more consternation than a herd of war elephants'. The *Diana* led the attack, and the occupation of Rangoon was one of the few moments of glory in what was otherwise described as 'the worst managed war in British history'.

---

13 later to become a successful novelist; *The Children of the New Forest* may be familiar to you

A paddle steamer, possibly the Diana, *of the Bengal
Marine used in the Anglo-Burmese War 1824–26.*

The invasion of Burma by sea rather than the more dangerous overland route across Assam was the culmination of 30 years of clashes along the border between the territories of the East India Company and the Kingdom of Ava, in the centre of what is now Burma. Since the rise of its Konbaung kings in the 1750s, that kingdom had embarked on an imperial journey that not only matched the glory of the Pagan empire that had dazzled the world 500 years before, but surpassed it in territorial gains. Conquering first the Mon kingdom of Pegu[14] and then absorbing much of Siam, in 1785, King Bodawpaya of Ava took the coastal region of Arakan, leading to a mass exodus of Arakan refugees into British Bengal. Further clashes occurred in Assam, Manipur and some other East Indian states claimed by the Burmese but under Calcutta's sphere of influence. The final straw for the British was the Burmese occupation of the Bengali island of Shalpuri in 1823, resulting in an ultimatum by Lord Amherst, the governor general of British India, to King Bagyidaw, demanding his troops' removal. This ultimatum was, however, taken by the Burmese as a sign of weakness, and it led to the kidnap of two British naval officers. Amherst's attempts to avert war by means of installing a boundary commission also foundered on Burmese imperial haughtiness, and war became inevitable.

Wars were expensive and at this point the British had no designs on acquiring great swathes of additional territory, which would prove costly to garrison and administer. The idea was to make a show of force and secure the existing borders. But Amherst had not reckoned with the fighting abilities of the Burmese and the tenacity of their

14   now Bago, and formerly Hanthawaddy

*Traditional Burmese barge on the Rangoon River c.1860s, a sight
soon to disappear with the advent of steam propulsion.*

general, Maha Bandula, a brilliant strategist who had been waiting for the British in
the Arakan, and managed to turn his army round and march it over the Arakan *yoma*,
mountain range, believed impassable, to counterattack in Rangoon. But then he fell
back to Donabyu, and Campbell moved his naval task force across the delta to confront
him there. Hit by a rocket, Maha Bandula died, and with the loss of his charismatic
leadership the Burmese army fell into disarray and withdrew.

With the Treaty of Yandabo of 1826, Ava ceded the coastal provinces of Tenasserim
and Arakan to the British, in the person of Sir Archibald. Despite the victory, this had
been a wasteful war for the British; of the 40,000 troops deployed 15,000 died, and of
the 3,586 troops who landed at Rangoon 3,115 died of disease. Only 150 made it into
battle. In addition, the British now had possession of two provinces that at first sight
would cost more to administer than could be collected in revenue.

As for the *Diana*, she was used for exploration of the Salween and Ataran river systems in Burma's deep south, where eventually the British were to profit from the great
teak forests, tin mining and rubber tapping. The Arakan was to prove agriculturally
rich, feeding Indian markets and producing a wealthy, educated Arakanese land-own-
ing class.

The Irrawaddy Flotilla proper was created for the Second Anglo-Burmese War of
1852 – which, like its predecessor, was the product of misunderstandings. The Burmese had not appreciated the power and might of the British Raj. The British were

A scene from the First Anglo-Burmese War of 1824–26.

equally ignorant in their failure to understand the complexities of face when dealing with official Burmese. A provincial warlord's attempt at extortion from two British sea captains in the southern city of Pegu led to the despatch of the 'combustible commodore', George Lambert, to demand compensation. Lambert ignored Governor-General Dalhousie's instructions to avoid conflict, and effectively started a war on the Rangoon river. Given the experience of the First Anglo-Burma war, on this occasion the campaign was far better organised and was in addition supplied with four steamers to be used on the rivers, under the command of Rear Admiral Austen (a brother of Jane Austen). The naval force arrived, and under a white flag of truce a steamer approached the Burmese fortifications to seek a response to a somewhat unreasonable ultimatum demanding compensation for military expenses incurred to date; it was met with fire from a battery. In consequence, the British annexed the province of Pegu together with the rich region of Myéde with its forests to the north and then retained them, even though no formal treaty was signed. It was not a very glorious war, and seizing and keeping territory without a treaty was a somewhat dishonourable action. Rangoon became the main hub of the British, and all Lower Burma was now under their yoke.

Meanwhile the four steamers that Austen had left behind – the *Lord William Bentinck*, built in 1832 in Lambeth, the *Damooda* and *Nerbudda* built in 1833 in India, and the *Jumna*, built in Lambeth in 1838 – the nascent Irrawaddy Flotilla, still manned by officers of the Bengal Marine and lascar crews, were mainly used for commissariat duties, supplying the garrisons at the frontier post of Thayetmyo. In 1885 two of the vessels were seconded to Colonel Phayre's mission to the Court of Ava, meticulously described by Sir Henry Yule in his published account of it. They proceeded upstream very slowly on a rising monsoon river, and reached Pagan, where they spent four days exploring and sketching the monuments: probably the first ever Western tourists. They were escorted up to Mandalay by 150 royal barges rowed by 9,000 men in full regalia. Thus the Irrawaddy Flotilla reached Mandalay for the first time in 1855.

A royal procession at Ava, 1856 from the Illustrated London News.

By 1885 relations had once again broken down between the British – now represented by a viceroy, following the dissolution of the East India Company in 1874 – and the Burmese, in the form of King Thibaw. During the 25-year reign of Thibaw's father, King Mindon, Burma had opened up to a considerable extent and, with regular river steamer services connecting Mandalay with the outside world, Burmese notables had been able to travel to Europe and see what they were dealing with. Likewise, there was now a sizable European expat community in Mandalay, which in 1855 had become the new capital. Mindon had promoted trade: he was particularly keen on seeing the Bhamo route to China reopened, and he had encouraged the IFC to start services to the Chindwin, opening up an agriculturally rich hinterland. (Meanwhile, he had ordered his own flotilla from shipyards in Italy in an attempt to compete with the IFC.) But whilst he had been a sagacious king and had managed to successfully play off British interests against the growing French influence at his court, Thibaw was less astute, and his veering towards the French only served to irritate the British. At the same time, under first Louis-Napoleon, and then the statesman Jules Ferry, France was building an empire in South-East Asia, and there was a growing concern in the British that Royal Burma was to become a French protectorate, as had Cochin China and Cambodia in 1862 and 1863 respectively (and, for that matter, Tonkin would in 1887). If so, not only would the Indian Raj have the French on its eastern border, but it would be the French who would control the ever-elusive golden road to China.

Fear of the French coupled with a fear of loss of trade was probably the main reason for the British annexation of Upper Burma in the Third Anglo-Burmese War, but there were several other more ostensible factors, including the breakdown of diplomatic relations, commercial extortion, and the issue of human rights. The debate over Burma in 1885 was not unlike the 2003 debate around the invasion of Iraq – the desire to remove an unsavoury regime, prevent further abuses of human rights, and seize great riches. There was no doubt that as atrocity heaped upon atrocity, the Thibaw regime, even by the practices of the day, set new standards for the abuse of power. Initiated by a massacre of the princes, in which over 80 rival claimants to the throne were clubbed to death in velvet sacks and then trampled upon by the royal elephants, the regime continued in that vein with several further massacres of would-be opponents. As corruption and the breakdown of order subsumed the country, Thibaw's queen, Supayalat, personally micromanaged every detail of administration whilst provincial warlords despoiled the country. Refugees, whether princes or peasants, fled south into British Burma. Agriculturally rich areas like the Mu valley went for several years without a harvest, all labourers having fled south.

In Glasgow and Manchester, the influential chambers of commerce clamoured for annexation, a call taken up by Lord Randolph Churchill, the foreign secretary. The final straw may have been an arbitrary fine placed on the Bombay Burmah Trading Corporation, which held teak concessions, but the decisive factor in the British decision to invade Burma was a Burmese diplomatic mission to Paris in 1883 and subsequent commercial concessions by the Burmese to the French. Thibaw and his ministers, encouraged by the French, had felt emboldened by recent British setbacks in Afghanistan and Zululand, both in 1879, suggesting that the British were not perhaps so invincible after all.

So began the third of the Irrawaddy Flotilla's wars. The fleet was seconded to the Burma Field Force for the transport of troops and supplies in what this time was to be a highly organised and meticulously planned campaign. The India Army had been training for this for some time before Britain's ultimatum to Thibaw, and the force had been assembled at Madras,[15] ready to sail at a moment's notice. Under General Prendergast 10,000 troops were embarked there in November, and within a week were transferred to the ships of the Irrawaddy Flotilla awaiting them in Rangoon. The steamers and flats had been fitted out as troopships with barracks, canteens, latrines, and stabling for the horses, and there were hospital ships. Guns supplied by the navy

were mounted on the steamers and along the sides of flats, and a small fleet of steam launches had machine-guns mounted on them. The IFC chartered its vessels to the Burma Field Force at Rs 45 per ton for steamers (with coal) and Rs 15 per ton for the flats, which at the time was felt to be exorbitant, and must have been profitable for the company's shareholders back in Scotland.

WITH LORD DUFFERIN IN BURMA—THE ADVANCE GUARD ON BOARD THE "SIR WILLIAM PEEL"—"NO DACOITS YET"
FROM A SKETCH BY OUR SPECIAL ARTIST, MR. F. VILLIERS

The Third Anglo-Burmese War of 1885 was to be a river war, with all movement and action confined to the waterway and its banks. To hold the Irrawaddy was to hold Burma, and the viceroy, Lord Dufferin, had given Prendergast strict instructions to attain the British goal of dethroning Thibaw 'by the display rather than use of force'. Speed was of the essence: the fleet rendezvoused at the frontier garrison town of Thayetmyo on 11 November, just one week after leaving Madras, and four days later the flotilla crossed into Burmese territory. Attempts were made by two of Thibaw's Italian military engineers, Camotta and Molinari, to sink two of the royal ships in order to block the channel against the invaders, but the men were captured by the *Kathleen* and *Irrawaddy*, sent ahead

THE STEAM-LAUNCH PEGU, UNDER LIEUTENANT TRENCH, R.N., IN SEARCH OF DACOITS.

Burma Field Force (top) Steam launch Pegu, *in search of dacoits, from the pacification of Upper Burma after the Third Ango-Burmese War, 1885.*

---

15   now Chennai

Sailors take the fort at Gwechaung. From The Graphic.

Scene from The Third Anglo-Burmese War, Naval Brigade.

to reconnoitre. Unfortunately for Thibaw, Camotta's diaries, detailing the Burmese defences, fell into British hands.

The main royal defences were two substantial forts built and commanded by Italian engineers at Minhla and Gwe Chaung. The latter was taken easily from the landward side by troops whilst being shelled by long-range guns from ships in the river, and its garrison of 8,000 Burmese troops disappeared into the interior. At Minhla the Burmese put up more of a fight; a Lieutenant Drury, lamented later by Kipling, and three sepoys fell on the British side, while 100 Burmese fell. This was the only real action of the war, and the flotilla sailed on to take Mandalay without a further shot being fired.

Deposing a king might not seem so easy. First, of all you have to find him in a labyrinthine palace city, and this task fell to the Irrawaddy commanders Terndrup and Morgan, who knew their way around the palace and court; Mrs Morgan was a great friend of Queen Supayalat. On 28 November Morgan led Colonel Sladen to the king, in order to handle the delicate negotiations surrounding his departure. The royal family departed the next day on board the *Thoreah*, which had been specially prepared for them, with an escort provided by the Liverpool regiment and the naval brigade. So as it turned out, within a month an army was able to sail from India, invade a sovereign state and depose its king. Such speed was almost entirely due to the efficiency and effectiveness of the Irrawaddy Flotilla.

The fourth of the Irrawaddy Flotilla's wars was as part of the First World War, when no fewer than 67 ships of the flotilla sailed from Rangoon to Mesopotamia[16] to assist in the campaign against the Turks there. The ships included paddle-steamers, sternwheelers, tugs, launches, flats and cargo boats – in other words a full flotilla in itself. The commanders and crew went with their vessels, which travelled in groups over the 1914–15 period, some under tow and some under steam, heading first for Bombay and then up to Basra, a total distance of over 4,200 nautical miles across the open sea. On the way three were lost: the *Tiddim* capsized under tow; the *Shweli* broke her back under steam; and the *Kelat* broke adrift in a cyclone and foundered. As Captain Chubb remarked, it was amazing that given the dangers of such an undertaking more were not lost.

On the Tigris the ships were used as troopships, hospital ships and supply vessels. Two vessels ran bi-weekly between Basra and Amarah, carrying mail and personnel. *Popa*, *Pima* and *Tamu* operated as canteen supply

King Thibaw's Italian steamers sunk at Nyaung U in the 1885 war. IFC ships are moored behind.

Elephant artillery with lascars, in the 1886 campaign. Many of the gunners were deployed from the Royal Navy. From The Graphic.

ships, bringing meals to the soldiers on the front line. Captain Woods wrote of how on his ship, the *Tantabin*, all the bed linen and tablecloths were cut up for use as surgical dressings. As General Townshend advanced up the Tigris in an attempt to capture Baghdad, the flotilla delivered supplies and support.

But the British were forced into retreat by the Turkish army under the command of a German general, Colmar von der Goltz, then were besieged at Kut without supplies. The paddle-steamer HMS *Julnar*, which had belonged to the Euphrates

16   now Iraq

and Tigris Steam Navigation Company, attempted to break through to Kut without success, and there were even attempts to supply Kut from the air. But Townshend surrendered and the British fell back. They were to regain Kut and take Baghdad in 1917.

The Mesopotamia campaign, as with the American invasion by the same route in 2000, was all about oil and, like the Third Anglo-Burmese War, was a river war, with all advances and retreats, supply and logistics happening on or along the banks of the Tigris. Sadly, it seems that few of these vessels made it back home to Burma. I wonder if any of them survive today along the waterfronts of Basra or Baghdad?

The Second World War was the fifth of the flotilla's wars, and the one when it met its tragic demise. It has been said that the scuppering of that fleet in 1942 was the greatest single loss of British merchant shipping ever. Over 500 of a fleet then constituting 600 vessels were scuppered or sunk in action, and then most of the ships that fell into Japanese hands were bombed or machine-gunned by the RAF in the reconquest. Had it not been for the Burma Road, built by the British for the Americans to supply Chiang Kai Shek's nationalist armies based in Chengdu, you might wonder whether the Japanese would ever have occupied Burma. Japan's war was primarily with the Chinese, so for the Japanese it was vital to cut off the supply of American materiel to Chiang. This, coupled with the Japanese fomenting of Burma's nascent independence movement under student leaders like Aung San, and training them in Japan in fascist military techniques – retained by the Tatmadaw to this day – spelt disaster for the British, who, totally unprepared, had traditionally garrisoned their colony in Burma with a minute force.

Rangoon suffered its first air raid on 23 December 1941, and the steamer *Nepaul* was attacked from the air, killing its commander and chief engineer. Thereafter one of the most rapid and dramatic evacuations ever of a country occurred. Once again, the river and its flotilla were the main conduit by which the European population, military casualties and retreating forces were evacuated, with the Japanese Imperial army hot on their heels. In some cases when the retreating British had pulled out of a town the Japanese would occupy it within 20 minutes.

The British operated a scorched earth policy, which they called the Act of Denial, destroying all infrastructure as they retreated. When they blew up the Burmah Oil Company refinery at Syriam it burned for days, casting a great black cloud over Rangoon. Port facilities, railways, bridges and of course shipping were all disabled, to deny their use to the Japanese.

Rangoon, a city of half a million people, became a ghost town, the Burmese heading off to the countryside. A million Indians attempted to make their escape from Burma, fearful of reprisals by Burmese nationalists and indeed the population at large.

Whilst the comparatively tiny European population of under 50,000 were evacuated by ship to Calcutta or upriver on Irrawaddy Flotilla steamers and out through the Chindwin valley, the Indian population had to walk out over the Arakan yoma to try and take ship from one of the Arakan coastal ports. The survival rate was appalling, and as monsoon rains broke, thousands died along the way from malaria and cholera. There were stampedes with many casualties, as they fought to get on board the few steamers available to take them across the Bay of Bengal. Those left behind mainly died of hunger and disease, abandoned by their British protectors. There is no accurate count of how many made it to India and how many were left behind, but more fell into the latter category than the former, and of those left behind more perished than survived.

Meanwhile, under the general manager, John Morton, a Glaswegian who had been 30 years in Burma with the IFC, a group of assistants and officers joined the 'last ditchers'. Having evacuated their families by sea, they moved into the company office in Phayre Street, conducting demolitions of the flotilla dockyards and port facilities. They co-ordinated the despatch of ammunition and coal barges upriver, as it was still hoped that the British would hold Upper Burma, in which case these supplies would be essential. In the end, however, they were to be later denied to the enemy. A small convoy escorted by the tug *Panhlaing* escaped by the sea route to Akyab[17] and then on to India. But the majority of the fleet, trapped in the Irrawaddy and Chindwin rivers, would be pushed further and further upstream as the Japanese advanced northwards. A great number of creek steamers and vessels were scuppered in Rangoon, as they lacked the crews to take them upcountry. Sir Eric Yarrow, of the Yarrow shipbuilding family, would often recount later how he, then a young officer in the Royal Engineers, gleefully blew up Yarrow-built ships, feeling sure that his family firm would get the rebuild orders after the war.

Morton then transferred his staff 180 miles upriver to Prome,[18] where a huge volume of stores needed to be transhipped from the railhead. Captain Rea of the *Hastings*, now commissioned by the army, managed to put a brave crew together at Prome and take his ship on a mission behind enemy lines to Henzada, carrying Sapper Major 'Mad Mike' Calvert, later a column commander of Wingate's Chindits, and a VC. Two of the *Hastings* crew were captured by the Japanese, and Rea was awarded an MC for his part in the action.

Captain Chubb, then commanding the *Siam*, describes how his ship, now painted grey, made a couple of runs up to Mandalay loaded with over 5,000 evacuees (she was licensed for 3,000); the journey time took fourteen rather than the usual five and a

---

17   now Sittwe, at the northern end of the west coast
18   now Pyay

half days, as the local Burmese villagers, at the time pro-Japanese, had cut the channel marker buoys, and he had to stop every four hours for reasons of sanitation. The ship's galleys were working round the clock to feed so many people, and outbreak of fire was a constant danger.

The *Nepaul*, like the *Mysore*, was converted into a hospital ship, transferring over the staff and equipment of the BOC hospital at Yenanchaung, and it carried nearly 900 casualties from this area to Sagaing for onward transport up the Chindwin towards India. Large red crosses were painted on their rooves, which the Japanese dive bombers respected. But other vessels were under constant fire: for example the *Sinkan*, under the command of a Chittagonian master, Bassa Meah, which was towing flats of ammunition; when one of those was hit Bassa Meah managed to cast it off as the ammunition exploded all around him.

In the retreat, many IFC ships had to be scuttled along the way as the Chittagonian crews deserted and headed for the hills, and on Chubb's last trip on the *Siam* a Lieutenant Robertson had his Sikh soldiers working as firemen. Seventy-five ships, mostly main line steamers with deep drafts, made it as far north as Katha, not far short of Bhamo. By now it was April, so the river would have been very low, and it is surprising they got that far, but amazingly there had been a sudden rise in the river which had allowed this. The Bhamo office still sent out the daily telegram with the water level, and it was this good news that enabled the great ships of the flotilla to continue north.

Morton and his IFC team were the last British to leave Mandalay, on 27 April, after ferrying the retreating army across the Irrawaddy at Sameikkon, 50 miles downstream of Mandalay. Meanwhile Bhamo was taken by a fast-moving Japanese force, and several paddlers fell into Japanese hands before they could be scuttled. The IFC agent there, Captain Musgrave, managed to escape overland to Myitkyina, 120 miles north of Bhamo, from where he was flown out to India.

Stern-wheelers with their shallower drafts made it up the Chindwin loaded with the wounded, and then acted as ferries to get the army across to the west bank at crossing points. The most significant of these was from Shwegyin to Kalewa, where the majority of General Slim's retreating army were taken across in the 11 sternwheelers of the Chindwin fleet. These were scuppered 60 miles further up at Sittaung, their officers and crews then legging it to Tamu in India.

On the Irrawaddy, the officers scuppered their ships by opening the injector valves, by putting gun cotton in the hulls as explosive, and by machine-gunning the waterlines from another boat. It is almost impossible to describe the emotion the commanders must have experienced as they sank the splendid ships they had loved and cared for. But they then calmly got into what cars were available and drove west on jungle tracks until their petrol ran out, then walked all the way across several mountain ranges and fast rivers till they hit the Chindwin, and once across that, over a further mountain range to Imphal, in India. Along these trails lay the dying and the dead. April is Burma's hottest month, with temperatures over 40°C, before the relief brought by the monsoon. John Morton's diary for 3 May describes the scene at Katha:

> Katha is a sight, vessels anchored ten abreast and all deserted. The last train has gone, the town is evacuated. Parties are told-off to sink every vessel, get our three cars ashore first, pay off our Chittagonians and free them to make for Manipur as best they can. It is at least 150 miles to the Chindwin – the cars will not get very far. The day is overcast and the rains not far off. We want low cloud for the Jap planes, but dry for marching – we can't have it both ways.

Again, the last out of Katha were the men of the Irrawaddy Flotilla, their sad duty done, with many a broken heart.

Captain Watts of the *Mindoon* wrote an account which describes a near three-week journey in which he and his men scavenged for food and water, even shooting a hen with a revolver, and sharing the water from their canteens with dying evacuees along the way. Most of the flotilla men got out before the rains of June, but thereafter malaria and dysentery took care of any stragglers. It was not just the greatest retreat in British military history but the greatest evacuation – far greater than that of Dunkirk, which was of course a defeat, but used by propagandists as a tale of British pluck. There was little opportunity for pluck, though, in Britain's retreat from Burma. It should be remembered that in the Burma Campaign, as with the First Anglo-Burmese War of 1824, there were far more casualties from illness than enemy action. In both these wars the real enemy was the mosquito.

On arrival in India nearly all the flotilla men immediately signed up for another tour of duty, and with their local knowledge and understanding of the country had a vital role in Field Marshal Slim and the 14th Army's reconquest of Burma in 1945. A number were decorated and attained high rank.

Following the retaking of Burma, one of the first priorities was to get what little was left of the flotilla running again to provide vital services, and former assistants of the company, such as Alister McCrae and Stuart Macdonald with military ranks, were tasked with this project. Tragically John Morton, the hero of this tale, who had returned to Scotland by air in 1942 to report to the directors and make plans for a new flotilla, was lost when his ship back to Burma went down.

During the war the company set up an office in the northern Indian town of Simla, where it planned the rebuilding of the fleet after the war, and indeed in 1947 over a dozen ships were ordered from Glasgow: six M-class main line steamers from Denny's, and a number of P-class sternwheelers from Yarrow's, no doubt to the satisfaction of Eric Yarrow. These were taken over by the IWT following the IFC's nationalisation in 1948.

The flotilla's wars were, however, by no means over, and after independence, as Burma collapsed into an array of civil wars in the 1950s – a number of which continue to this day – the spanking new P-class vessels that operated on the Bhamo run were frequently attacked by insurgent forces. One was lost in Bhamo's deep Second Defile, mortared by the Kachin Independence Army (KIA) from the clifftops above. When I travelled on that route in the mid-1980s, Bren guns were pointing out of the saloon windows, and when we acquired the original *Pandaw* in 1998 one of our first tasks was to remove the armoured plating that had been welded around the handrails. The wheelhouse up on its flying bridge was like a pillbox with steel plates welded all round, so it was quite difficult to see out.

In 2018 I was called by a representative of the then democratically elected government, who asked me to lend a ship for peace talks with the KIA, just over the Kachin state line, and I was happy to oblige. It is good to think that ships of the flotilla can be instruments of peace as well as war

P-class Ship Delivered In 1948.

3

The Steamers

By the late 1880s, the Irrawaddy Flotilla was the single most important instrument for the opening of Burma to economic development and the rule of law, and its people to the world at large. In no other country and at no other time has a single transport company come to dominate an economy and its administration to such a degree. With over 600 operational vessels covering just over 50 routeings or services, and with 60 sub-agencies in the port towns of this great riverine land, the flotilla carried the bulk of the country's rich produce downriver to ships sailing off to worldwide markets, then returned upstream with the imported goods sought by a prospering population. Over 6 million passengers were carried each year, a figure which represented half the population of the country. People who had never left their villages were now travelling up- and downriver on business, on Buddhist pilgrimage, and to attend college.

Unlike with some other great riverine systems, such as those of North America or indeed India, the construction of railways in the second half of the 19th century did not put the Burmese river steamer out of business but rather complemented it by running connecting services and assisting with the transhipment of goods. The fact that the system that had been established by the IFC by the 1880s continued into the second decade of the 21st century under its successor, IWT, with even the same routeings and timetables, speaks for itself. Whilst passenger transport has dropped off, the rivers of Burma remain the most economic method of bulk transport.

One secret of the IFC's success, as vital as its canny management and commercial opportunism, was the naval architecture and the rapid improvement of boiler technology between the 1880s and the early 1900s. With constant experimentation and some notable failures, the company, in conjunction with Denny's shipyard in Scotland, evolved the river steamer to a degree of perfection that has never been surpassed. Certainly, efficient management and burgeoning demand will have contributed to the company's success, but without the right sort of ship none of this would have been possible.

Such ships had to have sufficient power to carry enormous loads up rivers against a flow of 10 mph[19] or more, and to maintain control with similar loads going with a fast flow downstream. In one season, a ship might be grounding in 3 feet of water and by the next season, in the same place, caught up in a torrent 200 feet deep. How do you maintain your vessel's stability when it's hit by a 100-mile-an-hour cyclone and it has a flat bottom? How do you get it alongside a riverbank almost anywhere, without jetties or port infrastructure? The solutions attained had consequences not just for the opening of Burma to the world, but for other rivers and other continents. Denny's, Yarrow's and the other Clyde yards which specialised in river vessels were to take the experience of Burma and the designs they had evolved for that country, and apply them to the great rivers of South America and Africa.

Although the IFC's original four ships had been found unsuited to the Irrawaddy and turned out unprofitable, the potential of river navigation had been realised, and in the 1860s the IFC ordered from A. & J. Inglis in Glasgow its own two, slightly larger, ships: the *Colonel Fytche* and the *Colonel Phayre,* Fytche having been another prominent early colonial administrator in Burma. But the ships had design faults, with incorrectly shaped bows, and made poor headway in strong waters. In 1868, the side-paddler *Mandalay* was ordered from R. Duncan's of Glasgow, and was considerably larger, at 250 feet long and 24 feet wide with a hull depth of about 9 feet, drawing about half that again when laden. The *Mandalay* worked well, so throughout the 1870s as many as 20 paddlers of this type were ordered.

Colonel A Fytche: *built by A & J Inglis, Glasgow, 1867.*
The first ship ordered by the IFC and, in 1868, the first
steamer to run from Mandalay to Bhamo.

---

19   On inland waters land miles, rather than nautical miles, are used.

In these ships, the early design flaws were ironed out. With the exception of the triple-decked *Thoreah*, all were double-decked, with cargo, boilers and fuel storage in the hull. Decks were open to reduce windage – a real danger in a land of cyclones – and the openness was well suited to the haphazard placing of the third-class passengers, who preferred the floor to a chair, their dunnage arranged around them. First-class cabins were on the upper deck forward, second-class upper deck aft, and the third-class area was the open deck space between. There was no wheelhouse; the wheel stood open to the elements, just aft of the bow area on the main deck. The rest of the ship was roofed with corrugated iron like a great barn, keeping all below it dry in the monsoon and shaded in the hot season. Jalousies could be rolled down the sides to keep the sun or rain out. Some ships had rather attractive rattan matting around the handrails which, allowing air to pass, must have worked well as ventilation.

This design remained the prototype for most Irrawaddy ships from the 1870s to the time of writing; our own Pandaw ships have followed it in principle, retaining the same shallow draft and reduced windage despite the bulk of additional cabins. In the 1930s, the M-class ferry service ships began to feature flying bridges above for greater visibility, and this practice has continued to this day on nearly all Irrawaddy ships. Of course, the side-paddles have gone now, greatly reducing the beam which, including the sponsons,[20] would originally have been as much as a third of the ship's length.

Those 1870s ships were quick – far quicker than anything on the river today, such was the power of steam and efficiency of a paddle-powered craft. Take a trip on the PS *Waverley*, the last sea-going paddler in the world, built in 1947 and still sailing the Clyde. The speed will take your breath away! The fastest ships on the Irrawaddy achieved 15 mph on still water, so on a rapid downstream current would have been hitting speeds of nearly 30 mph over the ground!

In the 1880s there was a sudden leap in confidence and ambition in Irrawaddy ship design under Peter Denny of Dumbarton. This began with larger main line steamers of up to 300 feet in length and grossing over 1,000 tons, which were faster and could carry more people and goods than anything before. With the annexation of Upper Burma in 1886, these ships were established into what became known as a main line or express service, carrying mail. The first of these was the *Beloo*, or *Ogre*, delivered in 1886; it had the fine lines that continued through Irrawaddy ship design.

At around the same time in North America, the river boats on the Mississippi were attaining similar sizes, but were very ugly. Given the greater depth of the Mississippi, they could go deeper in draft and wider on the beam and thus provide far more space below deck for cargo and accommodation– but this made them very heavy and cumbersome, and not particularly fast. By contrast, the Irrawaddy designs spoke of élan, flair and top

---

20   paddle housings

Beeloo: *built by Denny 1886, it boasted a traditional Burmese carved-wood saloon with the heads of Queen Victoria and Peter Denny over alternate cabin doors. Used by the Duke of Clarence on his visit to Burma in 1889.*

Fig 18 P S ***Mindoon***, 1886. She and her sister *Yomah* were rated as fast cargo steamers. They were similar to the *Beeloo*, but not so fast. *N M M Negative B 1978 (F)*

PS Mindoon, *Denny's 1886, was the first ship to exceed 300 feet long.*

speeds. The *Beloo* class could carry 3,000 passengers, plus 500 tons of cargo in its holds, and a further 1,200 tons of cargo in two side flats. Denny's solution for how to carry great loads at speed was to use far lighter steel, from Bessemer or Siemens, rather than the heavy iron plates normally used in ship construction at the time, and the IFC was the first shipping company in the world to use steel widely. The paddle floats were made from teak so that if they hit debris, usually sunken logs, they would deliberately shatter, whereas a damaged steel paddle might twist and distort the mechanism within.

The second jump in ship design under Denny was the development of the shallow-draft sternwheeler. These vessels were intended for the Chindwin river, reconnoitred on a steam launch in 1882 by Fred Kennedy of the IFC and Annan Bryce of the Bombay Burmah Trading Corporation, who had timber concessions up there from the Burmese king, and declared fit for navigation. Upper Burma was then ruled by King Thibaw whilst Lower Burma was British, so the Chindwin, flowing near the border of British India, was of considerable strategic and commercial interest to the British. However, the main barrier to any development of these opportunities were the water levels, with an average dry season depth of about 3 feet and in the monsoon a flow rate strong enough to stop any ship.

Kennedy returned to Scotland, sat down with Peter Denny and worked out a radical solution, resulting in the shallowest-draft vessels ever constructed – and never achieved since. The *Kha Byoo* was the first of this class, at 170 feet long and 279 gross tons, and drew just 2 feet! Nicknamed 'lawnmowers', these sternwheelers were not the prettiest of ships, but in their marvellous simplicity they were extraordinarily clever. The boiler was a locomotive type and placed in the front to balance the weight – when you're hitting sandbanks you really do want the weight up front. It was followed by several smaller ships, at around 120 feet and far lighter, some with a gross tonnage of just 100; the lowest draft achieved was just over 1 foot, on a hull depth of just 5½ feet.

The furnace was wood-fired and fuelling took place at stations along the way on a daily basis to reduce weight and save space; plentiful chopped jungle wood was stacked ready at each station. The loading was done by girls who would sing as they daintily stepped down the gangplank with stacks of wood beautifully balanced on their heads, then flirt mischievously with the male crew and passengers, so a refuelling stop was a highlight of any Chindwin voyage.

The Chindwin sternwheeler was to evolve to be about 130 feet long with only six first-class cabins, but licensed to carry 800 deck passengers, not to mention cargo and of course the stacks of firewood for her boiler. Yarrows on the Clyde came to specialise in these ultra-shallow-draft vessels, though in the First World War due to shortages of steel, four were built at Yarrow's yard in British Columbia. Canadian ships on the Chindwin!

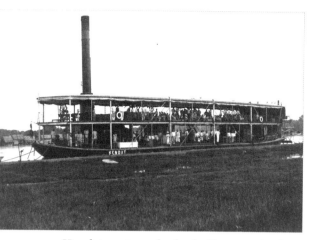

Kendat, *a sternwheeler by Yarrows, built in 1886, and with its minimal weight was highly successful.*

Hata, *a sternwheeler built by Denny in 1888; in 1900 her upper deck was blown away in a cyclone.*

Known as the K-class, these were probably the shallowest draft vessels of such a size in the world, and their success was in their simplicity. At Pandaw we attempted to revive this class and built the *Kalay*, *Kha Byoo* and *Kannee* in emulation of this concept, though sadly with diesel motors rather than steam-driven paddles, but achieving drafts of just under 3 feet – not bad when you have the weight of a dozen or so ensuite cabins to carry. All the names we used were original IFC names; I think our *Kha Byoo* is the third vessel of that name.

In 1886, the IFC fleet stood at 40 steamers and 64 flats, and by 1888 the flotilla had grown to over 80 steamers and in excess of 100 flats. The capital investment over just three years was over £1 million, which now, in the early 2020s, would be £130 million; a single Glasgow-built steamer would now cost just over £2.5 million, which seems like good value.

Back on the Irrawaddy, the *Beloo* was followed by the *China* of 1888, wider on the beam and 200 tons heavier, with a single boiler and a draft of just 3 feet 5 inches. With the rapid improvements in the efficiency of the navy-type boilers at this time, the single boiler would reduce weight and free up space. So there was no longer any need for a second funnel – but the company continued with the second one, because this was popular with their Burmese passengers who might otherwise have doubted the power and speed of a puny single-funnelled vessel. River ships then still had masts, although these were more symbolic than functional. At the same time, searchlights were introduced, enabling night navigation and almost halving journey times.

Then in the 1900s, something really dynamic happened – the introduction of the Siam class; the *Siam* was launched in 1903. At 328 feet long – the exact height of the Shwedagon Pagoda – and with a 47-foot beam and a draft of 9 feet 7 inches, these monsters carried 4,200 passengers (some accounts have it at 5,000) and 2,000 tons of cargo in holds and in flats. They were beautiful, too, with pure, clean lines incorporating the sponsons in an elegant flow. There was nothing in the world to rival this class of steamer in speed, efficiency and majesty. These were the riverine equivalent of the Flying Scotsman, the Blue Riband transatlantic liner, the Zeppelin airship.

Each Siam class ship had eight hydraulic lifts to the cargo deck, at first steam, later electric; they had restaurants and canteens, shops and a post office, like MacBrayne's West Coast services back in Scotland – and as with MacBrayne's, a postmark from the ship's post office became a collectible item. The flotilla post offices also acted as saving banks for villagers up and down the river. The 24 first-class cabins situated up front on the upper deck were state of the art in comfort and elegance, and came with electric fans; they would have been filled with colonial officials, IFC men on business and globetrotting tourists. Second class was favoured by Indian and Chinese businessmen.

There were seven Siam class ships built, all named after other Asian countries or regions: *Japan, Siam, Java, India, Assam, Ceylon* and in 1909 the last one, *Nepaul*. With a twice-weekly service from Rangoon to Mandalay and vice versa, there were always four ships operating, so the turnaround in port for unloading and reloading would be a couple of days between each voyage. With increased power and speed coupled with a searchlight and improved channel buoying, not to mention the widening of the Twante Canal[21] in 1935 to allow the main line steamers through it, the journey time from Rangoon to Bhamo was reduced to five nights; an average of just over 200 miles a day with sometimes two or three quickish stops in a day. (In 2022, we allow for ten nights sailing with a stop a day, but alas no night cruising.) Villagers could set their watches by their arrivals and departures – amazing, considering the number of potential impediments to any river journey. Local life revolved around the

R. Talbot Kelly, 'Express Steamer Passing Sagaing', 1905, from his book.

21   providing a shortcut between Rangoon and the delta

excitement of the steamers' arrivals and departures; whole towns would come alive when a steamer came in, and then go back into deep slumber until the next ship called.

PS India, *Denny's 1903, slightly smaller than the Siam class vessels, used on the Rangoon–Mandalay express steamer service.*

Fig 26 P S *Japan* 1904. Painted white for the visit of the Prince and Princess of Wales.
N M M Negative B 2726 (F)

PS Japan, *Denny's 1904, which, along with the Japan, Java and Ceylon, constituted the largest class of express steamers at 365 feet long, and licensed for just under 3,000 passengers. Here painted white for a royal visit.*

Although there was a railway with an overnight sleeper service from Rangoon to Mandalay, many people, whether on business or travelling for pleasure, preferred to go on the week-long river voyage simply because it was such fun. The author Desmond Kelly, who had grown up in 1930s Burma, told me that when the government moved to the hill station of Myamyo during the summer heat, most official families opted to go by steamer as it was something of a pleasure cruise through the colourful heart of the country. Nearly all travel writers commented on the excellence of the accommodation and messing on board.

It is interesting to note that from the completion of the *Nepaul* in 1909 to the flotilla's demise in 1942 no further ships of this size were ordered. Given the company's high standards of maintenance and care, it was often remarked by travel writers of the day that ships 20 years of age appeared new (something guests on our *Pandaws* often remark on, too!). These ships would have a lifetime of at least 50 years. If the company had survived, we might have expected a new class to emerged in the 1950s when, curiously, the ever-innovative Denny's were busy inventing the hovercraft!

Palow, Denny 1879, with flats. Note that these flats have, unusually, an upper deck for passengers, possibly used for the floating bazaar service operated by the company on the upper river.

The use of the flats was very clever, and anticipated the age of the shipping container as a way to reduce the time spent in port, hence money lost. The flats, with the bulk of cargo in them, could be dropped off at ports for loading and unloading more leisurely, over a longer period of time. By the heyday of the 1920s there were 200 flats, which tended to be known by their numbers, in the fleet. Each flat had its own crew and *sukani*, helmsman, and two sukani would steer in concert with the mother ship, which must have been quite an operation. Stories abound of flats being parted as a result of unfocused sukani, and axes were kept ready to cut the hawsers in an emergency. In times of low water, it might be necessary for the steamer to drop a flat and carry on with one, then return for the other. The combined beam of a Siam class ship across the sponsons and flats was 150 feet – imagine trying to steer *that* when bombing downstream at 20 mph! If you were puttering upstream in your country boat and met this floating metropolis, you got out of the way fast. A speck on the horizon would soon be bearing down upon you, rapidly getting bigger and bigger.

The flats had other uses too: in the Third Anglo-Burmese War some had batteries of guns mounted on them, and others were used as floating barracks for the soldiers or stables for the cavalry. Later came the idea of a floating bazaar, which I will describe in more detail in Chapter 5.

Snipe, *a Delta inspection launch in which a young assistant would*
live for months on end, patrolling the creeks and backwaters in order to check tickets.

The creek steamer, designed to operate in the vast 10,000-square-mile Irrawaddy Delta, was the most prolific of all the company's ships. Over 170 were built, and in 1941 there were no less than 60 services or routeings offered to the delta towns. These double-decked ships ranged from 80 to 115 feet long and were twin-screwed, as the creeks were often too narrow for paddlers. In addition to these steamers, a number of local operators, such as Chandra Pal, which ran single-decked launches, were absorbed into the fleet, and a wide array of vessels were used as ferries and for short-distance services between villages, as tugs and as inspection launches. For more about these, see Chapter 7.

Up until the 1930s, when the IFC started building ships in Burma, the bulk of the fleet had been built at yards on the Clyde, with Denny's of Dumbarton the main builder, and with Yarrow's and other yards specialising in river vessels building a number of shallower-draft vessels. Though a few of these sailed out to Burma under their own steam, boarded up along the sides, most were sent out as kits, and reassembled in the IFC dockyard at Dalla – 'reassembled', because they would have been assembled first on the Clyde for classing, and it should be noted that all IFC ships had Glasgow as their port of registry. Port side plates were painted red and starboard side plates were painted green, and of course all were numbered corresponding to the blueprint plans sent out with them. This was Airfix modelling on a grand scale! The boilers and engines would follow on a later ship and, by using the ship's davits, would be lifted from their holds straight into the steamer's hull, which had been floated and brought alongside, moored midstream in the Rangoon River. Such clever, simple, typically Scottish solutions saved enormous amounts of money.

Kobe under construction at Dalla in 2019. The parts were shipped out from Scotland, and the ship was assembled in the IFC dockyards.

The Dalla dockyard was a vast complex on the bank of the Rangoon river, facing the city. Ships had been built at Dalla right back to Portuguese times in the 16th and 17th centuries, and it should be remembered that Europe's interest in Burma was for its teak; by the 18th century, when both England and France had cut down their own forests to supply centuries of naval warfare, each country's motivation in gaining a foothold in Burma was for its shipbuilding. The IFC acquired the lease of the land at Dalla in 1874, and in its heyday employed over 2,500 workers.

In addition to the reassembly of the ship kits sent out there, Dalla undertook the repairs and refits of all ships, and given their longevity this must have been done to a high and exacting standard. Engine failures were virtually unknown. The dockyard offered ship repairs to ocean-going vessels, which could fly a particular flag in port to summon a standby engineer who would appear on a fast launch. The company took over the Rangoon Foundry at Athlone in 1904, with a further 1,000 employees, and had dockyards at Moulmein and Mandalay, the latter built by King Mindon for his fleet of Italian steamers, mostly sunk in the Third Anglo-Burmese War. In 1933, the Pazundaung Foundry was purchased from Bulloch Brothers, with the result that the IFC had a near-monopoly not just of river transport but also ship building and repair. This was what was needed to keep 600 ships up and running – dockyards, foundries and literally thousands of workers under a team of Dumbarton men.

By the 1930s, the IFC was building new ships at Dalla rather than shipping them out from Scotland, and that doubtlessly would have been the direction in which the company moved had it not been for the Second World War. As mentioned earlier, during the war most of the facilities were destroyed by the IFC officers, along with most other infrastructure, as part of an earth-scorching retreat. But Dalla is still on the go, run by IWT, and I have stood there under many a ship pulled up on the slip, sparks flying as welders patch a hull.

Back in the 1930s, most of the fleet ran on coal, and whilst there were coal mines up country, the bulk of coal was shipped into Rangoon from coal mines in India, via Calcutta. The IFC had been one of the first to burn oil in its ships' boilers, as it was readily available as a waste product from the mid-Burma oil refineries. However, after the refining process had improved by 1924 this was no longer available, and the company reverted to coal. In the First World War, however, with a shortage of coal, boilers had been converted to burn oil cake, an agricultural product from the Dry Zone of Middle Burma made up of compounded groundnuts and usually exported as animal fodder. So another first was the use of biofuels!

As mentioned earlier, the Chindwin sternwheelers with their locomotive engines ran on firewood, but with the construction of the Ava Bridge in 1931 their funnels had to be shortened and fitted with cowls or nets to catch the sparks. This certainly improved the appearance of the older sternwheelers, which had disproportionately tall funnels. All funnels were painted black and red – the IFC house colours – apparently because these were the cheapest colours of paint available. The IWT has continued with these colours on its ships to this day, and when we used them on our boats we got into a spot of trouble, and had to cover the black with navy blue.

In addition to the main line or express steamers, cargo steamers plied the same routes; they were the slow boats, stopping at every village. Many tourists preferred the cargo service, which had a first class, as a way to really get to know the country; in 1941 it took eight days up and seven days down between Rangoon and Mandalay, rather than four days on a main-liner.

There were also the ferry services which operated between various Irrawaddy towns; the 400-mile ferry journey from Prome to Mandalay took three nights. Interestingly, the timetables of the ferry services were arranged around the lawcourt timetables; more about that in Chapter 5.

The ships on the ferry services evolved into the M-class of 1927, which were about 200 feet long and fast and efficient – and the half-dozen delivered shortly after the war were still running till in the 2010s. The Ms were proud, swift vessels with their flying bridges and elegant lines, and their hulks can still be spotted laid up and forgotten along the fringes of IWT dockyards.

The other river system where the company operated was out of Moulmein on the Salween, going up to Hpa-an, and up the Ataran to Kyondoe, both deep in Karen state.

Telegraph by Mechans of Scotstoun – still in use!

These services were on launches 100 or more feet long and, given the local competition, they were designed to be very fast.

It is curious that the company never traded in the western coastal region of the Arakan – surely a perfect location for IFC activity with its numerous rivers connecting a rich agricultural hinterland, not to mention a labyrinth of coastal creeks and estuaries. There was, however, an Arakan Flotilla Company which, like the IFC, was nationalised in 1948 after independence, and it ran numerous services along the coast and backwaters of this riverine state. The IWT Handbook of 1962 has the timeta-

Mail drop for The Prince of Wales 1934.

bles for those services, which must have been identical to those of its predecessor; but I know little of this company and its ships, and would welcome any information. I have a hunch that it may have been an offshoot of the multitudinous British India,[22] whose ships called at Akyab, in the Arakan.

In the 1930s the main direction in which the company moved was aviation, with the formation of Burma's first airline in 1934 – Irrawaddy Flotilla and Airways. This was managed, and its pilots provided, by Imperial Airways (which became BOAC and was later merged with BEA into BA). The IFC also acted as Rangoon agents for Imperial Airways. Four Short Scion seaplanes were ordered from Northern Ireland, the intention being to provide an airmail service up and down the river, but the expected government contract was never won and the service remained unprofitable.

In the end, this novelty became popular with Burmese keen on joy rides and pleasure trips. There was one occasion when a plane was overloaded and could not take off, and after it had taxied back, a lady got off to lighten the load. It was then rumoured that the airline would not carry women, and the company had to offer several Burmese ladies free trips to dispel this myth. A popular trip was a pilgrimage flight to the Magwe Pagoda, where the aircraft auspiciously circumflew the pagoda seven times. Eventually, however, after the loss of two aircraft, it was decided to disband this unprofitable venture. Interestingly one of the pilots, Captain Esmonde, went on to win a posthumous VC for his part in the sinking of the *Scharnhorst*.

In its nearly 80 years of operations, the IFC and its shipbuilding partners remained at the forefront of naval architecture and technical innovation as applied to inland-water steamers. Burma was no backwater: here on the rivers, creative minds and

22   the British India Steam Navigation Company, founded in 1862 by William McKinnon of Glasgow

innovative spirits were at the cutting edge of technical developments, which, as mentioned earlier, had ramifications for the shipping industry across the world and set design prototypes for river navigation on all continents. On these Burmese rivers, great loads and large numbers of passengers were carried in challenging conditions in safety and considerable comfort. Although inevitably there were occasions when ships foundered on rocks or grounded on sand, collided with other vessels or even caught fire, the point I made at the start of this chapter bears repeating: the company successfully carried 6 million people a year for the better part of a century without loss of life.

Advertisement for the Irrawaddy
Flotilla and Airways, 1930s.

4

The Commanders

When you step on board this great boat [you are] expecting to find an imperious man with eyes alight with power, and the consciousness of power, and the knowledge that he is playing a great part. But you are disappointed, for you find a plain man, very simple in his habits and ways with weariness round the corners of his red eyes. Ah! they know their work these men … And I say nothing of the Clydesmen who rule the throbbing engines.

V.C. Scott O'Connor, 1904.

Little is known of the early commanders, around the time of the flotilla's arrival as a naval task force and in the Second Anglo-Burmese War of 1852. Nearly all records of those early days were lost either during the Japanese occupation of 1942, or to the work of ants following the nationalisation of the company in 1948. We do know, however, that a Captain Sevenoaks joined the company from the Indian Navy when his ship was sold to the company in 1864, and near Thayetmyo there is a Sevenoaks Channel, which must have been named after him.

By the 1880s a number of dynamic captains had emerged. In a famous silk shop in Mandalay was a sign reading 'By Appointment to the King and Queen of Burma and Irrawaddy Steamer Captains', such was their prestige. By 1884 the company had grown to 31 steamers and 65 flats, the largest of the steamers, like the *Mindon* and *Yoma*, 300 feet long and with a capacity, you will remember, of 3,000 passengers and 500 tons of cargo, plus 1,200 tons of cargo in its flats. D'Avuz's *Burma Pocket Almanac and Directory for 1893* lists 36 captains with their ships.

The IFC enjoyed good relations with King Mindon, and it ran regular steamer services between Rangoon, the capital of British Lower Burma, and Mandalay, the capital of Royal Burma. The IFC agent at Mandalay was a figure of some importance, a focus of business interests and intelligence. The first agent, Dr Clement Williams, had previously been the resident,[23] then became equivalent to a consul before resigning to take up the position as the IFC agent at Mandalay. Williams was close to the king, having carried out a successful cataract operation on him. He was followed as IFC agent by the Italian consul, Count Andrieno, who managed to stay close to power during the dark days of Thibaw and Supayalat. Thanks to Dr William's diplomacy, IFC services were extended as far north as Bhamo in 1868, and to the Chindwin around the same time.

We know of the Danish captain Jan Terndrup who at the age of 24 commanded the *Kha Byoo*, the first of Denny's ultra-shallow-draft steamers designed for the upper rivers. His family, apparently of Icelandic origin, had settled in Schleswig Holstein, then part of Denmark. At the age of 15, during the Prussian invasion of 1864, Terndrup had run away to sea and ended up in Rangoon, where he joined the flotilla. Steamer captains at that time were glamorous figures, as ships' captains are still; this handsome young Dane caught the eye of Queen Supayalat and became a favourite at court until the king put his foot down.

In 1884, when a Chinese warlord invaded, threatening Bhamo, Terndrup was sent upriver on the *Kha Byoo* to rescue its expat community, and successfully evacuated 600 Europeans after personally negotiating a ceasefire with the Chinese commander. The British government awarded him a gold watch for his efforts. Hugh Fisher, in his book *Through India and Burmah with Pen and Brush*, recalls meeting him in 1911 when Terndrup recounted to him the atrocities committed by the Burmese against the Kachins, describing over 30 crucified Kachins floating down the river. Writing in the 1970s, Captain Chubb recalls Terndrup sailing with him on the *Nepaul* in 1919. By then Terndrup had become flotilla commodore, which post he retained until he retired at well over 70; thereafter the company decided to bring in a retirement age of 55.

In October 1885, one Captain Cooper was sent up from Rangoon on the *Ashley Eden* to deliver the ultimatum, and his ship stood off Mandalay with banked fires whilst he delivered the document to the palace. Clearly it was preferable to use a man who was known at court and could access the king. The following year, however, Cooper, whilst commanding the *Thoreah*, hit a rock off Minbu, sinking the prestigious vessel. Despite this, he was later promoted to marine superintendent.

During the Third Anglo-Burmese War, the flotilla commanders took an active role in the campaign. The fleet had been requisitioned; the steamers were armed, and the flats were fitted out as mobile barracks. The triple-decked *Thoreah* alone transported, with her flats, 2,100 men upriver. General Prendergast's army of 10,000 with 7,000 followers were transported upriver to Mandalay with barely a shot fired. The only serious engagement was the aforementioned attack on the Italian-built Gwe Chaung and

---

23   a British diplomat whose responsibility mainly lay in keeping the local ruler on side

Minhla forts, which guarded the Irrawaddy just north of the border of British Burma at Thayetmyo, outgunned as their defenders were by the Royal Navy.

Meanwhile, Captain Redman on the *Okpho* had been despatched to Bhamo to rescue the Europeans there, but was captured at Moda and taken to Mandalay, where he and his officers were subjected to mock executions. Only the intervention of the IFC agent, Andrieno, saved them. There's clearly far more to being an IFC commander than sailing its ships.

No one knew Mandalay better than Andrieno and the Irrawaddy commanders, who visited regularly. As they knew how to move around the palace city subtly, there was no need for force. So Captain Terndrup acted as a guide to the British military, and Captain Morgan escorted Colonel Sladen into the palace to interview the king and persuade him and the royal family to go into exile.

Finally, on 29 November 1885, the royal family was escorted on board the *Thoreah* under Captain Patterson, who took the royal party down to Rangoon, where the king and queen and their children were transferred to the RIMS[24] *Clive* to sail to Madras and then on to Ratnagiri, where they were to live out the remainder of their lives in exile. The Queen Mother and Queen Supayargyi were exiled to Tavoy, far on the south coast. A further 41 princes and princesses were later carried to Rangoon later in December on the *Alaungpaya* and settled there on government pensions. The normal messing allowance on board for company officers was one rupee a day, but Captain Patterson claimed Rs 10,000 for entertaining the royal party.

Captain William Beckett had escaped from Mandalay on the *Palow* at the outbreak of the war, flying a royal peacock flag handed to him by Andrieno, who visited the ship in disguise late at night with a warning. Dressing up his clerk as a Burmese *wun*, official, and sitting in full rig at the fore of the ship, he disguised his ship as a Burmese prize, and sailed off unchallenged to run the gauntlet of the border forts, back into British territory. There, the *Palow* was fitted out with guns and manned by Royal Navy gunners; with almost Elizabethan bluster, Beckett came back upriver, firing broadsides at the royal forts.

Beckett seems to have been something of an institution in the flotilla, and stories of his eccentricities abound. Shortly after the searchlights were installed for the first time in 1889, he crept up on Thayetmyo and, sounding his horn, switched on his searchlight, which was turned on the town. Fearing a *beloo*, monster, the populace took fright and ran away into the jungle. Clearly, he was in favour of searchlights, and after their introduction insisted on sailing by night and remaining moored up all day. With a taste for pyrotechnics, perhaps acquired in the Third Anglo-Burmese War, he was famous for firing off a brass cannon each time he sailed into port. Perhaps he is best remembered

---

24   Royal India Marine Ship

for Beckett's Bluff near Magwe, where he had managed to lose a flat in deep water; there's no doubt that Beckett's Bluff continued to cause chuckles amongst fellow captains for years to come. A number of other features on the river are also named after embarrassing moments, such as Macfarlane's Folly. However, Beckett's most enduring legacy was the Beckett buoy; more about that in Chapter 6.

Most IFC captains were less flamboyant than Beckett, and probably (unlike the assistants) rather dour characters, habituated to spending 16 hours or more each day at their post whilst never losing focus. Their seemingly unmanoeuvrable monsters – 300 feet long, and 150 feet wide when towing flats – would entirely fill channels while there were hazards all around: rudderless teak rafts with entire villages on them drifting down; loose logs clanging into the hull and endangering the paddles; fishing nets strung out across the channels; and at night canoes whose single navigation light would be the oarsman's whacking great cheroot.

In 1888, Captain Clausen spent three days on the *Kha Byoo* trapped in a powerful whirlpool in the Second Defile, and his hair turned white. Such whirlpools were not uncommon during the monsoon floods. In contrast, in the low waters of the dry season groundings were frequent, as they still are today. Most captains could work their vessel off by using its paddles to displace sand. If that failed, they would drop kedging anchors and winch it off or, if the situation was particularly bad, get help from one of the super-shallow-draft (2-foot!) IFC tugs that patrolled the river. But there were several instances of long-term groundings, such as the *Momein*, left high and dry for nearly a year in 1919. In such cases, their commanders were required to stay on board until they floated off. There are stories of captains cultivating little gardens to grow vegetables in the lee of their ships.

In 1904, V.C. Scott O'Connor wrote:

> Some of the steamers that come this way are of the largest size; mailers on their way from Mandalay; cargo boats with flats in tow, laden with the produce of the land; and when they come round into the view of Maubin, the great stream shrinks and looks strangely small, as if it were being overcome by a monster from another world. Three hundred feet they are in length, these steamers with their flats in tow, half as wide, and they forge imperiously ahead as if all space belongs to them, and swing round and roar with anchor chains, while the lascars leap and the skipper's white face gleams in the heavy shadows by the wheel – the face of a man in command.

The company tended to recruit its captains in Scotland and send them out to Rangoon, where they would spend a year as a second officer on a main line steamer and then as a chief officer on a smaller ship. They then sat the exam for the First Class Inland Master's Certificate and if they passed it were appointed to their own command and higher pay. There were additions to their pay for passing the language exams in Hindi necessary for dealing with the Indian crew, and in Burmese for communicating with passengers. All IFC commanders came from a seafaring background, as did its other European officers. Main line steamers had a European commander, chief officer and second officer, and chief, second, third and fourth engineers. Smaller ships had a European commander and engineer. However the captain had sole responsibility and would be at the helm constantly, rarely handing over command to a subordinate.

The deck crew on all ships were almost entirely Chittagonian lascars under a *sarang*, foreman, most of the crew being his kinsmen, or at least from his home village, usually in the Cox's Bazaar area of what is now Bangladesh. Whenever a sarang transferred to another ship, the crew would go with him. Present-day Burmese rivermen still use many lascar words, such as *sukani* for the helmsman, who is now more a chief officer and a particularly important member of the crew. Smaller vessels such as the delta creek steamers were commanded by Chittagonian masters. Pursers on the larger ships tended to be Burmese clerks and as with the Burma railways by the 20th century, the engineers were Anglo-Burmese, taking over from the Scots.

The captains were well paid and in addition received a 2.5 per cent commission on a vessel's earnings; a powerful incentive to ensure efficient loading to increase cargo tonnage and make sure every passenger had a ticket. Damages were deducted, which made the captains very careful. One captain broke the mirror of his searchlight and rather than pay for a new one, acquired a replacement from a bar in Rangoon; when the light came on, 'Younger's Indian Pale Ale' was flashed up in brilliant technicolour on the passing riverbanks. A teetotalling company director out from Glasgow happened to be on board and made a fuss, and the captain was forced to replace it.

The company also had a very generous provident fund, which provided healthcare and insurance. There were officer's clubs in Rangoon and Mandalay, and a company newsletter, *Flotilla News*, kept everyone in the loop. There was even a company football league, which was based on the Scottish league with teams of company employees from the different offices – Bhamo Rangers, Pakokku Thistle etc – though there were murmurings from head office in Glasgow about the teams travelling gratis up- or downriver to away games.

Irrawaddy commanders were provided with a valet to ensure that uniforms were pressed and laundered. E.M. Powell-Brown describes her husband, the captain of an oil steamer, rising at four and, never having time to change out of his pyjamas, keeping a uniform jacket handy for acknowledging other ships passing by. She wrote the best account of the life of an Irrawaddy captain in her *Year on the Irrawaddy*, published in 1911; the Skipper, as she always referred to her husband, would be at the wheel for 20 hours a day, drinking coffee and smoking cigarettes. Describing the Skipper at work, the tension is palpable:

> Picture for yourself a vessel of tremendous beam with an equally broad flat on either side streaming through a zig zag channel scarcely wider than the steamer and flats, with a hurrying tide helping them along and tantalizing little boats scudding across the pathway. Imagine what endeavours are needed to prevent the flats smashing into the banks they swing round a sharp corner. Think of the accumulated difficulties when the Commander sees a similar vessel bearing down on him from the opposite direction and a warning 'by your leave' from another ship overtaking him and you will get some faint idea of the state of mind of the skipper as he steers his vessel through the creek.

These oil steamers towed flats of crude oil from the oil fields at Yenanchaung to the Burmah Oil Company refinery at Syriam near Rangoon. Given their inflammable nature, they were not allowed to go alongside other ships at the ghauts, and had to moor midstream. It was a lonely life for the captain so, unlike in other types of ship, his wife was allowed to live on board.

Steamer towing oil flats from the up-country oil fields at Yenanchaung to the refinery at Syriam.

The wives of other captains lived in Rangoon lodgings. There was a famous one run by a Scots widow where these lonely ladies awaited their men's return, which in the case of an express steamer captain would be roughly every three weeks. There were good moments, though. E.M. Powell-Brown describes their vessel being tied up for the night on a remote riverbank with a group of other ships, and the captains getting together round a saloon piano to sing sea shanties until late in the tropical night.

In 1895, John Innes, one of the company's directors from Glasgow, wrote:

> Next to the style of our steamers was the superior type of our Captains … to this no doubt due to the almost complete immunity of accidents we experienced. During my stay of nearly two months in Burma not a single accident took place, and this in the face of rivers with barely 6 to 12 inches spare water in places, and torturous navigation which one requires to see in order to appreciate.

It is this tradition of good seamanship and safety that is perhaps the flotilla's greatest legacy in post-war Burma. Although the European captains and their lascar crews have long gone, their legacy lives on in the near-supernatural ability of men to read the river.

Today, however, the IWT runs very few services, as people travel in their cars and buses on the fast, new roads that run up and down the Irrawaddy valley. On the river the only movement is China-bound bulk freight on great barges, and a few river cruise ships carrying tourists. When I signed a deal with IWT for the charter of a ship in 1996, it had a fleet of over 500 vessels, including a dozen built in Scotland just after the war, which were still running until the end of the 2010s. Tragically, most of that once great fleet has been abandoned and is turning to rust and rotting away. Young rivermen coming up will never know the bustle and excitement of serving on a line ship, trading from port to port up and down the river. Curiously, we at Pandaw follow in the footsteps of the IFC, running the exact same routes on the Irrawaddy, Chindwin and around the delta as they did in the past.

Headstone of Charles Smith, commander, who died aboard the Hindostan *in 1903.*

An aerial view of a steamer and flats alongside a pontoon on the Rangoon River.

A typical scene from the Rangoon River in the late 19th century.

5

A Voyage on an IFC Ship

'River travelling is monotonous and soothing'
W Somerset Maugham
on the Irrawaddy, 1929

By the 1920s travel to Burma had become all the rage. To give an idea of the destination's popularity, over 100 books were published about Burma travels, lapped up by the armchair-travelling public. There were lavishly illustrated books describing journeys through river valleys and coasts; books about plant-gathering in the mountains, from which came so many of our garden rhododendrons and azaleas; books about sporting in Burma, with its big game hunting that was said to rival that of Africa; there was even a book about mahseer fishing on the Upper Irrawaddy. Burma came late to the empire and, with its magical atmosphere and pristine ancient culture, it called out to those seeking the mystical east, with great unexplored tracts of country and of course great rivers that offered that soothing monotony.

After disembarking from a Bibby Liner or a Paddy Henderson steamer at the Rangoon docks along the Strand Road after a three-week voyage out, the traveller would transfer to one of the great Rangoon

> **"A WORD TO TOURISTS."**
> ### Irrawaddy Flotilla Co., Ltd.
>
> WE would call your attention to one of the most fascinating and beautiful trips to be found in your whole Eastern tour. What could be more delightful than to travel in one of our modern palatial steamers up the world-famous "Irrawady" of "Kipling" renown. Make the entire journey on our steamers, leaving Rangoon for Mandalay, stopping to sight see at several places *en route*. If your time is limited, the journey can be made by our express steamers, but the more preferable way to travel to get a comprehensive idea of Burma and all its beauty is to take our slower boats, stopping at all the Burmese villages and seeing the different tribes of natives, all in their own tribal dress. Especially the trip up the Irrawaddy from Mandalay to Bhamo, practically on frontier of China,
>
> **Cannot be equalled in the East.**
>
> For general information apply at head office of Company, and we will be pleased to extend every courtesy to prospective passengers.
>
> **IRRAWADDY FLOTILLA Co., Ltd.,**
> **4, Phayre Street,**
> **RANGOON, BURMA.**

IFC advertisement: 'A Word to Tourists', typical of the 1920s.

hotels, many of which were owned by the Armenian Sarkies family. The Strand survives, tragically 'restored' so badly that little of the original, either architecturally or atmospherically, remains. Other options for accommodation were the Minto Mansions, British India or Oriental hotels. There was a Thomas Cook office on Phayre Street, close to the IFC office, and there mail or telegrams could be received, traveller's cheques cashed, and onward travel arrangements made.

Any trip to Burma would include a voyage on an IFC steamer. Some visitors chose to go all the way to Mandalay from Rangoon on a great line steamer which took eight days in the 1920s, while others booked a Rangoon–Mandalay cargo steamer, a slow boat which provided more time ashore in the many fascinating ports of call. Some would take the train to Prome and join the ship there, cutting the journey down to five days. Those wishing to go to Bhamo might take the train to Mandalay or even up Katha and jump on one of the weekly smaller shallow-draft steamers that plied this route. Whichever route was chosen no one 'did' Burma without a cruise on a flotilla steamer, which was a real highlight.

Irrawaddy Flotilla Co., Ltd.

Time taken on Rail journeys.

Rangoon to Prome or *vice versâ* -	-	9 hours.
,, ,, Mandalay ,, ,, ,, -	-	20 ,,
.. .. Katha .. .. ,, -	-	1¼ days.

Some tours by Steamer or Steamer & Rail.

I.

Rangoon-Mandalay by Steamer -	-	9½ days.

II.

Mandalay-Rangoon by Steamer -	-	8 days.
or		
Mandalay-Prome ,, ,, -	-	4 ,,

III.

Mandalay-Bhamo by Express Steamer -	-	3 days.
or		
,, ,, by Cargo Steamer -	-	5½ ,,
Bhamo-Mandalay by Express Steamer -	-	2½ ,,
or		
,, ,, by Cargo Steamer -	-	3½ ,,

IV

Katha-Bhamo by Ferry -	-	1 day.
Bhamo-Mandalay by Express Steamer -	-	2½ days.

V.

Rangoon-Bassein by Steamer -	-	1½ days.
Bassein-Rangoon ,, ,, -	-	1½ ,,

IFC advertisement: journey times up till the 1930s. Now, in the 21st century, the voyages take a lot longer.

Handbook: a guide book for tourists produced by the IFC in 1935. Burma's most famous artist, U Ba Nyan, was commissioned to illustrate the cover.

*The Strand Hotel, built in 1901 by the Armenian Sarkies brothers; it was the first stop
for any Burma traveller before embarking on a flotilla ship from an adjacent jetty.*

Major Raven-Hart made the trip in 1939 on his way up to Bhamo to paddle back
down in his famous *Canoe Errant*, which flew the red ensign and travelled with him to
various continents in order for him to canoe their great rivers. Raven-Hart remarked
that 'the food was good, and very Scottish with Dundee marmalade and Crawford's
biscuits and porridge daily and most of the officers were Scottish'. Raven-Hart loved his
voyage, sailing on the *Java* from Rangoon to Mandalay and changing ship at Bhamo.
He describes how on the *Java* between the first-class section upper deck forward and
the second-class on the upper deck aft sat the deck passengers on their woven mats with
their baggage and goods piled around them, puffing on their cheroots, playing cards
or chess as children ran riot and monks sat meditating. Raven-Hart happily kicked off
his flip-flops to take up invitations to join groups on their mats, share cheroots, chew
betel and play chess. Old India hands could not believe how open and friendly the
atmosphere was – so unlike India, as here in Burma a Westerner could be accepted
and join in so easily. Raven-Hart would spend more time on deck getting to know the
Burmese than up front with the Europeans with their 'drab clothes and drab faces and
raucous voices and yelling laughter':

At first, I thought I must have aboard a Burmese equivalent of a Sunday school picnic: everyone was in silks and fine linen, and everyone seemed to know everyone, and to like everyone, and children wandered from one family circle sitting on one cane mat to another party sitting on each other, each entirely 'at home', boxes and pillow marking off and comfortably furnishing each temporary abode.

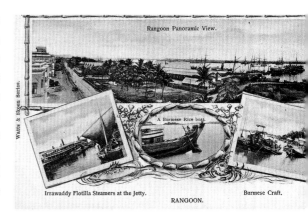

Rangoon postcard.

Likewise, for many a traveller an Irrawaddy voyage was not just a voyage through a country but a revelation of Burmese life and character. Everyone agreed that there was no better way to understand Burma and the Burmese than by going on a steamer voyage, and this continued until very recently. Much of my own travelling up and down the country in the 1980s was by line ship, where I made countless friends and really got to know the country – regrettably, though, without the benefit of the full Scottish breakfast. Stopping off every day to explore often charming little port towns or sitting on deck with a good book, this was the ultimate in relaxation.

Life on board: colonial officials are entertained by a pway *or theatrical troupe. From* The Graphic, *1880s.*

Scotsman Richard Curle, publisher and friend of Joseph Conrad, describes being cooped up on board:

> The happy-party atmosphere draws all together, the honeymoon couple, the tired engineer from Rangoon, the American oil driller … the man like a Cambridge don who is arranging the census and discusses music, the major on a tour of inspection, the young officers of the ship with their realistic talk and sentimental love of banjo melodies, the robust missionary who looks at you as if he knew something about you not at all to your credit, the fever-stricken youths down on leave from the jungle …

No you can't escape your companions on an Irrawaddy steamer, construction of all of which, whether large or small, seem to be exactly the same. The first-class accommodation is shut off entirely from the vessel; it consists of one long saloon, with cabins opening out to either side and a table down the centre, a saloon which bulges at the end, where cabins cease, into a sort of drawing room with easy chairs. Then through sliding doors you come to the bow of the ship, the observation post from which the expanse of the river opens before you. A cramped life, you will admit, in which one might be excused for sleeping too much.

Curle, like Raven-Hart, would escape this stuffy colonial atmosphere in the passenger decks:

Were it not for the comfort of the IFC steamers and the varied life that is about you on the third class deck and on the towed flats, one would miss nothing by the experience. But that life is Burma in little. The Burmese love to travel on the river. They compose themselves in huddled rows till the whole large deck resembles a tropical bean-feast. They squat down contentedly with their bundles and their merchandise, with their food and their cooking stoves, in a fantastic medley of gay colours. They talk, they sleep, and the subdued hush of that drowsy life passes over the ship sweltering down the Irrawaddy beneath her awnings. The smell of the tethered cattle in the flats, going to the delta for the rice harvest, mingles with the smell of curries and fruits, and chickens and dogs pick their way amidst the recumbent passengers.

As at that time the IFC ships did not have wheelhouses, the commander was able to move around his open foredeck and look up- and downriver without being closed in. But having the first-class travellers observing from the saloon and constantly popping out to ask questions must have been a mixed blessing. Some captains and their first officers were full of local information and colour, but others were somewhat more taciturn. There was a second steering position on the main deck below, which was mainly used at night as the searchlight was situated on the upper deck and it was necessary to get below it to see well.

Though quite small, the cabins were comfortable and well fitted out in teak and brass, and one photo shows an IF-monogrammed carpet. In the central saloon, gargantuan meals were served by a Madrassi[25] butler and Burmese mealtimes were followed with an early light snack, followed by the 'full Scottish' at about 11 a.m., which is when most

---

25   from Madras, now Chennai

Burmese have their main meal. Then there would be afternoon tea and a late supper accompanied by copious amounts of beer. I have a small collection of IFC tableware salvaged from ships sunk in the war, and a mint-condition water jug that Alister McCrae gave me, all of the best quality and emblazoned with the company logo.

After supper a dram or two would be poured and the ship's officers, all recruited from seagoing backgrounds, would sing shanties, accompanied no doubt by their banjos. Curle was perhaps being a little superior in his treatment of his fellow passengers – it might be that quite a jolly time was had as the ships moored up on a remote

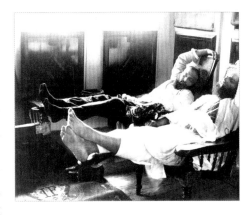

Indian passengers: the first-class saloon with Indian gentlemen snoozing in their steamer chairs. Note the 'IF' carpet.

bank in the cool of the night. Captains of ships moored nearby would pop over for a game of cards and join in the sing-song. Up-country colonials, bored stiff in their riverside bungalows and desperate for news and companionship, would wander on board to join the fun for an evening.

The saloon of a typical express steamer, with the tiny cabins off to the sides. The saloon would be ventilated by air blowing through from a forward opening when the ship was in motion. Note also the electric fans.

Saloon of Rangoon-Mandalay Express Steamer.

The second-class section was situated in the aft section of the upper deck. Whilst up front was strictly for the European businessmen, civil servants, army officers and well-heeled tourists, the second-class section would be where Indian money lenders, Chinese pawnbrokers, Armenian bankers and German-Jewish merchants would be found. Then there were the 3,000 or so deck passengers, who would sit on their

On deck: Europeans travelling on the river in the 1930s.

bundles of luggage on the open deck in the central section, picnicking or visiting a canteen in the aft section. Thus, on any steamer you had a microcosm of colonial Burma's political, economic and social hierarchy: the European administrators and representatives of global business lounging serene with their chota pegs[26] on steamer chairs in front; the Indian and Chinese money makers wheeling and dealing at the back; and the Burmans squatting on their mats, squeezed in the middle, chatting away and puffing on their cheroots.

As Walter B. Harris was to comment of his Irrawaddy voyage in *East for Pleasure*, 'It would be ungracious to omit that the comfort of the traveller is studied in every way and that every consideration is shown to him.' Indeed, the flotilla, along with the travel agency Thomas Cook in Rangoon, was responsible for opening up Burma to tourism as the Edwardian romantic travel writer of the 1900s gave way to the American globetrotter of the 1920s, for whom a voyage to Bhamo was a must. Actually, the first American tourist was probably Ulysses Grant, recently retired US president, who visited Rangoon in 1877 as part of a retire-

Polo was a popular pastime in colonial Burma, and here a match is photographed from a passing steamer in the 1930s.

---

26   half-size whisky and sodas

ment world tour. (In 1904 a future American president, Herbert Hoover, who was a mining engineer reopened the silver mines at Namtu, prompting the British administrator Maurice Collis's remark, 'he ran off with the silver'.) The majority of American travellers were, however, neither past nor future presidents, but rather prosperous adventurers in those carefree times in the decade preceding the Wall Street Crash.

Sportsmen (as they were known at the time) came to Burma in great numbers, and it was often said that for big game Burma rivalled Africa. There were wild animals everywhere. Tigers pestered villages which, per tradition, were encircled with thick thorny hedges and stockade-like fences with gates bolted at night to keep these great beasts out. Owners of orchards in the Mandalay suburbs complained of wild elephants trampling their crops at night. Everywhere jungle fowl abounded. Maurice Collis, at the time a magistrate, would, after closing his Sagaing courthouse each day, wander off into the bush and bring back a bag of game. The flotilla officers shot duck on the riverbanks. Famous sportsmen, like John Hanning Speke of the Nile, visited Lower Burma in the 1850s whilst serving in India. The best book on the subject was by Colonel Pollok and W.S. Thom; it provides practical information on all aspects of hunting big cats like the tiger, leopard and panther, as well as buffalo, rhinoceros, gaur, gayal, tsine[27] and several types of deer, hogs, wild dogs, jackals and of course elephants. Upon seeing an elephant grazing in a field in 1894, one flotilla captain took up his rifle and shot it dead; then, on discovering it belonged to the Forest Department, he was fined £60 and lost his gun licence. Tamed working elephants, with a working lifespan of around 50 years, were worth a tidy sum, and thereafter the shooting of animals from moving steamers was banned. The keen sportsman could jump on a Bibby liner out to Rangoon and then on up the Irrawaddy on an IFC steamer and bag anything from a tiger to an elephant over a winter season. Today it is unlikely that you will see any of these animals running wild, but that may be as much due to the pressures of a population that has grown eightfold as the depredations of the white hunters.

The flotilla, privately owned, had a quasi-official status and took on many of the functions of government organisations, from sorting and delivering mail to undertaking river conservancy to ensuring the free flow of transport for all users of the river to providing ships in time of war. In addition to this, the IFC carried an assortment of royalty and important personages. Dalhousie, Curzon and most successive viceroys did a Burma tour and of course travelled on the Irrawaddy amidst great fanfare and pomp. For these voyages the ships would be repainted white and the funnels yellow, the official government colours. The first royals to travel on a flotilla ship were of course poor King Thibaw and his family, taken away into exile in provincial India. Then there was Prince Albert Victor, the Duke of Clarence, who was packed off on an imperial

---

27   gaur, gayal and tsine are types of wild cattle

tour in 1889 following a hushed-up gay scandal, and it was even rumoured that he was Jack the Ripper. He travelled on the *Beloo*, or *Monster*, under Captain Hole (whose descendants I am in touch with), and his last official act before leaving Burma was the opening of the Rangoon sewage works. Who says the colonial administration lacked humour?

The future George V and Queen Mary, as Prince and Princess of Wales, travelled on the *Japan* in 1906, and can be seen relaxing on deck in this photograph. It was said that the prince was fond of oxtail soup and the commander, the well-known Captain de la Taste, instructed the butler to buy half a dozen Later, the captain found half a dozen oxen tethered in a pen on the lower deck.

These royal cruises were splendid affairs with much pageantry as the ship called at ports along the way; triumphal arches of welcome would be specially erected, with military bands, guards of honour and local dignitaries of all races lined up for presentation. Think of Captain de la Taste at the summit of his career commanding the most splendid of all the company's ships, commodore of the greatest privately owned flotilla in the world, with royal guests on board whose safe carriage was his sole responsibility.

The Crown Prince of Siam travelled, appropriately, on the *Siam* in 1906, and Lord Mountbatten of Burma made his first visit to Burma in 1921, travelling on the *Nepaul* in the company of the then Prince of Wales (who later, as Edward VIII, was to abdicate). Alister McCrae, then a young manager with the IFC on the *Nepaul*, was presented by the prince with a silver cigarette case as a thank you for taking care of the no doubt very smooth arrangements. On that cruise, flying boats belonging to the recently formed Irrawaddy Flotilla Airways met the ship along the way to deliver despatches and mail. Ashore, sycophantic banners read 'Tell Daddy We are Happy Under British Rule' whilst the police kept independence agitators well away from the royal entourage. On returning to Rangoon the prince reviewed a regatta on the Royal Lakes from Scandal Point.

The last of Mountbatten's many Irrawaddy cruises was on the *Mingyi* (built by Denny in 1947) during the 1960s, when he visited as a guest of General Ne Win. The general kept the *Mingyi* as his private river yacht, and for that reason she retained her steam boiler and side paddles when in the 1970s all the other ships of the fleet were converted to diesel and outboard propeller propulsion.

But what of the 6 million or so Burmese passengers who travelled up and down river in a year? As has been noted the Burmese adored river trips; it was very much in their character to waft down a great river in a party atmosphere. As Norman Lewis noted in the 1950s, often people going to see friends off would impulsively decide to come along too. I have seen an upbound steamer meeting a down steamer and when they we heaved to for the exchange of provisions and information, people would spot friends,

The Prince and Princess of Wales (later George V and Queen Mary) and their entourage relax on the deck of a launch-type vessel.

jump over the rails to join them and go back the way they came. Here were a people who for millennia had never strayed far beyond their village boundaries taking trips to the sacred city of Mandalay that they had only ever dreamed off. When I travelled down the Chindwin in the 1980s, if I asked anyone why they were going to Mandalay they would say '*Hpaya-pu* ', pilgrimage, as they sat on great bundles of contraband.

The spiritual and material could happily co-exist on these journeys. Back in the 1880s, the river opened the country up to possibilities not just of pilgrimage and trade, but of ideas. As colleges and universities opened, bright village boys could travel to distant cities to be educated and learn about the world beyond Burma. For the hermit kingdom, as Burma had been, the opening of the rivers was surely the single most important factor in the opening of the country.

And all aspects of Burmese life could be found on these decks – groups of toga-clad *hpongyis* who always seemed to be travelling around visiting other monks in distant monasteries; prisoners shackled to their police escorts, who were generally to be found fast asleep and often had to be woken up by their charges when the ship arrived at their destination; ladies in their Sunday best holding up a tiny mirror and forever working away at their toilette with hair-combing and *thanaka* rubbing; the 'a-smokin' of a whackin' white cheroot', which was communal and passed around even to children and babies, with a tin underneath to catch the sparks.

There would be the colourful, exotic sight of travelling circuses and *pwe*, theatre groups, ever on the move to various festivals. As each river town had a pagoda festival, there was a terrific movement of people up- and downriver visiting each other's festivals. Annually there was a massive migration of peasants together with their bullocks from upper Burma to work the delta rice harvest. Lawyers in black *taipon* jackets together with their ever-hopeful clients would be making their way to provincial capitals on the ferry services timed around court opening hours; this in a country that had happily embraced the British legal system to the point where litigation became something of a speculative hobby for many. F.C.V. Foucar, a British lawyer practising in 1930s Burma, describes how many of his Indian merchant clients would always have several lawsuits on the go at any one time in the hope that at least one would be successful. Happy times for lawyers!

Alister McCrae and Alan Prentice in their book on the flotilla describe first-hand experience in checking tickets when they would make a surprise boarding from an inspection launch:

> Obtaining tickets for the check was not always easy. For this operation passengers could be divided into different groups. First there were those who did not know where they had put their tickets and could not find them. Next there were those who thought they knew where they had put their tickets, but still could not find them. Then there was the distrustful citizen who kept his ticket in some secret place which required a long search for recovery. There were also those who had temporarily moved down to the lower deck for social or toilet purposes and had left their ticket on the upper deck. Finally, there were those who had actually lost their tickets through misadventure of having them blow overboard…
>
> Elderly passengers often wore jackets with many pockets both inside and outside the garment, all of which had to be searched before a ticket would be recovered … Matchboxes were for some reason considered to be safe places to keep tickets, but frequently in river breezes both matches and tickets were blown overboard when tickets were presented. It was common to find groups of passengers who kept family tickets in tiffin carriers (food containers), sometimes immersed in the wet contents for added safety, but illegible and sticky when handled. Dainty Burmese women with pocketless *eingyi* (muslin jackets) often kept their tickets skewered to their tight under-bodices by a safety pin that gave an added security if the pin was rusty. But at least they knew where their tickets were.

The birth of a baby on board was a common occurrence, giving rise to much joking over whether it had a ticket or not. Childbirth was said to bring good luck to a ship, and was therefore encouraged with the offer of rewards. Soon the IFC found it was effectively running floating maternity homes, and had to withdraw the offer.

Whilst chickens and dogs roamed the upper deck, the lower deck and flats might contain pens of cattle, horses and sometimes elephants. The transport of elephants was a profitable income stream for the company, as the timber firms moved working elephants from area to area. This was never easy as it was extremely difficult to coax an elephant – averaging 8 feet high and 3 tons – on board. In 1884 there was the case of six elephants carried across the mile-wide river at Prome. Having managed to get them onto a flat and across the river, the steamer returned to the other side and sounded its horn. The elephants, clearly thinking this was a mating call, dived into the river and swam back across.

This ticket, dating from 1942, was salvaged by the author from the safe of the Japan sunk at Katha in 1942 and rescued in 1998. One side is in Burmese and the other in English, and the river stop paid for would be clipped.

I have seen elephants standing on deck whizzing down the river, and it's quite a sight. On one occasion an elephant fell through the wooden deck into the hold below and the only way to get it out was to employ villagers to fill up the hold with sand. On other occasions, to induce elephants to go on board, they would create tunnels of bamboo fronds and leafy branches to disguise a flat. In 1908 the company developed a special elephant flat with extra thick teak planks (steel decks being too hot for them) with piped water supplied to keep them cool. These flats were towed on the port side, avoiding the noisy engine drains on the starboard side, as it was essential to avoid anything that might disturb the elephants and cause a stampede.

Nearly all early 20th-century travel writers embarked on a voyage to Bhamo enthused about the fortnightly *zay-thinbo*, bazaar boat, slower than the express steamer but far more fun. In essence, this was a huge mobile floating market, the steamer and flats filled with market stalls selling all manner of produce. These stalls were prized possessions and handed down from generation to generation and would have long-standing business connections in the villages. Scott O'Connor explains:

> Thus if the headman Moung Bah, of Moda village, wishes for a new *putsoe* (sarong) of fashionable dog tooth patter, or his wife a *tamein* (lady's sarong) of the new apple green and pink tartan, or Ma Hla, the village belle, a necklace of Birmingham pearls, they go down to the steamer landing and with much detail describe their requirements to Ah Tun the Chinaman, or Sheik Ibrahim, the Mohammedan trader … and in the fulness of time, the 'fire boat' trumpeting its advent, brings to each of them his heart's desire.

The great excitement of such a voyage to Bhamo was the fact that you were sailing upriver on what was effectively a floating market full of bustle and excitement in port and then serenely indolent between ports. O'Connor captures the market at rest between stops: 'seated on gay carpets, reclining on soft quilts, slumbering under silken tartans, flirting, gossiping, smoking contentedly, or playing animated chess' and this was in 'a bountiful land where there were no paupers or poor law; in a smiling land where it was always afternoon'.

With the blast of the ship's whistle a village and its surrounding area would suddenly awaken and become frenetic as people rushed in excitement down to the landing stage. Even before the gangplank was down, people were wading into the water and clambering aboard. The ship would be invaded by the entire local population, bartering would begin, and the babble would get louder and louder. When the whistle for departure sounded the transactions would reach a climax. Then the people disembarked and according to McCrae and Prentice, there would be 'restoration of peace in the village again – until the next Bazaar steamer'.

A postcard showing Strand Road and typical craft found along its jetties, c.1900.

6

The Hazards

At Bhamo, 1,030 miles from Rangoon, the river gauge can still be seen on the riverbank just below the old IFC agency. The gauge is not very exciting or beautiful, looking like a giant concrete ruler plunged vertically into the shallows, tethered by a gantry. The agent would regularly check this and communicate any significant rises or falls to head office in Phayre Street by telegram. This was particularly relevant at the end of the low water season in April, when the first snow melt would be coming down from the Himalayas with the arrival of spring up there. A rise in the water at Bhamo would take exactly 11 days to reach Rangoon, and those days could then be used to load ships and prepare for departure with the backlog of the goods held back by the low waters.

Such simple solutions embodied the IFC approach to the navigational challenges of the Irrawaddy. Taming the river with locks and dams, as has been done on most European waterways and the Nile, would be impossible given the river's scale and volume. No construction would last very long with such forces applied to it.

Any other river would be mapped or charted, and surveyed by boat regularly to update these charts. But on the Irrawaddy this would be a pointless exercise, as any survey would be more or less redundant within a few days as sands shifted and channels changed their course. I was approached quite recently by a NGO, lavishly funded by the World Bank, with a project to install fixed buoys on the channel. When I showed our captains its stylish online video presentation on how it would all work, they laughed. What was the point of sinking great concrete blocks and attaching heavy chain when they would be out of date in a week – and, immovable, present a considerable hazard to ships? When we experimented with echo sounders, we found them pretty useless as firstly they were distorted by so much sand, gravel and debris in the murky brown regurgitating water, and secondly, you would feel the ship hit a submerged ledge of sand just *before* the alarm went off.

The IFC realised all this. On the Irrawaddy it fell to its staff to assist navigation with buoying and pilotage, and only on the Chindwin did the government shoulder the cost. Other users of the river got the benefit of this for free. Ever with an eye to the bottom line, this was something that the company did not want to exhaust its profits on, but at the same time vessels needed to be guided safely through challenging and dangerous waters. In fact, the company achieved this with great efficiency and considerable economy. There were three pillars to the successful navigation of these tricky waterways: ship design, discussed in an earlier chapter; buoys and markers to indicate where the channels were; and a beat-based system of pilotage.

Buoy boats remain in operation today, little changed from IFC days.

As early as the 1850s, buoys had been used to mark hazards or channel entrances, and by the 1870s this had evolved into a simple system whereby a local country boat was part-filled with sand and allowed to drift on the current and bump along hitting the banks. Whenever it got stuck, a marker pole was stuck into the bank, some sand was shifted off over the side, and the boat floated off, to repeat the operation.

By the 1880s the company had invested in proper buoying launches that to this day are called buoy boats. The *Apollo* and *Echo* only drew 2 feet, and had detachable boilers and engines to lessen the weight in the event that they became well and truly stuck. Their heirs can still be seen puttering up and down the river, decks and wheelhouse festively festooned with piles of bamboo poles and paper balloons. Of course during the monsoon all their work is swept away, and with the fall in the river in October and November they start again. Beckett's Buoy, mentioned earlier, was an ingenious system consisting of a gunny bag filled with sand attached to a 10-foot bamboo pole using a rattan rope, and an old condensed-milk tin used as a reflector after the advent of searchlights and night navigation in 1886. The cost was small, but the saving in time lost when ships got stuck was huge. The bamboo buoy sticks were painted red and green for port and starboard; consistent with the system for entering a river from the open sea, the port buoys would be on your left-hand side when you were going upstream.

In the absence of echo sounders, all Irrawaddy ships still retain the simplest and most efficient system of gauging depth – leadsmen poling with lengths of bamboo and chanting the depths up to the wheelhouse. Today the unit of measurement is the elbow, which is about a foot and a half. A leadsman on either side of the bow will chant 'port side six elbows' to be met with 'starboard side five and half elbows'. It is a lovely-sounding chant and, to me, the music of the river. The poles are painted red and white to denote elbow lengths. In IFC times, the lascars chanted in Chittagonian Hindi and their unit of measurement was hands.

The pilot service was divided into 13 beats with 15 pilot launches, and each beat could be anything from 40 to 80 miles long depending on its complexity. Each pilot would have up-to-date information on the channel movement for his stretch. The pilot would not take the helm but stand by the master, offering advice. In King Thibaw's time a pilot who lost a ship would be beheaded – and even today, under the military, he would go to jail, so for that reason pilots can be somewhat reticent. The best time to be a pilot was probably under the IFC. Some were lascar, but many Burmese. Pilot launches were between 50 and 60 feet long with twin screws, like the *Tay*, delivered in 1911, which went to Mesopotamia and never came home. There was a smaller class of pilot launch for the Bhamo beat delivered in 1916: *Dart*, *Dee*, *Devon* and *Don*. There was also an *Ayr*, operating in the delta. The superintendent of pilots had his own launch, the *Lanpya*, pathfinder, well kitted out with decent accommodation, on which he lived for nine months of the year; during the monsoon he was sent back to Glasgow for three months to report to the board. This system continues unchanged to the time of writing, apart from the fact that the current superintendent, from the IWT, does not get an annual free trip to Glasgow. During the economic anarchy of the 1980s and 1990s, pilots were paid per beat with a gallon of fuel, and it was normal to see them leaping on board with an empty jerry can in hand.

The company also operated a number of dredgers used to maintain channels, and a curious sternwheeler called *Pounder* that in low water would be pulled by four anchors over rocks and then hit them with a giant hammer; it also had giant scoops to lift the fragmented rocks and enormous pumps to shift sands. There was some blasting done, too; for example, the once-hazardous Koonawah rock channel and reefs above Pakokku, which in King Mindon's time had its own pilot station, were blasted away by the Royal Engineers in the Third Anglo-Burmese War.

A common hazard were tree trunks and branches washed away during the monsoon, and *Rescue* had a 45-ton crane to lift out any such snags. We once had two ships moored alongside each other at the Mandalay docks; they were damaged when a massive banyan tree bough snapped off, crushing their wheelhouses at the same time.

Lanypa *or* Pathfinder, *used as a launch by the superintendent of pilots, with comfortable accommodation, built in 1915. The superintendent would live on the launch for several months at a time.*

Although attempts to tame the river on a permanent basis proved futile, seasonal works intended to direct a flow in order to clear build-ups of sand or unblock a channel opening were constantly being undertaken. Bandallings, named after a Colonel Bandall who had developed the idea in India, were an economic solution using locally available materials; stakes with rattan matting between them, which formed a barrier to divert flows. Of course, these would be lost in the monsoon and had to be re-established annually. After the experiences of King Thibaw's sunken ships blocking channels in the third war, there were various similar attempts to use blocks to shift sands; whilst initially successful they resulted in further blockages downstream so were abandoned.

Markers, usually paper balloons, were attached to trees or poles along the riverbank to indicate to masters where to make a turn, but as they were never lit they had to be picked out by *se-like*, searchlight, at night. (On our expeditions we would often find ourselves knowing there was a marker up there somewhere, searching along the banks with our searchlight.) Fixed lights presented considerable problems in maintenance, as was the case at the Hole in the Wall near Maubin, where a light was needed to indicate an elusive channel opening. A villager had been appointed lightkeeper but on one occasion, when the path from his house to the light was inundated after heavy rain, he moved the light closer to home. The next morning four steamers were grounded opposite his house.

Searchlights – which arrived in 1886, and which Captain Beckett had so much fun with – made a huge difference, and it became possible to night-navigate consistently the deeper stretches in the long straight between Prome and Magwe and in the delta. This was to knock a day off the voyage between Mandalay and Rangoon. Later a night commander was introduced; he would join the ship at Prome or Magwe, taking her through the night and giving the permanent commander a rest. On our first ship, *Pandaw I*, built by Denny in 1947, we had an original searchlight made in Glasgow. It was an enormous thing, controlled by a cog system attached to wheels on the bridge, which would be turned to elevate it or swing it to the side. When we ran out of filaments and asked for replacements, IWT shrugged its collective shoulders as if to say that was the end of an era – but we tracked down a company in India that made them for the old-fashioned film projectors still used in Indian cinemas, and I was able to stockpile them.

Despite the thoroughness of pilots and buoying, despite the commander's wisdom and experience and despite the clever designs of vessels, accidents did happen. Today, for mainly environmental reasons, river conditions are far worse than they were 70 years ago. No Siam class vessel would get very far along any stretch of the river these days. Groundings are a regular occurrence, and at low water they happen almost daily on the Chindwin and Upper Irrawaddy. On our voyages we advertise these as part of the excitement, and I think our passengers would be disappointed if they did not experience a bump or two. Most of the time we shoogle off, but sometimes we have to hail another vessel or send for a tug, which takes longer. Falling rivers are the most dangerous as the channels have not yet formed, or if they have, have not yet been identified. A grounding going downstream is far more dangerous than upstream, as we come downriver with a considerable momentum, which will carry a vessel further over the bank. Going upstream, a vessel is travelling over the land much more slowly, and on feeling a bump a rapid shift into hard astern can avert disaster.

In the days of the IFC the same risk was ever present, and it was not unknown for ships to be grounded for several months, as was the *Taping* in 1912, or even for a whole year like the *Momein* in 1919. Bearing in mind that a commander was paid a percentage of freight carried, this would have resulted in considerable loss of earnings. There was also the danger that a beached ship might be so stranded for several years if a channel were to move off in a different direction and take its time to come back. For that reason, when ships were truly grounded, work would begin to dig trench-like channels around and leading to the ship so as to return the flow on the next rise.

Interestingly the company was developing new technologies to deal with the problems of grounding. The twin-screwed vessel *Thumingala* of 1939, which was the first larger vessel entirely built at Dalla, had forward and aft ballast tanks with electric pumps so that it could raise or lower its forward or aft draft. Had not world events intervened, this system would have been the way forward.

When channels were particularly narrow a commander could drop a flat, anchoring it or mooring it to a riverbank, and then take one flat through, drop it and return for other one. In some cases where a channel was narrow and the current fast, a master might, on going downstream, anchor then roll down astern on the chain, which would act as a brake and offer considerable control. The anchor would then be picked up by the ship's boat once the tension had released. A marker buoy might be attached with a rope to lift it and then the chain unshackled to be winched back on board. Often kedging anchors were dropped by boat, as well.

Kedging was another technique used to get off a sandbank, but I am not sure how much it was used. I have tried it on several occasions without success, and I wonder if back in the day they had similar problems. The ships are just too big and heavy – and, being flat-bottomed, too stuck – to be pulled off with their single windlass.

Despite the company's reputation for safety and efficiency, ships were lost. The most common causes, apart from war, were fire, collision with other vessels, and striking rocks. Looking at Chubb's list of the 543 powered vessels owned by the company over its 80 years, 21 units were lost – 3 to fire, and the remainder wrecked after collisions or foundering on rocks. Most of these losses were in the early period; but after 1910, as ship safety and navigational support improved, losses were few. There was the tragic loss of the brand-new *Kashmir* on its maiden voyage in 1910 when the fuel oil caught fire, causing considerable loss of life. When the tug *Ngatsein* foundered in the Gulf of Martaban, it was abandoned by its crew, leaving its master and chief engineer to drown. Other types of accidents happened, too; when the 1930 earthquake struck lower Burma the *Pugno* fell over on the Dalla slipway.

When ships got too old to operate efficiently, usually after about 30 to 50 years, they were used as pontoons at landing stages, some with offices and even agent's houses on them. Vessels that sank, given the shallow depths, would normally be easily salvageable, but there was a real danger that if capsized they would quickly fill with sand and in themselves become sandbanks, making salvage impracticable. The funnels and wheelhouse of the *Thoreah*, the only triple-decker ever built, which had carried off the royal party from Mandalay in 1886 and which had sunk off Magwe the following year, protruded from a sandbank into the 1930s. This formation of sandbanks was exactly what happened after 1942, when the bulk of the fleet was scuppered in the Act of Denial before the advancing Japanese. When Norman Lewis came down in the 1950s he could see the ships' upperworks sticking out of the sand at Katha– but when I visited Katha for the first time in the early 1980s I had no idea that the great mounds of sand midstream contained ship's graves. Only in the 1990s, with the arrival of the inflatable airbag, cheap Chinese pumps and an awful lot of labour, were the ships salvaged, and it is from the salvagers that I collected my IFC-monogrammed cutlery, cups and plates, and a ticket that had been submerged in the ship's safe for 50 years. Incidentally, many of those ships, their steel hulls in pristine condition, would sail again.

The company does not seem to have had many of its own dredgers apart from the *Pounder* mentioned above, but was contracted to assemble and deliver dredgers to the Chauk oilfield area, where they were used by companies drilling for oil in the river bed. Today there are no longer any oil rigs midstream, but contemporary photos show fields of them up and down the river between Chauk and Yenanchaung.

The construction of the Ava Bridge in 1931 created a new hazard, as its massive columns created new and unpredictable eddies and drags. Although it was 227 feet high from the river bed, a number of ships had to have their funnels reduced to get under it in a high water. Only on one occasion in IFC times could a ship not pass, and it happened to us as we were going upriver in the early 2000s. Fortunately we had an empty ship just above the bridge and disembarked our passengers, bussed them round, and reembarked them on the spare ship on the other side.

There is no doubt that navigation today is far more restricted than it was before the war despite the fact that in that era drafts were deeper, ships much bigger and speeds greater. Some argue that the paddles themselves helped to maintain the channels by gouging out the sand, but I am not so sure about that. The crucial factor in the changes in the river's behaviour is the massive deforestation that occurred through the 1990s and first decade of this century. During that period, under the State Law and Order Restoration Council (SLORC) military regime, desperate for dollars as the circle of sanctions tightened, felling licences were handed out to cronies. Whereas until then the highly professional forestry department had maintained the British system of conservation, using elephants for selective extraction and planting a dozen saplings for each tree felled, this sustainable system was abandoned in favour of mechanised clear-felling that turned rich rainforest habitats into desolate scrub deserts.

We are talking about vast tracts – each concession the size of an English county. With no root systems to hold soil in place, each monsoon would wash it away and it ended up in the river as silt. For each of those two decades as I worked on the river, I saw log raft after log raft – and later, when the timbermen had acquired barges, barge upon barge, year on year, heaped with teak and other hardwoods. Nowadays a log raft is a rare sight, and the same big barges all seem to be carrying Indian coal upstream to China.

Pot rafts being assembled at Kyaukmyoung. The largest pots are used for flotation and the smaller ones are placed within them.

Rafters using poles to punt their way down river.

The greatest threat the river now faces is the proposed dam at Myitsone, the confluence where the Irrawaddy proper begins. This joint venture between the China Power Investment Corporation and its Burmese crony company Asia World would create the 15th largest dam in the world, at 1,300 metres long and 140 metres high, and produce 6,000 megawatts of power destined for China. If built, it will be of little benefit to the Burmese, most of whom are still not connected to the electricity grid. It would flood an area of nearly 500 square kilometres where there are currently 45 Kachin villages, whose inhabitants would be forcibly removed.

Worse than this would be the ecological devastation to the Irrawaddy valley, which depends on the seasonal flood and flow for irrigation, fishing and of course transport. Similar dams on the Chinese Mekong have resulted in droughts in Cambodia and the abandonment of traditional fishing activities in Laos. As a result of those dams our ships can no longer travel upstream from Thailand to China, and navigation through Laos has become restricted. The Myitsone project was first mooted in 2001 and has been resisted within Burma by the NLD[28] and by environmentalists internationally. Fortunately, despite intense diplomatic pressure from China in 2011, the prime minister U Thein Sein suspended the project in the name of the 'will of the people'.

Despite this promise, the Chinese and their Burmese military partners have continued to pursue this project, and villagers in the projected dam area have since been evicted. The Kachin Independence Army has taken action against the Burmese army in this area in an attempt to derail the project. With the February 2021 military coup, which would have been rubber-stamped by Big Brother in China, there is now a real fear that this insane project will be back on the table. (One wonders even if this is why the Chinese approved the coup – this project is really important to them.)

It beggars belief that the Burmese military would literally turn the tap off on their country's heartland with its rich agricultural resources – the true wealth of Burma – and transform it into an arid, waterless desert. They would be consigning tens of millions of their own people to extreme poverty and even starvation, not to mention the devastation to waterlife and wildlife. All so they can profit from selling cheap electricity to China, then go out and buy more massive SUVs for themselves and their families. But they have already cut down vast swathes of trees for the same reasons, so anything is possible.

---

28   the mainstream political party National League for Democracy

PART TWO:

A
River Voyage
in the
21st century

7

Rangoon and the Delta

The street became my religion. The Burmese street and the Chinese quarter with its open-air theatres and paper dragons and splendid lanterns. The Hindu street, the humblest of them, with its temples operated as a business by one caste, and the poor people prostrate in the mud outside. Markets where the betel leaves rose up in green pyramids like mountains of malachite. The stalls and pens where they sold wild animals and birds. The winding streets where supple Burmese women walked with long cheroots in their mouths. All this engrossed me and drew me gradually under the spell of real life.

Pablo Neruda, 1928

When we launched a Pandaw river expedition across the delta in 2017, I was being a bit naughty: we had a ship resting in Rangoon and not enough time to run a voyage up and down to Mandalay, so I offered our members a week's cruise across the delta, thinking that although it might be a bit dull, if we gave them lots to eat and drink they would be fine. When they got back to base, I was overwhelmed by emails saying how wonderful it had been. Our members found the maze of creeks and channels fascinating, the pristine little delta towns buzzing with life. No one there appeared to have seen tourists before, and our members were warmly welcomed everywhere. There was great birdlife in the rich and verdant vegetation along the riverbanks. We were running a couple of delta expeditions now every year, and they were fully subscribed.

The Irrawaddy Delta covers an area of 5,000 square miles, and in addition to the four main Irrawaddy channels there are several hundred lesser ones. Prior to the arrival of the British, the delta had been an area of jungle and swamp, but with Chetty[29] finance and Tamil seasonal labour, the settlement of Karen[30] communities, and investment in canals for drainage, irrigation and transport, the delta was to develop into the rice bas-

---

29   a southern Indian caste, often Tamil, resident in south-east Asia

30   an originally Sino-Tibetan group, who migrated into south-eastern Burma

ket of Asia. There are now roads and bridges connecting the main delta towns, mostly built by the SLORC regime in the 1990s and 2000s to facilitate troop movements as much as trade, but the bulk of this enormous tonnage of produce is still carried by paddy boat.

In colonial days over 1,000 such boats were operated by local owners, bringing the paddy from outlying villages to rice mills. Once the rice was bagged up, the IFC transported it to seagoing ports such as Rangoon and Bassein[31] to be shipped abroad. In its heyday in the 1920s, the IFC ran 57 different services with 100 double-decker steamers and 10 single-deckers: they all had names ending in an o: *Cato*, *Plato*, *Pluto*, *Grotto*, *Zero*, *Braco*, *Porto*, *Bello* etc (the last two named after the home town of the company's marine superintendent – Portobello!) and I recall finding a *Braco*, named after the Perthshire village of that name, still running in the 1990s. The Rangoon–Bassein night express was the only service to offer first-class sleeper accommodation; this continued running under the IWT, and until about 2000 remained the usual way of travelling to and from that important town.

Gozo, a typical creek steamer built by Denny, 1923.

The creek steamers tended to have Chittagonian masters rather than Europeans, and as there were considerable problems with lost earnings in the delta, the company deployed a number of inspection launches designed for high-speed chases through the tight, winding delta channels. On board each of these patrol boats would be

31   now Pathein

an assistant (which is what, if you will remember, the young Scots managers were called), who would be quartered for months on end in a cabin screened against mosquitoes, which in the delta are said to be amongst the virulent in the world. His job was to pounce on the delta steamers for ticket checks and cash counts; more about this below.

As our passengers noted, the delta people are friendly and welcoming, and there was a glowing feeling that this was the real old Burma, untrammelled by modernity. This had not, however, always been the case. With the absorption of Lower Burma into the British Empire in 1853, the delta presented one of the greatest agricultural opportunities ever known. At that time it was sparsely populated, and mainly jungle and swamp: tigers and crocodiles, not humans, were the main inhabitants. In 1830, only 66,000 acres were under cultivation, but by 1935 there were 9.7 million acres planted with paddy. To put this in perspective, by 1940 there were 18.5 million cultivatable acres in Burma, of which two thirds were planted with paddy, 80 per cent of that in the delta.

The clearing and cultivation of the delta between the 1860s and 1880s saw a transition from the traditional slash-and-burn farming, where land was abundant and famers scarce, to what amounted to one of the world's first great agro-industrial experiments. With the opening of the Suez Canal in 1869 the demand for Burmese rice in Europe hugely increased, as did the prices paid and profits made. Prior to that date rice had been something of a luxury, perhaps confined to European rice producers in Italy (for risotto) and Spain (for paella). Suddenly, rice was available in quantity. Rice pudding became a staple British dessert, and curries, made popular by Queen Victoria, an integral part of the British diet. This meant that Lower Burma had become part of a globalised market.

Following the repeal of the British Corn Laws in 1846, a liberal economic philosophy that was to become known as *laissez faire* triumphed. This discouraged any form of protectionism, and advocated freedom of movement – in other words, tariff-free trade and the free migration of peoples to fill gaps in the labour supply. In Burma, to stimulate the development of the delta, the government exercised a policy of encouraging Upper Burmese peasants to migrate down to the delta and settle there. Anyone could stake a claim, and if they paid taxes for several years could then claim title to it. In a society where there was very little private ownership of land, such concepts were alien. But during the disintegration of government under King Thibaw in the 1870s, the economy of Upper Burma had collapsed and there were several years when crops were not harvested. Hence a flow of willing cultivators from that region to settle in the delta, seeking a better way of life.

It would, however, take at least ten years of hard graft before a plot could produce a profitable rice crop and the Burmese peasants were forced to take loans from the ubiquitous Chinese shopkeeper for basic supplies to maintain them over this period. Usurious interest rates were as much as 35 per cent per year. Once producing paddy, the settler could borrow against the anticipated harvest, calculated at one additional basket of paddy to the value of each basket borrowed – tantamount to 100 per cent annual interest. Not surprisingly the Burmese peasant became swamped by debt, and usually what happened was that once he had cultivated the land and a title could be produced following payment of tax (for which the funds had been borrowed) he would mortgage the land, at equally usurious rates, to an Indian *chettyar*, moneylender, who would become the de facto owner. As soon as the peasant defaulted the chettyar would repossess his property and evict the peasant, who would move on to a more outlying area, stake a new claim and repeat the process. Fights between rival claimants of newly settled land were common and in the remoter Laputta area of the south-west gangs fought each other as they seized land.

The chettyars thus amassed considerable holdings of land. However, as they were primarily bankers, not agriculturalists, they had little interest in the long-term development of the land. Worse, they sent their earnings back to India, and little of the wealth generated stayed in Burma. The chettyars were the buffer between the disreputable loan shark and the highly respectable British banks in Rangoon, who were part of international financial markets. Having amassed great swathes of land, the chettyars granted one-year tenancies to Burmese farmers, who would then move from place to place each year, with little long-term interest in enhancing the land by manuring or improving infrastructure such as the embankments. None of this was conducive to improving yields.

The chettyars, in fact, found it more economical to ship mass labour in from South India, whether as permanent cultivators or even as seasonal migrant labour. It was more cost-effective for them to transport Madrassi labourers across the Indian Ocean to harvest the crop, and then send them back afterwards, than to employ seasonal labour from Upper Burma. Early on, to stimulate the delta's development, the government had subsidised the steamer passage to assist with this. Something like 100,000 Indians, mainly Madrassi, crossed over every year for the harvest season, and Rangoon became the second largest port of immigration in the world after New York.

The Burmans, with their higher living costs, could not compete with this flood of cheap labour, and became marginalised. This led to a rootlessness amongst the Burmese who had settled in the delta. Crime was rife. Rangoon had the highest murder rate in the world as young Burmese men drifted there, having lost the social and cultural cohesion of traditional Burmese life. The colonial regime lacked the resources to police so vast an area, and there was considerable corruption when it came to registering claims and granting land titles. The jails, however, were two-thirds full of

Indians, and run by Indians too, so the Burmans found themselves outnumbered by Indians at every turn, even in prison. Dacoity[32] raised its ugly head, and on the rivers piratical boardings of IFC vessels were not unknown. All this came to a head in 1929 with the Wall Street Crash and the Great Depression. Overnight, mills and plantations in Burma closed down, the ships stopped sailing and there was mass unemployment. This led to rioting in Rangoon and the mass slaughter of Indians over a dispute about stevedoring in the port. A riot in the Rangoon jail led to its capture by its inmates protesting at the brutality of the Indian guards. Maurice Collis described how the colonial regime was powerless to control it, and resorted to the influence of a powerful Indian businessman who intervened and brought the situation under control.

Power in colonial Burma, particularly Lower Burma, was essentially divvied up between the European clubs, Hindu castes, Moslem sects and Chinese clans. The Europeans sat in their clubs and did not dirty their hands, leaving the castes, sects and clans to run things. European bankers, brokers and lawyers, and the great firms like the Steel Brothers or the Bombay Burmah, relied on Indians for their human resources. Being part of an international network, these powerful people and corporations could raise finance for investment within the country and export commodities to a globalised market. The big banks let the chettyars handle the unseemly side of finance whilst they handled top-tier investments and international transactions. The IFC, with near 100 per cent Indian crew on its ships, and financed by Glasgow money, paid its dividends to its investors in Scotland.

The Burmese were left out of all this. Their traditional village structure, based around the monastery, had collapsed and they were of neither the merchant class nor the official class. With the exile of their king and the collapse of their traditional feudal structure, they had neither status nor position in society. By the 1930s this was changing, but it was too late. They were victims of that *liberal laissez faire* philosophy, and the rootless bands of dispossessed Burmese paddling through the delta creeks were rendered landless by an over-rapid globalisation and a brutal system of agro-industrialisation.

Not all businessmen were heartless: the MacGregor, of the merchants Darwood & MacGregor, left half his vast fortune to the poor of Rangoon and the other half to the poor of Glasgow. Rangoon University, cradle of the independence movement, had been built with donations from the big European companies, and these then provided ready employment for its promising young graduates. The Indian civil servants did perhaps, however, represent the ultimate irony, as Maurice Collis pointed out; they would have been mainly Oxbridge-educated in the best of liberal traditions – but these essentially humane men, deeply sympathetic to the plight of the Burmese, were obliged to take

---

32   banditry

their orders from London, where the influential and powerful city directors ensured that colonial policy was entirely directed towards ensuring efficient trading conditions rather than development and self-determination. As Collis was to say, the patronising attitude of the colonial administrators was that they were 'trustees managing the estate of a minor'.

By the 1930s, however, many of the young ICS men, influenced by the rise of Fabian socialism, were dedicated to developing democratic institutions. They lobbied endlessly – and successfully, eventually, in 1936 – for full separation from India. Young British academics who had come out to teach in the new university in the 1930s were progressive rather than reactionary. The economist J.S. Furnivall set up a Fabian book club for his students, which had a considerable influence on the growth of Burmese nationalism; the fact that after independence the U Nu administration was a doctrinaire socialist government may be attributed to Furnivall's huge influence. Interestingly when on separation in 1936 members of the elite ICS were offered jobs back in India not one left, despite the career disadvantages of staying on with the inferior Burma Civil Service.

The ultimate demonstration of Burmese discontent was the Saya San rebellion, which started in Tharawaddy in December 1930 and continued well into 1932. This was a spontaneous outbreak, not connected with the intellectual nationalist movements in Rangoon that had shadowed the Indian Congress movement. Instead, it was ostensibly about tax demands in a time of dwindling income, and the Galon King, as Saya San styled himself, looked to the trappings of the old Burmese court and Buddhist mysticism. The rebellion quickly spread across the delta as Saya San's movement took on a messianic dimension. The government was forced to employ its entire garrison of just over 8,000 troops, supported by the Karens of the delta. Then a further 3,000 troops, including a British battalion, had to be drafted in from India to quell the outbreak. It should be noted that the majority of the Galon army was unarmed, and the men trusted in the power of their tattoos to protect them from British bullets. Eventually Saya San was captured and executed, but even after three years of mopping up, the movement fragmented into dacoit bands. In the post-war anarchy, these bands transferred their aspirations from celestial fantasy to the hard realities of the Burma Communist Party and its civil war with the newly independent Burma government.

Most Westerners find it difficult to understand the hatred of Indians in Burma today. Even the gentlest, most charming, most learned Burman is filled with what might seem like an irrational loathing for the Indian. In the 1960s when General Ne Win nationalised all large Indian businesses and seized their property, anticipating Idi Amin by a decade, there was an exodus of Indians to India. Soldiers stripped rich Indian ladies of their jewellery as they embarked on their evacuation flights: they were not going to be allowed to steal away the riches of Burma. Scores were being settled.

The worst manifestation of this hatred of all things Indian was the Burma army's 2017 counter-insurgent operations in the Arakan, not to mention the vendettas of the Arakan Army, who wanted independence from Burma, and the Rohyingya, as the migrants to Bangladesh have styled themselves, to be returned. Over 100 years since the Indian settlement of the delta, there continue to be violent outbreaks against Moslem communities of Indian origin. The worst was a massacre in Meiktila in 2013, and this problem has escalated under an unsavoury new movement of militant Buddhism. It is as though the ever-proud Burmese still seek vengeance not so much for the perceived Indian plundering of their country, but more significantly for the loss of face they endured in becoming the underdog. They had been swamped by a flood-tide of Indianisation which at that stage of their development they lacked the skills and experience to compete with.

Delta police post dating from colonial times and still in use.

Ultimately the British, with their liberal *laissez faire* economic and social absolutism, were to blame. Whilst the official colonial policy was to encourage Burmese farmers in the delta, the British did nothing to regulate the usurious exploitation of the Burmans by the Chinese and chettyar moneylenders. The land grab became uncontrollable, and policing ineffective. The Burmese, used to seeking swift, simple, clear justice before a village headman, found little, if any, redress in the British judicial system with its courts and lawyers – who were mainly Indians, anyhow, exacting high fees. Everywhere you looked were Indians. They tilled the soil, reaped the harvest and manned the flotilla boats, and they were the policemen, lawyers, sepoy soldiers, moneylenders and bankers, rice brokers and shop owners. By 1931 there were over a million Indians in Burma, equivalent to 10 per cent of the total population of Lower Burma, and in Rangoon over 50 per cent of the population were Indian. Of these, over 65 per cent had not been born in Burma, so within around 30 years over 650,000 had made the crossing. These figures do not include seasonal labour, not included in the census. The British had encouraged this Indian plantation as the quickest way to agro-industrialise this region, and the disastrous consequences are still felt today.

Rangoon, which has now reverted to its pre-British name of Yangon, is the most un-Burmese of cities. Laid out by the British and populated mainly by Indians, it was sister to Calcutta, to which it was linked by weekly steamer services of the British India. Many of the architectural practices of the 1920s and 1930s in Rangoon were sub-offices of practices in Calcutta, and most of these were Scots concerns anyhow. In those decades a second Rangoon had emerged, replacing the lower-lying neoclassical city of the 1860s with bold steel-framed commercial buildings, like those in New York. In the down-

Scots Kirk, Rangoon

The Scots kirk on Signal Pagoda Road, now a Methodist church.

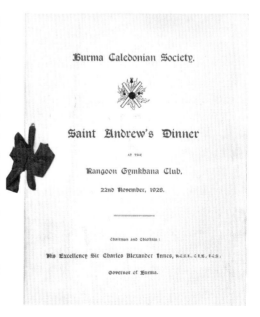

Burma Caledonian Society, St Andrew's dinner menu, 1928.

town commercial centre little of the Rangoon of the late Victorian age has survived, and now in the 21st century we see a third Rangoon, of concrete and glass, shattering in its ugliness, which has replaced the art deco of that second Rangoon.

When I first went there in 1981, Rangoon had clearly barely changed from the Rangoon the British had left in 1948. Other than that, standing still in time, an all-engulfing decrepitude had subsumed the city; on the one hand nothing had been changed, but on the other nothing had been maintained. Buildings were coated with a green slime and abundant plant life. In some places trees sprung from ledges and gutters. The city was quite smelly, as the Victorian sewers had long been clogged up and slabs were often missing from the pavements, with great chasms lurking below. The electric supply was erratic and power cuts could last for days on end. In such murkiness few would venture out after dark, not so much for fear of rats the size of cats or packs of rabid dogs as because of the risk of disappearing forever into one of those black holes.

Scene from Rangoon River.

Downtown had been laid out after the British occupation of Lower Burma in 1854 according to a grid plan, filling a peninsula fronting the Rangoon river and defined by the Pazundaung Creek to the east and the Hlaing River to the west. With three sides facing the water there was ample space for wharfs, and the entire front along the Strand Road was the Rangoon port, lined with godowns. As many as 30 ships at a time could berth bow to stern along the quayside here. Along the Strand were also the jetties of the IFC where steamers came and went daily, whether one of the many creek steamer services into the delta or the great line steamers heading up twice a week to Mandalay.

The waterfront was then, as indeed it is now, a hive of activity and excitement. It was no place of beauty – there was no corniche to stroll along at sundown as you find

Scene from the Rangoon River.

in Saigon or Phnom Penh – but rather the grime of commerce, with rail tracks crisscrossing the road leading to marshalling yards. On the flanking watercourses of the Pazundaung and Hlaing were the gigantic rice mills of Steel Brothers and the other Scots rice traders, and it was to these that the flotillas of sail-powered *hnaw* drifted after the annual rice harvest. Sampans darted from shore to ship, bearing supplies and returning crew to their moored ships, always a tricky trip given the velocity of the tides here, which rise and fall 50 feet, and the threat of tidal bores. In bygone days brave Burmese had raced canoes perched on these tidal walls. Pilot launches would meet ships entering the river at the Hastings shoal, and guide them through terrifying currents. The pilots were usually master mariners who had settled for a shore-based life with their families, but their task was no sinecure. Shalimar, in *Down to the Sea*, wrote of Rangoon's pilots, and must have served as one himself, describing so vividly the terrors of the passage.

The broad streets named after colonial officials such as Fytch, Phayre, Fraser, Montgomery and Dalhousie have been renamed after Burmese heroes. In those streets were the offices of the great colonial enterprises; the IFC had its new office, completed in 1933, on Phayre Street, just a short walk from the river. The Secretariat was the centre of colonial administration and, like most of the government buildings, was finished in an un-stuccoed red brick which is very warm and attractive. From here all Burma was run, and there were no other executive offices in the capital. But after independence numerous ministries popped up all over the city, usually in former commercial buildings. In 2006 these were relocated to the new capital at Naypyidaw, and at the time of writing most of these former ministries sit abandoned, but being government-owned, have been spared the developer's wrecking ball.

Downtown's religious edifices do perhaps tell the city's story best. Around the centre point, marked by the Sule Pagoda, mosques and Hindu temples jostle amicably. Just down Merchant Street is the Armenian Church of St John the Baptist, the oldest church in Rangoon and probably the oldest surviving church in Burma. The Jewish synagogue is the oldest in South-East Asia, and is a popular attraction for Israeli tourists. The Roman Catholic Cathedral of St Mary is the largest Christian church in all of Asia, and the Anglican Cathedral, founded by my (adopted!) ancestor Bishop Strachan in the 1880s, is a very fine example of a Gothic revival church building. On Signal Pagoda Road was the Scots kirk (conveniently, if you remember, just across from Belwood, the IFC assistants' compound, and the Steel Brothers chummery). There were the enormous Baptist churches with their American pastors for the Karens; and Catholic nunneries and mission schools like St Paul's and St John's that

Rangoon street scene, c.1900.

did so much to create a cultured, highly educated Burmese intellectual elite. In addition, the Methodists and all the other offshoots of Protestantism had their places of worship, and there was a Greek Orthodox church, too. Every Oriental religion, cult, sect and society was represented; Sikh temples, Parsee shrines, Zoroastrian ziggurats, all dotted the Rangoon skyline. In Chinatown, huge temples known to the colonials as joss houses served not just as shrines but as martial arts schools, casinos and opium dens.

Chinese secret societies and triads flourished, and the British remained conscientiously oblivious to Rangoon's criminal underworld. Pathan gangsters fixed the horse races, and Shalimar describes a pilot who had done a ship-owning Pathan crime lord a favour being rewarded with a racing tip. When Indian prisoners rioted and ran amok in the jail the British were helpless, and Maurice Collis had to ask an Indian mafia boss to intervene and settle matters. In fact, it becomes patently clear that the British grip on Burma was both weak and tiny, and the British and Indian garrison there was just as small. What held the colony together, then, was not firepower but a web of mutual interests spreading from the British multinationals of their day to the various spheres of commercial interests – not just Scots, but Chinese, Indian, Armenian, Jewish and (up to the First World War at least) even German. In Upper Burma, as we shall see, there was clearly a Burman interest as well, as the locals enjoyed an unprecedented prosperity protected by a relatively fair rule of law. I recall the Burmese writer Ludu Daw Amar saying to me 'the British ruled Burma on bicycles; the Japanese, trucks, and the Burmese with tanks'. Maurice Collis describes how he and a colleague in their baggy white suits and solar topees, unarmed and unsupported by any police or military, were able to confront an angry mob of several hundred and politely ask them, no doubt in Burmese, to go home, please – which they did!

Like the religious edifices of downtown Rangoon, so too the clubs told the story of an ethnically diverse community. At the peak of the club pyramid was the Pegu Club, exclusive to members of the India Civil Service, which became the Burma Civil Service. Here in the vast billiard hall, members could relax with their chota pegs amidst their 'own sort'. Clubs, then, like today, were all about keeping together with your own sort and keeping people of any other sort out. No civil servant would want to be tarnished with the presence of a vulgar businessman, no matter his or his company's wealth and power. Like all the European clubs in India and Burma, the Pegu Club had a strict colour bar, and one distinguished young Burmese barrister, who had a rugby blue from his Oxford college and captained the Pegu rugby team, was not even allowed to use the showers there after a game, let alone have a drink in the bar.

The rival Gymkhana Club was for the big company men, and beneath this were dozens of other clubs representing various interests: IFC officers; merchant officers and pilots; army officers and NCOs; Anglo-Burmese railwaymen; police officers; and various minority groups. They all had club houses in the city where they could discuss mutual interests and policy, including a splendid German Club built in the style of a Bavarian schloss, which was confiscated at the outbreak of the First World War. Then there were sports clubs, the most famous being the Rangoon Golf Club of 1893; a swimming club at Kokkine; a rowing club on the Royal Lakes, or Kandawgyi; a riding club at the Kyaikkasan Race Course; a dinghy sailing club on the Inya Lake; all these are – at the time of writing at least – still going strong, supported by a sporty Rangoon populace.

Downtown, the Indians tended to live on the eastern side towards Bohtatung and Monkey Point, and the Chinatown, or Tayok-dan, was to the west side. Across railway tracks to the north of downtown were the suburban areas, which spread out around and beyond the great Shwedagon Pagoda and the Kandawgyi. These areas mainly contained Buddhist monasteries, as they still do, and beyond them in the Winkaba, Maze, area stood the great villas and bungalows of Rangoon's elite. Not just the white colonials, but rich Indian and Chinese merchants too. The older ones, dating from the late 19th century, were of wood and raised high off the ground on stilts. Later ones were made of brick and stuccoed and painted white with drive-through porches and loggia terraces running around them. Most had tennis courts and well-stocked gardens.

Only one or two of the timber houses survive now around the Kandawgyi, and of the villas, the embassy ones seem to be the only survivors. Back in the 1980s there were still thousands of them, but they were mostly demolished in the 1990s to make now shabby apartment blocks. It is hard to convey now just how beautiful Rangoon actually was, and of course when I was first there we took it for granted. Before the roads were all widened in the 1990s, suburban Rangoon was a web of single-track country lanes, overhung with bougainvillea, and with all that mock Tudor architecture one felt one was lost in a sort of tropical Surrey. When the bulldozers moved in and I would try and explain to Burmese friends just what they were losing, they looked at me as if I were insane. A one-acre plot, as most were, was suddenly worth a million dollars, and having just come out of 25 years of socialist poverty, who was going to say no to that? Realising just what was happening before my own eyes as a frenzy of destruction went on all around, I borrowed a motorbike from a friend and spent a couple of weeks driving around photographing these houses. A number of these photos are in my friend Noel Singer's book *Old Rangoon*, which I was later privileged to publish.

Rangoon, with its deep-water port, was connected to an inland waterway system that extended over several thousand miles and was thus the perfect entrepôt for this rich land. Before the British established their capital there in 1852, the then Yangon was the seat of a governor, and the Shwedagon, a national shrine, was of considerable importance as a centre of pilgrimage. But other than the governor's stockade and the shrines and monasteries that adorned the Shwedagon hill, the place was of little significance, and as has been shown, the power of the Burmese empire was inland and insular. Yet in the 1920s it was to grow into the Pearl of the Orient, as a regional hub outshining Bangkok and Singapore, and people came here on leave from all over Asia to enjoy themselves in the music halls, to shop in one of several state-of-the-art department stores such as Rowe & Company, and to stay at the Strand or another of the several luxury hotels.

As mentioned earlier, the port of Rangoon had the highest number of immigrants per year in the world after New York, which is some indication of what was going on. The British had encouraged Indians to live and work in what had been a totally depopulated country, as Lower Burma had then been, and over a million came. Contemporary accounts describe thousands of poor Madrassi sleeping in the streets of Rangoon after arrival before moving off to the delta.

Meanwhile, Rangoon's Burmese population – very much the minority – tended to live in the Sanchaung area. Up till the 1990s, it had a very Burmese atmosphere with wooden houses all jammed up against each other, and lots of tea houses and bustling markets. It could have been any small Burmese town set in the midst of this great alien city of Palladian villas and Anglo-Indian tenements. But tensions could run high between the Burmese and the Indians; in 1930 an angry Burmese mob systematically butchered hundreds of Indians over a stevedoring dispute at the docks. On another occasion, the predominantly Indian prison warders started systematically picking off

Burmese prisoners in a prison revolt. Such tensions were to climax with the expulsion of Indians under Ne Win after the 1962 revolution, and indeed continue to this day with the irrational and near-pathological hatred of Indians borne within each and every Burmese.

Until Rangoon's fall in 1942, the Rice Board monitored the export of rice and took a levy. This revenue having been entirely spent on infrastructure development, it would be wrong to say that colonial policy was necessarily exploitative. Whilst little was done to protect the Burman from usury, considerable investment in education resulted in a country-wide high school system which – displacing the village *kyaung*, monastic, schools – equipped the Burmese for the modern world. In Rangoon, the elite schools like St John's and St Paul's were run by Catholic orders for predominantly Buddhist pupils. The development of Rangoon College into a university in 1920, the expansion funded by donations from British companies, led to a boom in education, with young graduates entering either the big companies or the government administration. Ironically, it was from this that the nationalist movement arose, leading to eventual independence and the nationalisation of the commercial concerns that had fostered the rise of a westernised class of Burman. Wealthier students studied in the universities of India or the United Kingdom, many choosing law and being called to the bar. Of these a number came from landowning delta families who had amassed fortunes and moved to Rangoon.

In London, deep in a City office building, was the Rice Room. Here, in secrecy, white-coated scientists awaited samples of each year's crop, flown in from Rangoon, for analysis of quality and yield. The offices belonged to Steel Brothers, the largest buyers of rice in the delta, with their great mills along the Pazundaung Creek. Founded by another Scot, William Strang Steel, this company traded in other commodities as well, including oil and teak. After the harvest, over 1,000 barges under sail would drift along the Rangoon river in the moonlight, laden with the year's crop. Along the jetties, Indian brokers auctioned off the contents to the European rice buyers for milling and export abroad, much of it to India. To give an idea of the scale of this operation, in the 1920s Steel Brothers would have 28 seagoing cargo ships in the Rangoon port simultaneously loading rice. Without this rice, India would have starved.

Steel Brothers expanded into what might today be called a multinational with operations all over the world and thus survived independence and the subsequent collapse of trade within Burma. Yet despite its scale, it was perhaps more sympathetic to the Burmese peasant than the chettyar. As many smaller localised mills were set up across the delta by independent operators, taking a large share away from the greater Rangoon mills, the young European assistants were despatched across the delta to set up rice-buying stations to buy direct from the cultivators, missing out the Indian brokers and millers, who had been offering lower prices. Speaking Burmese and living amongst the Burmese, the assistants were in tune with the land. In fact, one group of young assistants took up paddy farming for themselves as a hobby, and thus had a first-hand understanding of forthcoming yields and harvest dates – something no chettyar in his counting house could ever have achieved.

The strength or otherwise of the Burmese claim to Lower Burma remains in question. The Burmese, or Mien, of Tibeto-Burmese stock, having migrated down the Irrawaddy valley from south-west China in the early centuries CE, had occupied the Irrawaddy valley from the north of the delta at Prome, as far north as Tagaung on the Upper Irrawaddy, and, of course, the rich Chindwin valley. Southern Burma was, however, occupied by the Mon people, who had been there long before the Mien made their entry into the Irrawaddy valley. The Mon city-states along the southern seaboard traded with India, and it was through them that Indian religious sects, including Buddhism, permeated South-East Asia. Over a period of about 750 years power swung from the Mon to the Burmese and back again like a pendulum: when the Burmese were on the up the Mon were down, and vice versa: Anawratha of Pagan in the 11th century invades the Mon country and captures Thaton; Pagan falls to the Mongols in the 13th century, and the Mons enjoy a cultural renaissance under the Hanthawaddy kingdom; in the 16th century the Burmese resurge and crush the Mon again; in the mid-18th century the Burmese kingdom implodes and a second Hanthawaddy kingdom emerges with the assistance of the French, and sacks Ava in 1752; but this success is short-lived and in 1757 a new Burmese dynasty, the Konbaung, invade and decimate the Mon south.

Thereafter follows a period of enslavement and genocide when, with the exception of pockets on the Martaban coast and in the Siamese territory of Tenasserim, the Mon all but disappear from Lower Burma. Yet, other than investing the port of Rangoon with its famous Dagon shrine, the Konbaung Burmese apparently felt no need to settle the region. This was because wars were fought not to gain land but to gain people. As with the several Burmese conquests of Siam, no attempt was made to colonise or even administer captured territory; rather, the objective was the mass transport of the surviving populace back to Burma to maintain an ever-dwindling labour force. Ever-dwindling in the face of ever-prevalent tropical disease, megalomaniacal pagoda building, and incessant warfare.

The French had been in Syriam or Thanlyin since 1727, when Dupleix, the governor-general of French India, had realised the possibilities of shipbuilding in Burma, with its abundant supplies of teak. With the Mon rebellion of 1740, the French were forced to withdraw, and in 1752, following a Mon diplomatic mission to Pondicherry canvassing for support, a French envoy, Sieur de Bruno, was despatched with warships, musketeers and artillery to assist Mon and seize the Irrawaddy Delta for the French. But much to the ire of the French, the British had established a foothold on the edge of the delta, on the island of Negrais, in 1753. So the French did perhaps back the wrong horse, and Sieur de Bruno was captured and roasted alive by the victorious Burmese. His troops were treated more humanely, however, being absorbed into the Burmese army and eventually given Burmese wives and land in the Mu and Chindwin valleys, where there are still Catholic villages to this day.

But neither the French nor British were the first Europeans to meddle in the affairs of Burma. From the 16th century onwards, Portuguese mercenaries and adventurers had been active in the area, the most notorious of them Felipe de Brito, appointed by the Burmese governor of Syriam in 1599. He subsequently rebelled against his masters, desecrated Buddhist shrines, and was eventually captured and suffered impalement. The Portuguese were at the forefront of the Toungoo king's extensive military campaigns to re-establish the Burmese empire that had fallen in the 13th century, including the conquest of the Mons and Siamese. The Portuguese influence at the royal court was considerable, and it is estimated that over 5,000 Portuguese were settled in Burma under the *ahmudan* system, under which regiments lived on estates provided for their support. They were encouraged to marry locally, and by the mid-17th century the men of these regiments of artillery and musketeers were of mixed blood, known as Bayingyi (from the Persian *feringee*); they are still listed as one of Burma's official ethnic groups. The Bayingyi continued as an integral part of the Burmese army until the fall of the Konbaung in 1886, and remained staunchly Catholic, as their descendants are today. Their regimental banners even had a cross on them. I recently stumbled on a Bayingyi 'city village' in the suburbs of Mandalay, arranged around a church and convent. The residents were prosperous, their main business activity appearing to be as undertakers. Sadly, when Ne Win banned foreign names in the 1960s and forced all non-Burmese to take Burmese names, they lost much of their sense of identity, and when in 1997 I asked if they remembered their family names, expecting a chorus of de Souzas, Pereiras and Coelhos, they took to scratching their heads.

With the widening of the Twante Canal in 1935 to allow larger steamers through, two days were knocked off the express steamer voyage from Rangoon to Mandalay, bringing it down to five days. Steamers no longer had to make a great detour round the edge of the delta to reach the main channel taking them north. There are in fact four large channels, the Bathein, Pyapone, Bogale and Toe rivers, and each of these can be a mile wide. Interconnecting channels and creeks are uncountable. (Interestingly, with the dumping of silt the delta gets larger each year by 1,000 hectares.) The great arms of the delta are actually quite boring to cruise along, but the lesser interconnecting channels fascinating. The region is densely populated, and these channels are full of life with nearly all movement of people and goods by waterborne craft of various sorts. Scott O'Connor, who travelled with the Irrawaddy Flotilla in around 1900, describes the popular pastime of everyone from kids to old folk getting into their tiny canoes and surfing on the wake of a great 300-foot paddle-steamer. These mighty vessels, with their flat either side, filled the channels from bank to bank. Imagine the shock and excitement of seeing one of these coming around the bend! Whether in a canoe, country boat or creek steamer, you got out of the way fast, as such a thing is unstoppable, particularly when racing downstream on a 12 mph current.

Today our Rangoon to Mandalay ships follow the same route as the express steamers, stopping at larger delta towns of Maubin and Donabyu which are full of buzz and so typically Burmese with their markets, teashops and monasteries. It is hard to believe that 100 years ago they were hubs of Indian counting houses and brokerages, the shops all owned by Chinese, and that 200 years before that you were more likely to meet a Portuguese bearing an arquebus than a Burman wielding his *dah*, sword. (Donabyu, if you remember, is where the great Burmese general Maha Bandula fell to a stray British rocket in the 1824 war. Had he been luckier, Burmese history might have taken a different course.)

As William Somerset Maugham was to write of his voyage by IFC steamer 'the immense violence of slow-moving water gave me an exquisite sense of inviolate peace'.

But for the young IFC assistant, not long out from Scotland and sent for six months to learn the delta, there would have been a lot less inviolate peace and quite a lot of excitement. *Rover*, the company's fastest inspection launch – indeed, the fastest boat

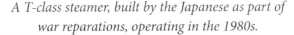

A T-class steamer, built by the Japanese as part of war reparations, operating in the 1980s.

in Burma – could hit 35 mph. Hiding up creeks in it, or in one of the other three launches, *Snipe*, *Hawk*, and *Wren*, the assistant could pounce on passing steamers and be alongside and on board before the lascar master and his purser had time to sort their ledgers. With the collusion of passengers, sometimes the entire complement, the purser would undercharge for passage and, not issuing tickets, omit the entries in his ledger. It was a matter of a simple ticket check and cash count, but with over 100 vessels running in and around the delta it was a constant game of cat and mouse. Although a highly efficient bush telegraph extended right across the area and the masters were well informed of the launches' whereabouts, the point was that it kept the pursers on their toes and stopped them going too far.

During the Second World War much of the delta was abandoned, and in its aftermath, as civil war raged through the land, the Karen took control of much of the area as part of its rebellion. There had been Karen Christian villages in the delta since the earliest days of British rule, and in the land grab of the 1860s and 1870s, when pitched battles were fought between rival gangs, these villages, under the strict discipline of their pastors, had been oases of law and order.

On independence in 1948 a large part of the Burma army was in fact Karen, trained by the British and well led by battle-hardened Karen officers. They formed the forerunner of today's KNU or Karen National Union, in an attempt to carve out a Karen Free State within the delta area. At one point the front line between the Karen and Burma armies was drawn through the Rangoon suburbs with the Karen in Insein and the Burmese controlling the city, lobbing shells at each other. Then, in 1948–49, came the insurgency of the Burma Communist Party; today as you drive through delta towns and villages you will see every police station is a mini-fortress dating from the days when the government's sway was light and Communist guerrillas were at large.

Following the 1962 revolution, when Burma under General Ne Win embarked on one of the weirdest socialist experiments the world has yet seen, the delta lands were nationalised into cooperatives and land ownership was abolished. During that period Burma ceased to be the largest rice exporter in the world and was even said to have to import rice. This was mainly because the Burmese cultivator did not take to a communal system and, disincentivised, reduced his output to the needs of immediate family or hoarded rice to sell on the black market. Other factors came into play in the decline of Burma rice production. Other rice-producing countries, like Thailand or Vietnam, were mechanised and took advantage of new developments in fertilisers and higher-yielding new strains of rice, whilst Burma fell behind during its three decades of self-isolation. A further 20 years of sanctions, vociferously advocated by Aung San Suu Kyi, in my opinion did more damage to the country than Ne Win's Burmese

Road to Socialism. India, having been the largest single importer of Burmese rice, was to become self-sufficient in rice thanks to the post-war agricultural revolution that Burma missed out on. Another consideration in the decline of Burma as a rice exporter is demographic. Between the 1931 census and the time of writing, the population of Burma has more than quadrupled, so there are many more mouths to feed at home.

The landfall of Cyclone Nargis along the delta coast in May 2008 brought Burma to the world's attention. A million people were made homeless overnight, their livestock lost, their farmland and wells flooded with salt water. Over 138,000 people died. The military government did little to help, and the world grew angry. The wife of the country's senior general announced in public that this was the working of divine karma on the wicked Christians, who still occupied much of the delta. The Americans sent warships, genuinely wanting to assist. The Burmese generals hid in their bunkers. But the pressure was on to allow aid agencies access, and the sanctions and embargos were lifted. Eventually, under the pressure of the UN secretary-general, the generals were persuaded that the Americans were not going to invade, and aid was allowed to flow in.

Nargis changed much in Burma: with the easing of the Suu Kyi sanctions the country became more prosperous overnight. Aid agencies opened up all over Rangoon, and foreigners started pouring in. Whilst it is arguable just how effective such aid programmes are, the point was that Nargis had opened the door. The generals became less paranoid, and a more moderate and reforming administration under General Thein Win, the unsung Gorbachev of Burma, paved the way for a return to the democratic process.

Our Round the Delta expedition, which lasts a week, weaves through connecting channels, creeks and rivers, visiting the main delta towns: Pyabone, Bogale and Bassein. It is hard to believe that just 12 years ago all this lay in ruins. The ever-industrious Burmese managed to get back to some form of normality remarkably quickly, mainly through their own efforts and the help of their compatriots. Pandaw passengers donated funds for a Nargis orphanage, and now most of those kids have grown up and gone off to college or got jobs. During the emergency period our crews took two of our ships down to the delta, where they were converted by a UK medical charity into floating hospitals; three babies were born on *Pandaw IV*.

8

Middle Burma

A few miles downstream from 21st-century Prome stands the Akauk-taung, Customs Hill, looming over the river, its cliffs filled with niches containing Buddha images. Here the Irrawaddy proper begins for those heading upstream, and ends for those coming down. Below this point, the river splits into myriad channels, and the delta fans out towards the ocean. Above it, the river forms a single course. Here was the ancient border post that marked entry into the real Burma, and even today you feel spiritually as if you are in a land of mysticism and magic, wizardry and trance, where things are done somewhat differently from any other place settled by humanity.

Breasting the current we are in hills now, lowish and undulating with teak forests on the east bank and market gardens specialising in *aw-za-thi*, custard apples, on the west bank. A bridge built by SLORC in the 1990s spans the river just below Prome, built for a road which takes one on to the Taungup pass road leading to the Arakan, now passable by car. Prome itself was a classic British Indian grid-plan town – a mini-Rangoon, just as Rangoon was a mini-Calcutta. There are still a good few Indians living in the downtown tenement blocks; those who stayed on for one reason or another after the end of empire. There was also an Indian community here that had settled long before the coming of the *kala pyu* or 'white Indians'. These were the Kathay, who had been brought here in the 18th century following King Bodawpaya's invasion of Manipur. They were weavers of fine silk *putsoe*, sarongs, but their craft was in decline when Scott O'Connor visited them around 1900, unable to compete against cheaper Manchester imports.

Prome was in many ways the template for the colonial river town, developed after the second annexation of 1854, with its administrative buildings and churches strung out along the river bund: the courthouse and the club; the Anglican church and Catholic cathedral; and, of course, the agency of the Irrawaddy Flotilla Company, below which, along the ghauts, steamers moored and loaded or unloaded. Burma's first railway linked Prome to Rangoon in 1877 and, for urgent freight or passengers in a hurry, cut out the four-day river voyage via the delta. Prome remains a city of the stevedore,

Watching the steamer come in. After 150 years of river navigation, this is still the most exciting part of any villager's day.

with great gangs of strong young men jogging in files as they heft sacks and bales up and down the banks from ship to shore, and shore to ship. I became great friends with one of the gangmasters in the 1990s; Ma Cho was a very bright young lady, not averse to leading from the front with a box or basket on her head, and she commanded a cohort of over 100 men that she cajoled with ribald banter. Upper Burma is run by such women.

Scott O' Connor describes a mixed community not just of Manipuri weavers but of a Chinese community of shoemakers, split between the Long Coats and the Short Coats with their respective joss houses or temples that acted as schools teaching Chinese calligraphy. There was a cigar-making quarter and an artisan's quarter where the traditions of court painting and wood carving continued, their products now destined for the Western souvenir market. With the fall of the court at Mandalay in 1886 and the decline of patronage, many craftsmen turned their hands to the tourist trade. Indeed, much of the Burmese art that turns up in UK auction houses labelled Konbaung Dynasty or Mandalay Period was actually made around the turn of the 19th/20th century for the Western market; every large country house in Britain has its Burmese dinner gong.

Further up the river bund were the splendid houses of the colonial officers, the grandest being that of the district commissioner, and of course the residence of the IFC agent. Prome had its famous shrine, the Shwesandaw, looking over the town from its steep little hill, with a monumental seated Buddha of 20th-century construction opposite. The Shwesandaw, enshrining a hair of the Buddha, is one of Burma's great urban shrines, and revered nationally.

In 1981 I spent three months in Burma working as an apprentice on a power station being built by the Scottish company John Brown Engineering. I was cooped up in a heavily shuttered bungalow with a bunch of engineers from the Clydebank area, and we were the only foreigners Prome had seen since the war. There was little to do in our free time, so having acquired a bicycle I began to explore the area and came across a fascinating group of temples in the countryside to the east of the town. Little did I realise that this was one of Burma's most important archaeological sites, Thareyakittiya, which dates from the 5th to the 10th centuries CE and was the forerunner of Pagan. I made local friends, and we would go on treks through the jungle, swimming in ponds and eating curry picnics. This was the 'Burmese arcadia' described by so many colonial books.

Prome was famous as the birthplace of one Shu Maung or, as he later styled himself, Ne Win, Shining Star. General Ne Win, as he became, did more to shape Burma than anyone else in post-war Burmese history. As this was U Ne Win's town, and he was liable to visit at any time, the road between Rangoon and Prome was definitely the best road in Burma and in the days before traffic you could do it in four hours – but now, in the 2020s, it takes about double that.

District Court, Prome. As litigation grew to be a popular activity for Burmese river dwellers, ferry schedules were arranged around court sitting times.

I remember on one occasion we were told by our Burmese government liaison that U Ne Win would be visiting the power station. so all of us foreign workers were confined to barracks, out of sight, the power station construction being a solely Burmese effort. Throughout the previous month, engineers had constructed a jetty on the riverbank and remade the road leading up from it. The jetty was painted white, as were the trunks of all the trees lining the road. Military intelligence officers in fake Ray Ban aviator glasses were everywhere for weeks in advance, and on one occasion when a Bangkok-bound jumbo jet passed overhead, there was great excitement and much pointing at the sky: it was a CIA spy plane! In the end, however, the general did not arrive by boat, but flew in by helicopter.

Prome had been the northernmost outpost of the Mon kingdom, conquered in 1551 by the Burmese King Tabinshwehti and his general, Bayinnaung, who succeeded him. The Portuguese writer Fernão Mendes Pinto, with the Burmese army, described how Tabinshweti's war elephants were fed on a mash of bran and chopped-up babies and then plied with alcohol to get their energy up before battle. Terrifyingly, they wielded great swords with their trunks. Despite this, the outcome of most 16th-century battles in Burma hinged on foreign mercenaries, who supplied firepower in the form of musketry and artillery. There were Portuguese on both the Burmese and Mon sides. Since that time Prome has been Burmese, and indeed until the development of Lower Burma in the 19th century it was the first port on the Irrawaddy for travellers coming from the sea, the gateway to Burma. Likewise, as the river's first chokepoint, it was of strategic importance to the ancient Pyu, whose city-state had traded here with Indian merchant travellers, and it acted as entrepôt to the land beyond.

In addition to the main line and cargo steamers that stopped here on the run from Rangoon to Mandalay, Prome was a hub for the ferry services – much more, though, than just cross-river ferries. They linked Prome with Magwe and Mandalay on three-day sailings which, as mentioned earlier, were timed according to the opening times of the lawcourts. Between here and Magwe the channel is narrow, just half a mile wide, and therefore deeper. This makes night navigation a possibility, though now, due to silting and lack of buoying, it is far riskier than back in colonial days.

*The evening bath – the river remains the bathing place for most
river dwellers, and clothes are washed at the same time.*

Sailing upstream from Prome into sunlight and blue skies after months of overcast monsoon sky in muggy Rangoon, you feel the heaviness lift and your soul can breathe again. For here, we are entering the Dry Zone of Middle Burma, where the annual rainfall reduces from the 75 inches a year of the delta to just 25. Suddenly, everything changes. The landscape becomes buff-coloured, arid, almost desert-like, with scrub and thorny bushes, in dramatic contrast to the verdant greens of the delta with its lush palms and fronds lining the riverbanks. Rice cultivation gives way to groundnuts or peanuts, Burma's other great crop, introduced by the British and its second-largest export after rice. In colonial times, this great harvest of peanuts was compressed into oil cakes and exported as winter feed for British livestock. Think of generations of British children nurtured on their pint of milk a day connected to Burma through the food chain. Historians tend to focus on the dynamics of the rice trade and forget about the groundnuts, which by 1940–41 were cultivated on an area of 781,000 acres, much of which had been marginal land and not previously cultivated. Prior to this terrific expansion of land use, the Middle Burma landscape must have been very different to what it is in the 21st century, with its teeming villages. Back then, human activity would have been confined to the riverbanks and islands where people could fish and grow seasonal crops. Millet was the main source of sustenance rather than rice, as that was limited to fertile flatland pockets that could be irrigated from surrounding hills, such as the rice bowl around Kyaukse and the plain south of Mandalay, around Ava and Amarapura, and the flat areas of the Chindwin and Mu valleys. Beyond these rice pockets, there was wilderness.

On the section of river between Prome and Magwe there is a succession of quintessentially Burmese towns. A favourite is Allanmyo,[33] named after a General Allan, and to step ashore here is to step into the Burma of eccentrically decorated merchants' houses, where neoclassical symmetry meets the florid world of Burmese courtly decoration, where the side-car[34] sayas snooze in their ranks, and Burmese heavy metal blares from an empty teashop. Low-lying lush green hills, now denuded of timber of any value, still form a pleasing backdrop as we chug in to moor against the glimmering sands that stretch out at low water from the town straggling along its strand.

Thayetmyo, or Mango Town, the former frontier post of British Burma, was a garrison town between the first and second Anglo-Burmese wars and until recently contained many an architectural gem from those early days of British occupation. Sadly, most of these have been bulldozed to make space for various conglomerate-owned banks, covered in mirror glass and grimy ceramic tiles, resembling 1970s public lavatories turned inside out. It was here that I discovered the Turkish cemetery, where I was taken mistakenly in a pony trap when I was trying to find the British cemetery. During the Mesopotamian campaign of the First World War, 12,000 Turkish prisoners were shipped to India and Burma. The Thayetmyo camp was the largest of all the camps, with 3,500 prisoners; in total, over 1,000 Turks died in Burma, mainly of

---

33   now Aunglan

34   as trishaws are known in Burma

malaria. Interestingly, a number were sent up to Maymyo to work on landscaping the botanical gardens there. When I was there, much of the cemetery had been reclaimed by scrub jungle, but I understand that in 2012 Burma and Turkey formed diplomatic ties and it has since been restored.

I never found the English cemetery, but one favourite excursion for Pandaw passengers is the Thayetmyo Golf Club, founded in 1876 and the oldest in Burma, which proclaims itself, on a large painted sign, to be twinned with the Royal and Ancient Golf Club at St Andrews. We featured this in an early Pandaw brochure, and received a sharp note from the secretary of the R&A declaring that there was no such connection. After an enjoyable ride one day in pony traps out from the river port to the golf club, under the shady rain trees[35] that line the roads, marvelling at the well-kept greens and pleasing fairways, we spotted a chain gang of prisoners in white longyis[36] and shirts with their rakes and hoes, the greenkeepers of Thayetmyo.

Colonial merchants' houses in Thayetmyo, 1990s.

It was to Thayetmyo that the earliest IFC services ran, connecting with the seagoing services to bring mail up to the troops and supply them with provisions and munitions. It was from Thayetmyo that the Third Anglo-Burmese war of 1885 was launched, and it was here that the great flotilla assembled with its troopships and gunships firing broadsides, not to mention floating stables, hospitals and all else amphibiously borne in a near-bloodless invasion.

Half a day's sail upriver and we reach the Burmese royal frontier, with its imposing forts at Gwechaung on the east bank and Minhla on the west bank. These were the state-of-the-art constructions designed by King Mindon's Italian military engineers, but which turned out to prove fairly useless in the event of troops coming up from the rear and surprising them, as happened at Gwechaung. The Battle of the Minhla

---

35   *Samanea saman*, called rain trees because their leaves fold up just before rainfall
36   the Burmese equivalent of the Malaysian sarong

Thayetmyo Golf Club; note its affiliation!

Redoubt was the only serious action of the war, with one British casualty and a number of Burmese who had heroically made their stand. Gwechaung is well worth the walk up, and is really quite impressive with its deep magazines and star-shaped gun emplacements commanding a marvellous view up and down the Irrawaddy valley.

After seizing Upper Burma with barely a shot fired and sending the royal family into exile, the British discovered they had a problem on their hands. Whilst their military planning had been impeccable, their political planning turned out to be a disaster: Upper Burma very quickly collapsed into the hands of dacoits and warlords; pretender princes flourished and commanding guerrilla armies formed from remnants of the royal army; former ministers were reinstated by the British under Commissioner Bernard, but were powerless to control the ensuing anarchy. Only in 1890, after several years of military policing supported by over 40,000 Indian troops often stationed in posts only 15 miles apart throughout the country, was the rebellion contained.

The river bank at Thayetmyo; boats and pagodas everywhere.

Whilst Thibaw, or at least his ministers, may have been disliked by the populace, the British had miscalculated the symbolic importance of the king and his court. A Burmese king's primary role was the defence and propagation of Buddhism; compared with this, all other matters, such as foreign affairs and trade, would pale into insignificance. So Thibaw's years of misrule were soon forgotten in the spiritual vacuum into which Burma had fallen. Without that symbol, all order collapsed. Some of the rebels were dacoits onto a good thing, while others were militant monks saving their religion, and others proto-nationalists, piqued that they had suddenly found themselves living in a province of India.

In its first year the pacification cost more than the actual war, and costs were to double the year after. Ironically, far more people were executed during the pacification, whether in palace purges or settling scores in the districts, than had lost their lives to the vagaries of Thibaw's henchmen. Yet the restoration of human rights, high on the British agenda, had been part of the moral argument used to justify the annexation. Admittedly, the distinction between dacoits raping and pillaging their own people and patriotic freedom fighters may have been blurred.

After five years of mayhem there was a move amongst the more educated Burmese – former bureaucrats, merchants and senior monks – towards cooperating with the British administration. However, in some regions, such as the Kachin country, the rebellion continued through the 1890s, and had even out of sympathy spread across British Lower Burma, where the Karen were called up to protect British interests.

Despite this anarchy, what the British found in Upper Burma was a developed state with proper institutions and a legal framework. Burma was not like Afghanistan, where the British had met with similar challenges not long before. Here in Burma was a highly educated people, arguably with a higher rate of literacy than in most of Europe, with proper institutions of government. There was a *hluttaw* or parliament, *wungyi* or ministers, a judiciary, and a national revenue-collection system, all marks of a developed state that had transcended feudalism. There was also a functional system of regional administration. The weakness of the Burmese state lay in the system of individual monarchs who, if strong personalities like King Bodawpaya of Mingun Pagoda fame, might become megalomaniacs, or if of a feeble character might be dominated by palace cliques (or, in the case of King Thibaw, an alliance formed between his chief queen, Supayalat, and certain ministers). Furthermore, in any reign there was a prevalent sense of insecurity; even a strong, respected king like Mindon was vulnerable to palace plots, coup attempts and armed rebellions. Thus, each reign began with the ritualised extermination of siblings and other possible rival claimants, as when Thibaw had his 80 siblings bludgeoned to death in velvet sacks, and successive purges continued through his reign as paranoia took hold of his domineering queen. Indeed, despite his position of authority, his father Mindon would not even name an heir for fear that he would not have the patience to wait for his death.

Commissioner Bernard was succeeded by Sir Charles Crosthwaite in 1887 who undertook the reform of the country's administration in the wake of the rising when many of the *myothugyi*, headmen, had sided with the rebels. Crosthwaite introduced a new system of village headmen who were responsible for tax collection, policing and justice. This innovation was to radically change the way in which the rural areas were administered.

Much of cultivable Upper Burma consisted of royal lands divided into *ahmudan*, estates occupied by people who owed the crown service; thus army regiments would maintain themselves from the revenue of an estate, as would senior officials, or the descendants of courtiers who had been granted these estates. In the latter case, you might find after several generations the entire population a village belonging to such an extended family descended from a single courtier and the land divided up between individual households. Monasteries also had estates, the revenue again being used to support them, and worked by hereditarily bonded pagoda slaves.

Outside the core royal lands were administrative areas called *athi* from where taxes were collected and troops drafted in times of war. These were administered by a myo-thugyi, whose role was often hereditary. Anyone who developed new land would by rights be able to claim it as their own, so in the core lands there was little concept of land ownership with an attached monetary value. Land was held in common by groups and there was no hereditary aristocracy. Members of the royal household might be made a *myo-sa*, town eater, as governors were known, but for life only. Courtiers could be drawn from all walks of life and were promoted on the basis of scholarship, so were more akin to the Chinese mandarin. Many of the most talented came from rural villages, rising up through monastic schools, educated in philosophy and poetry; they were men who attained high office on the basis of scholarly attainment. On our river journey we encounter numerous splendid, lavishly endowed village monasteries offered by sons of these villages who had risen high in government. They employed court artists and artisans skilled in the latest styles to build these dazzling schemes in their home villages.

This was all very different from India or indeed Britain, where the most cultivable land remained in the ownership of a hereditary aristocracy. Indeed, the absence of such an aristocracy made Burma a very different sort of place from anything the British had previously encountered in their imperial mission. There was no caste system like that in India, and, as many an Irrawaddy traveller noted on the decks of the Irrawaddy steamer, everyone chatted and interacted with each other on equal terms regardless of status or wealth. Ashore in a riverside village, Raven-Hart was spellbound by the dazzling elegance of a young lady in her silks and rubies. She then disappeared into a hovel, and Raven-Hart realised that in Burma where you lived mattered not; rather it was *how* you lived. It is much the same in Burma today, which is why it is such a great place to be. Everyone is gregarious and there is a distinct lack of pomposity, even amongst high officials, rich traders and powerful monks. Norman Lewis noted this on his tour of 1952 after an audience with a Shan *sawbwa*, hereditary prince: 'I must confess a preference for the easy-going affability of the Burmese notables by comparison with the well-bred Shan aloofness.' I have known impoverished old couples rattling around in great mansions and busy millionaires thriving in the domestic squalor of a shophouse. This has changed now, with a new rich, crony class living in the suburban mansions of Rangoon and Mandalay, but out in the villages of Burma that happy egalitarianism remains.

In addition to mass literacy, a meritocratic administrative class and the unimportance of land ownership, the other aspect of Burma the British found that was very different to India – or, again, even Britain – was the role of women. Unlike in India there was no harem or seraglio, and women did not go around covering their faces, but rather revelled in their beauty, set off by silks and jewellery, the store of family wealth, ethereal and majestic. Then, as now, Burmese women had a considerable cultural and economic role. Most business was in the hands of women, something that may have originated from women being market stall holders but grew with the economy to include general trading and most wider aspects of business. Indeed, to hold a market stall in any village is still a considerable sign of status, a place where the women sit all day in their finery chatting, playing cards, indulging in business speculations far beyond the front of selling of fish paste or betel nut.

A business might be fronted by the man of the house, but the decision making was done from within. Widows or *a-pyo-gyi*, who might have been consigned to the fire in India, had the most important role of all, becoming matriarchal figures commanding dominion over extended networks of terrified male relatives. When a hereditary headman was under age or incapacitated, his mother or wife would happily conduct the town's business in an efficient manner, dispensing justice, collecting taxes and arranging public works. A strong personality like Queen Supayalat soon had her husband and his all-powerful ministers well under her thumb, and until recently another powerful lady was at the centre of all political life. As with the former Warsaw Pact countries, in Burma during the socialist years women were trained as engineers and electricians, and did a variety of jobs seen previously as the preserve of males; it was not unusual to see girls in hard hats and boiler suits up telegraph poles or popping out of access holes in the street. Sadly, that seems to have disappeared now, and women have reverted to a more traditional role of marketing and managing their domestic and national economy.

It is also interesting to remember that one of the central figures of the international women's movement of the 1930s, the forerunner of feminism and even the Me Too movement, was Daw Mya Sein, the first Burmese woman to go to Oxford University. She was Burma's representative for the League of Nations and the Geneva Women's Conference in 1931; a historian whose works remain key resources to this day. Daw Mya Sein moved easily in international circles, mixing with the European intellectual elite; when in London she would pop into 10 Downing Street for tea with Ramsay Macdonald, the prime minister, and she knew George Bernard Shaw and other great writers of the day. Daw Mya Sein was probably the most famous Burmese lady until the arrival of another Oxonian, Daw Aung San Suu Kyi. In 1930s London she was the face of Burma, raising awareness and interest in an otherwise little-known country, till then considered an appendage to India.

Magwe is the quintessential Middle Burma town, hot and dusty in summer, muddy in the monsoon, and cold to the point of crispness in winter. Your ship moors below towering banks, and highest of all is the venerable Myat-tha-lon Pagoda, which is constructed of gold bricks, or at least bricks coated in gold, rather than the flimsy gold leaf used on other pagodas. Here, resplendent, is the ineffable wealth of Burma – unspendable, unthievable, for who would dare either? The pagoda has always been a focus for mystics, and you will find an army of wizards, magicians, alchemists, fortune tellers and herbalists offering their services and wares at her *chinthé* (lion)-guarded, guardian gates. This is the real Burma, the magic Burma that Maurice Collis wrote of, comparing it with a classical arcadia where people cohabit with the spirits who live in trees and various nooks and crannies. These ethereal beings were visible to country folk untainted by modernity, and who regarded them with a neighbourly affection. Indeed, they would get along quite happily with them so long as steps were taken to placate the more difficult ones. It was here at Magwe that the IFC Airways discovered its lucrative sideline, the pilgrimage flights, each auspiciously circumnavigating the pagoda seven times.

The town is vibrant and bustling, the teashops full of men idling whilst their womenfolk are off at the market, the sidecars and pony traps having given way to mopeds and tuk-tuks making an infernal din. Burma, once so tranquil, is now a roar of traffic. Pop music blasting from the teashops competes with the chants of monks and interminable sermons by the great *sayadawgyi*, abbots, from Tannoy speakers strung up high in

Daw Mya Sein in London 1932 on her way to the Geneva Women's Conference.

the palms, set to repeat endlessly 24 hours, day and night, for the public's greater edification. One thinks wistfully of the black-outs and brown-outs in the days of erratic power supply – what peace!

It is in these big river towns that you can feel the great wealth of Burma. Not the rubies and jade, the copper and silver, and the oil and gas offshore and onshore – but the sheer scale of agricultural produce that shifts from a broad hinterland where bullocks still plough and many hands harvest, transported to the river, stacked in sacks and bales on trusty bullock carts, carried down the banks on the backs of stevedores and up wobbly gangplanks into the holds of the thousands of ships that will carry this bounty south to the seaports and onward to foreign shores. It is India that now, in the 21st century, is the main buyer of Burma's groundnuts.

Sailing on, up, deeper into Middle Burma, we see farmland giving way to desert, and we enter the *Tattadesa*, Parched Land, as described in 11th-century Mon epigraphy. The land is rocky; only scrub and cacti grow here, and it seems unlikely that it would have yielded much in the way of a living. But Burma being Burma, it did. We are now in Yenanchaung, Smelly Water Creek, and that smelly water was crude oil. These were the oilfields of Burma, stretching north to Chauk. In the 1900s over 50 per cent of the world's oil came from here, and yet another of those sobriquets like 'Rangoon, the pearl of the orient' or 'Burma, the rice bowl of Asia' was applied this time: 'Burma, the petrol pump of Asia'.

The largest producer of oil was the Burmah Oil Company, founded by David Sime Cargill in Glasgow in 1886. Cargill, the son of a Montrose farmer, was born in 1826 and had made his fortune in Ceylon with the department stores bearing his name and known as the Harrods of the East, which have continued to flourish there. Having invested in the Rangoon Oil Company – yet another of our friend James Galbraith's many ventures – Cargill visited Rangoon in 1874 and formed an association with the Glaswegian Kirkman Finlay, who had realised the potential for oil in Burma. Buying out Galbraith in the failing Rangoon Oil Company, Cargill persevered for another ten years, losing money but not optimism.

Following the 1886 annexation of Burma by the British, the Rangoon Oil Company, renamed Burmah Oil, secured the rights to purchase oil produced in the Yenanchaung area by *htwinza*, local families with a concession to drill, usually by hand, for oil. Cargill was careful to protect their rights in a sort of compassionate colonialism. But later the company started buying out these concessions, and American drillers – mainly Texans who had had originally been Ulster Scots – were brought in in some number. The Texans in turn trained young Scottish drillers and engineers. The American presence in Yenanchaung was maintained right up till the evacuation in 1942, and there was even an American Club in Yenanchaung, which must have been interesting. The Middle Burma desert remains dotted with nodding donkey oil rigs, their technology dating from about 1900, and at one time there were even drilling rigs in the middle of the river, or at least scattered across the sands; but those are long gone now, washed away by a river that takes no prisoners.

Burmah Oil, or BOC as it was known in Burma at that time, was the first ever global oil company, and was later to develop the oil fields of Iran, forming the Anglo-Persian Oil Company. It was through the Burma connection that many Scots became oilmen working all over the world, and this continues, with an oil services hub in Aberdeen. Burmah Oil merged with Castrol in 1966, and in 2000 the company was absorbed by BP. I am old enough to remember Burmah petrol stations all over Scotland.

The Irrawaddy Flotilla operated a fleet of river tankers and tanker flats to transport the oil down to the refinery that BOC had built on Syriam island, close to Rangoon. However, the flotilla lost this business in 1909, when BOC constructed a 300-mile pipeline connecting the fields with the refinery. BOC also operated a fleet of seagoing tankers that could go alongside at Syriam to take on oil. When the great power and wealth of this company is considered, along with the three other pillars of the Scottish commercial establishment – the IFC, Steel Brothers and the Bombay-Burmah, with their city directors and all their influence back in Glasgow and London – it is no surprise that the more liberal-minded administrators, keen to advance the Burmese cause, were held back.

In 1942, all this quite literally went up in smoke. From the great refinery at Syriam to the individual wells, all was put to the torch to deny them to the Japanese. A pall of thick black smoke hung over Middle Burma for months on end. Then after the war oil production never regained its former peak. In 1963 BOC in Burma was nationalised, and thereafter investment dwindled, along with the oil reserves; technology did not keep pace to drill deeper down. Today, the main production is natural gas from a deposit that runs beneath the river for 100 miles or so; the gas is used to power several power stations built up and down the river in the 1970s and 1980s by John Brown of Clydebank. It is curious to think that flowing beneath the Irrawaddy there is literally a river of gas, which was harnessed by Scottish expertise in the 1970s and 1980s just as the oil fields were 100 years earlier.

Logo of the Burmah Oil Company, once a familiar sight at petrol stations all over the UK.

Whilst at Magwe, you could pop over the

bridge to see the mud volcanoes at Minbu that make rather cheeky flatulent noises, and can be quite smelly too. Inland, passing the nodding donkeys still nodding as you drive through jagged crags and prickly cacti, there is this strange feeling you are motoring through Texan backwaters.

Once you are past the new bridge at Chauk you will find the river changes character again. From a well-ordered decent-flowing deep stream, it fans out into a wilderness of uncharted islands and sands in places where there can be several miles from one bank to the other. This continues for the next 50 miles or so past the Chindwin confluence, before the river starts behaving herself again on the final run between Myinmu and Mandalay. Little farms pop up on the islands where fisherfolk, trying their hand at nuts and beans to supplement their meagre incomes, retreat inland with the great rise in May or June, when those islands vanish again. Other, larger, islands such as Thi-ri-kyun have static populations with the houses perched high on stilts, and mounds for their cattle to retreat to when the waters advance. It is unsurprising that this region of middle Burma is known as the Dry Zone, for outside of the monsoon season it is like desert, the soil a sandy silt, fields shaded by thorny acacias with hedgerows of prickly cacti. Toddy palms – nature's great gift to humans – rise loftily above, and before the pressures of material demand one family was happily able to live off a small stand of such trees. The fronds provided building materials, the fruit food, the sap alcohol and jaggery – a sugar lump rather like a tablet. I love the Dry Zone, and will often set off across the fields walking for hours across the countryside exhilarated by the sheer aridity of it, with piercing blue skies above and mountain ranges framing the landscape to the east and west.

First stop on this section of the river must be the village of Pakhan-nge. This was an important centre of patronage for the wealthy cotton merchants of Salay in the early 20th century. Pakhan-nge had always been important as a spiritual centre, and its earliest monuments date from the late Pagan period, in the 13th century. In fact, these are the southernmost Pagan temples to survive. It is a mile or so's walk or cycle in from the riverbank, and well worth the foray. Nearly all the great teak monasteries are in a state of dereliction, with the occasional hermit monk occupying a chamber or wing that has not yet collapsed. Brick temples with splendid archways and painted narratives along the covered hallways fragment before your eyes as the banyans ensconce themselves. There is no greater testimony to Buddhist notions of impermanence than Pakhan-nge. The rich cotton barons of Salay reaping their rewards on higher planes of existence for their bountiful acts of merit have not been replaced, and post-independence, with collectivisation and a collapse in the cotton trade, new patrons have not emerged. It is Pakhan-nge's forsakenness that makes it so alluring.

And so on to Salay, just an hour or so upriver depending on which way the chan-

Wood carving at the Salay Yokesone Kyaung.

Surviving fragments of teak monastery complexes at Pakhan-nge.

nels have decided to turn. Salay is famed in Burmese literary history as the home of the poet and playwright U Ponnya, born in 1812 and often called the Shakespeare of Burma. In the 1850s he rose to become one of King Mindon's court poets, and received titles and estates in the Salay area. However, he later became involved in political intrigue and was murdered by a *myowun*, senior court official, loyal to the crown. An unhappy King Mindon, desolate at the loss of his favourite poet, described this act as a 'dog killing man'.

There are many splendid sanctuaries within the town area, mainly from the late 19th century and built in that happy mix of colonial classical adorned with florid Burmese stucco. Earlier than these is the splendid Yokesone Kyaung, an elaborate wood-carved monastery dating to 1882, just three years before the final annexation by the British. Standing on 153 teak posts, each a single tree trunk a metre thick, this is one of the finest surviving teak monasteries from the Konbaung dynasty – far better than anything to be found in Mandalay – and it is embellished with highly elaborate wood carvings in high relief that tell the tales of the Lord Buddha's *jataka*, former lives. In the museum attached to the monastery, amongst the statuary and ritual objects assembled here, are some of U Ponnya's original manuscripts.

Salay was a cotton centre long before the British arrived, and the harvested cotton, packed in great white bales, made its way upriver on country boats rowed, or towed from the bank, or at certain times of year under sail, all the way to Bhamo to be transferred to the backs of mules headed for China. With the establishment of IFC services to Bhamo in the 1870s, far larger shipments could be made and far faster: Salay boomed. This is evident not just in the extravagant works of merit we have just visited at Pakhan-nge but in the splendid mansions once occupied by Salay's cotton barons. In the town centre there are over 50 surviving mansions from the late 19th and early 20th centuries. They have something of the feel

Steelwork used on balconies at Salay, made by Cowie of Glasgow.

of New Orleans, with loggias running along at street level and verandas above. Much of the original filigree cast-iron work survives on these, and on close examination you will see they are stamped with the mark of Cowie of Glasgow, so they would of course have been carried upstream on the ships of the Irrawaddy Flotilla. One of the most splendid is the house of U Bo Kyi, where his descendants still live. He had two such houses, one for each wife and family, as according to Buddhist law the families had to be housed in separate but similar conditions. Clearly a rich man, U Bo Kyi was one of Salay's great cotton barons, and no doubt one of the many donors who embellished the sacred grounds of Pakhan-nge. Thankfully a number of local people have realised the importance of Salay, which is but a day trip from Pagan; the former tourist guide Daw Khine Win has, for example, created a lovely boutique hotel out of one of the riverside mansions. Salay House itself is part-museum, filled with memorabilia from Salay's heyday, and part-hotel. Another house has been converted into a stylish café, and Salay's potential for a smarter, sympathetic sort of tourism is huge.

Typical merchant's house at Salay; nearly 50 remain to this day.

Back on board, we cast off and sail on upstream. On our left, the west bank becomes even more barren, and steep jagged hills rise, culminating in the great holy mountain of Tan Chi Taung, which looks eastwards across several miles of river – a deep blue sea in the monsoon and a shimmering desert of glimmering white sands in the summer – to the plain of Pagan with its dazzling spires shimmering in the heat. It is here in the heart of Burma that the two great spiritual centres of Mount Popa and Pagan stand, just 20 miles apart. At just under 5,000 feet (1518 metres), Popa towers over the Irrawaddy valley and can be seen from every direction.

Mount Popa is often called the Mount Olympus of Burma, the seat of the gods – but actually the nats, gods, are everywhere – up every tree, in houses and barns, in springs and wells, and on every hill. On ships there is an engine room nat, and on the rivers various nats hold sway, commanding the currents and the destinies of the ships and their cargoes. The nats are a reflection of a people living in complete harmony with the natural world around them, in which everything is endowed with spiritual life and has a sentient existence of its own. The moment people enter a monetised economy and start getting televisions and smartphones and can travel around on mopeds, all this will go, as it has gone now throughout much of Burma due to the rapid transition to modernity of the 2010s.

Back in the 1920s, Maurice Collis observed the uniqueness of living in a world akin to that of ancient arcadia, a world where man (*sic*) and spirit could jostle together in harmony, and people could actually see a nat living up a tree. Collis assumed that he was observing the last throes of something very ancient, yet when I first went to Burma in the 1980s this was still the case, due to Burma having been locked in time for 50 years by the isolationism of General Ne Win and then the sanctions that Daw Aung San Suu Kyi had called for. On Popa there still resided the royalty amongst the nats: the Mahagiri Min, Lords of the Great Mountain. There are two Mahagiri nats, brother Maung Tin De and sister Ma Dway Hla. Her formal title is *Hnamadawgyi*, Great Royal Sister of the Mahagiri, and many of her devotees claim her as Mahagiri.

How the two came to preside over Mount Popa is a curious tale. They were from Prome in the south, where Maung Tin De was a blacksmith famed across the land for his strength. The King of Tagaung, far to the north, became jealous of his strength and plotted his murder. Maung Tin De got wind of this plan and ran away to hide in the forest. The king then married his sister and invited him to his capital, offering him a governorship. Maung Tin De arrived at Tagaung but was seized and tied to a tree trunk and set on fire. Ma Dway Hla, now queen, threw herself on the flames, and the king, now deeply in love with her and trying to pull her from the flames, was left holding her golden mask. For this reason, she is known as *Shwe Myet Hna*, Golden Mask. From then on, the brother and sister haunted a tree near where they had died, and any man or beast that came near it died mysteriously. So the king had the tree cut down and thrown in the river; it flowed down to Pagan, whose king was at war with Tagaung. The Pagan king had a dream in which he was directed by the nats to rescue the log; he did this, and cutting two four-foot lengths from it had images of the brother and sister carved and enshrined at Popa.

The premier nat is Thagya Min, or Indra, presiding over the national pantheon of 36 other nats. Thagya derives from Hindu cosmology, and Mount Popa takes on the hue of Mount Meru, the abode of the 37 principal Hindu gods. (There are other nats that come from Hinduism, such as Mahapenni, the Burmese Ganesha, but they are outside the royal pantheon.) All of the 37, like the two Mahagiri nats, suffered early deaths as a result of misfortune, sometimes from diseases such as dysentery or malaria, or from alcoholism, grief or misrule. Here in a nutshell is the Burmese condition: tropical maladies and a collapse into depression and addiction in the face of the monstrous injustice of government, not to mention an unfair and nasty early death at its hands. It is these victims, raised to the status of gods, who alone have the compassion and understanding to help steer mere mortals through a troubled world of evil government.

There is reference in colonial writings to serpent dancers living high on the mountain's slopes, writhing in ecstasy with their pythons and cobras to wild music, possessed by nats. Sadly, they seem to have moved on, and in my walks around the mountain I have found no traces of them. The *taung-lay*, Little Mount Popa, an ugly plug of rock on the south-east side of the main mountain, is the centre of today's cult. It is grubby and unpleasant with touts and thieving monkeys; a general sense of tackiness pervades. Yet it is here that people flock to from all over for the great Mahagiri festivals on the full moon of Nadaw (December) and the 9th to 13th days of the waning moon of Wagaung (August). On these occasions the little mountain resounds to multiple *nat-pwe*, a cyclical drama over several days and nights when each of the 37 is propitiated by *nat-gadaw*, nat brides. These are mediums, generally either old ladies or transvestites, and they perform as each nat, with its own dances and rituals, often for hours on end. These are wonderful occasions, when all the general wackiness of Burmese culture and life comes together. My favourite is the alcoholic nat U Min Kyaw, and when the medium is possessed, he or she will consume several bottles of rum, not to mention loads of cigarettes, and then, after writhing in a wild Bacchanalistic dance for several hours, snap out of it dead cold sober. In the Burmese nat cults you have a colourful cocktail of animism, shamanism and even voodoo all in one. It is the antidote to Buddhism, which in Burma takes the form of a dull, uneventful sort of religion. Its monks are forever being defrocked by the official monk police for embracing these cults too enthusiastically, and they end up as high priests of the cult, living in splendidly endowed shrines outwith the Buddhist mainstream.

The real Popa is well worth a climb, and there is a good path all the way. You can see a great crater with the north side collapsed to form a corrie. From the summit all Middle Burma lies before you, upriver and down, the Arakan *yoma* to the west and the Shan plateau to the east. There is an extensive artificial lake to the south, on the Kyaukpadaung side. It's really worth the effort. Thickly wooded, in these slightly cooler altitudes, the slopes have an abundance of flora, and it is here that rare herbs are gathered for mixing into traditional Burmese medicines. The air is good here, perhaps from the combination of so many balm-laden and healing plants and the cool after the heat and dust of the surrounding plain. The monkeys are better behaved up here than their spoilt cousins at the taung-lay, and shy spotted deer lurk in the glades. The villages around the foothills are hives of farming activity, and to trek through them is a delight. One time we were called into a monastery by a friendly monk to share a juicy watermelon with him. I asked if he was from Popa originally, but no, he was from Rangoon and had come for a weekend 20 years ago and never left! A couple of very good hotels have been built at Popa, and a golf course too.

Back on the river, the villages on the east bank from here up to the Pakokku area are very poor, as there is little that can be grown on this side. Huts huddle in shady creeks that break through the grey rock of these lifeless hills. Yet the ever-industrious Burmese have profited from a mix of hard work and cunning enterprise by hand-drilling 100 feet or so through down through the rock to find crude oil bubbling up. This was just what had been found at Yenanchaung by its *htwinza* people back in the 1870s. Nothing has changed. The oil is gathered in buckets and taken home to be refined on the kitchen fire, producing petrol and diesel. The local people have done so well with this that in one of the villages (which will remain nameless as such operations are illegal), when we set up one of our Pandaw Clinics to provide basic medical care to village people who otherwise would have no access to any form of healthcare, the local people rallied around and raised the money for its construction. This had never happened before in other villages.

On the approach to Pagan the river sprawls, miles wide. But in the dry season your vessel meanders through a transient archipelago of shimmering white sands with hazy horizons as if fumblingly lost in a desert mirage. Then round a great 90-degree turn, is the Tan Chi Taung mountain again, with its gilded summit pagodas twinkling in the sun, standing proud on the yoma to the west – and there is Pagan before you.

9

Royal Burma

As your steamer rounds the bend below the Tan Chi Taung mountain, you will see from the deck of your ship the great temples of Pagan soaring high. For the next few days on the river, you will pass five former capitals of the country. This is the heart of Burma, distant from the sea and the world beyond, but at the confluence of river routes descending from India and China. This part of Buddhist Burma remains its spiritual centre, and despite political and economic power moving south with the British and remaining there after independence, the great monastic centres and continuing traditions of artistic patronage continue to flourish here. Pagan is the oldest of these capitals, having consolidated control of the Irrawaddy valley from the 11th to the 13th centuries; then there was Sagaing in the 13th century; Ava in the 16th; Amarapura in the 19th; and finally Mandalay, from 1857 to 1885.

Cargo boat beneath the Tan-chi-taung monastery, across the river from Pagan.

Pagan at dusk.

There are about 2,000 temples at Pagan still standing – and four times as many which have been lost. The highpoint of Pagan architecture was in the 12th century, when the Pagan builder developed the pointed arch and clever systems to carry great loads whilst the builders of the great European cathedrals were doing the same thing. Pagan was the first truly great Burmese city. Prior to her ascendency, the early Burmese civilisations of the Irrawaddy valley had been small city-states ringed by walls to protect them from a hostile world beyond, but at Pagan many Burmese were able to live outside the city walls in urban villages, made up mainly of craftsmen employed in temple construction and maintenance. Whilst being a declaration of Burmese hegemony over the Irrawaddy valley, the creation of Pagan was an international effort. Indian monks, scholars, architects and craftsmen had arrived in numbers to take advantage of the Burmese king's patronage at a time when Buddhism in India was declining in the face of Moslem conquest and Hindu militancy. The Mon language was used for the narration of paintings in the temples, eventually to be surpassed by Old Burmese as it developed a script of its own. When it comes to art – whether the crisp stucco decoration on the temples, the great programmes of mural painting and sculpture within these temples, or the exquisite bronze figures that may be seen in the museum there – the Pagan period represented the high point of art in Burma, and nothing subsequent has surpassed it in terms of quality or beauty.

Perhaps Marco Polo was the first European visitor to Pagan, accompanying Kublai Khan's occupation of the Irrawaddy valley in 1278. If he didn't actually travel there, he would have learnt of it from his Mongol hosts, and in his *Travels* he described Pagan quite accurately, writing of 'little gilded bells that tinkled every time the wind blew through them'. Later, Portuguese mercenaries would have passed through, campaigning up and down the Irrawaddy valley. The early British envoys were dismissive, but in 1855 a Scot, one Henry Yule of the Bengal Engineers, accompanying Sir Arthur Phayre's mission to the Court of Ava, stopped off and together with Sir Arthur explored the monuments, later writing 'Pagan surprised us all. None of the preceding visitors to Ava had prepared us for remains of such importance and interest'. Yule made the first known drawings of the temples, and published them in his book on the mission.

Soon after this, weekly steamer services were established between Rangoon, capital of British Burma, and Mandalay, the new capital of Royal Burma. Nyaung-U was the main port for the Pagan area, with a steamer ghaut just where we tie up today. As in Bhamo, the IFC agency at Nyaung-U effectively became the tourist information office, the agent dispensing information, arranging guides and pony traps to take visitors seeking entertainment for a few hours while their ship loaded or unloaded cargo on its way to Mandalay. The only place for a foreigner to stay then was the Circuit House and I do not think there was a proper hotel there till the 1970s when the state-owned Thiripyitsaya Hotel opened.

I first visited in 1981 and then, apart from the ravages of the terrible 1975 earthquake, the site had clearly changed little since the time of Yule, and I was fortunate to spend a whole year there in 1987 as a graduate student studying its architectural history. But today, in the 21st century, Pagan bears little resemblance to the Pagan I knew in the 1980s. The reason for this visual transformation is that the military junta that came to power in 1988, known by the sinister-sounding acronym SLORC, embarked on a transformation of the site. First, it rebuilt nearly every monument using modern brick and cement in dubious interpretations of their original forms, sometimes verging on fantasy. Across the land, the military extorted 'donations' from people to pay for building materials from factories owned by the military to be used by military-owned contractors. In other words, it was a racket in the name of restoring the ruins to their former glory. Secondly, they turned Pagan green, by covering the area with trees, and there were draconian punishments for anyone who cut a tree down. Pagan went from being near-desert to near-woodlands and, laudable as this is in today's world, it completely altered the once open vista from which the monuments, larger and lesser, had so spectacularly risen from the empty sands. Thirdly, the military forcibly relocated the local community from a picturesque long-established village, well integrated into the archaeological area – and indeed one of its attractions – to a soulless new town some miles to the south. Finally, the military went silly building roads everywhere, including an ugly dual carriageway which ran straight through the heart of the site.

Despite these depredations I still like Pagan, perhaps because the people are witty and warm-hearted, and my 40-year association means that they regard me as one of them. When running Pandaw, we had our headquarters in an old Nyaung-U shop-house, and my wife Roser and I had a flat above the office. We would often rise early to mountain-bike across the plain, keeping off the roads and on the cart tracks. In the villages around Pagan not much has changed since Yule's time, with tourism having had little impact or benefit to the village people, other than the occasional minimal hotel wage coming in.

By the second decade of the 21st century new horrors had befallen Pagan. As, quite rightly, new hotels may not be built within the 30 square mile archaeological zone, new hotel zones have opened on the roads leading out of Pagan on the north and south sides. Identikit hotels with kidney-shaped pools and chalet-style rooms, like motels lining an American interstate, are strung out along these roads for miles. They are there in anticipation of a mass tourism influx that mercifully has yet to come. The bonanza of course would be hordes of visitors from mainland China, but so far there are neither the flights nor indeed the airports to handle this market in Pagan, and we have been spared.

Even so, going round the larger monuments such as the Dhammayangyi or Sulam-ani temples can now be a trying experience, with ranks of coaches outside them spew-ing diesel smog, guides with megaphones, touts everywhere and pestilent children trying to interest you in trinkets for sale. In fact, most of the tourism Pagan gets now is domestic, in the form of coach parties coming up from Rangoon; with its passen-gers nibbling away together in unison, a coach's path might be traced from the trail of sweetie papers and plastic wrappings ejected from the windows. Sometimes one is ankle-deep in throwaway plastic. Plastic pollution has become one of the greatest problems across Burma, yet is something that no one there seems to understand or recognise. It's a far cry from the 1980s and 1990s when I would prop my bicycle up against a pillar, not bothering to lock it, and be the only person wandering around within a great temple and not a sweetie paper in sight. However, it is still possible, using a bicycle or ebike, to get off the track at Pagan and be alone amongst great art, despite the taint of SLORC's corrupting hand.

How Burmese is Pagan? Up till the 11th century the early Burmans had no script of their own and relied on the Mon and Pyu writing systems. Portable images in bronze or stone were brought back after conquests of the Pyu in middle Burma and the Mon in the deltaic south. Statuary even crossed the sea from India and Ceylon, carried by sailors, traders and monks. As Pagan grew from city state to kingdom and then empire spanning the length of the Irrawaddy and absorbing all peoples and states within that reach, wealth accumulated and patronage increased. As with Burma today, surplus wealth was expended on religious works – whether feeding monks, or building and fitting out monasteries, or building temples. Despite SLORC's architectural meddling, these monuments can be profoundly beautiful and stir one to thoughts of how quintessentially Burmese they are in their aesthetic.

How ironic it is that with the collapse of Buddhism in 12th-century India in the face of the Muslim conquests of North India and the establishment of the Delhi sultanate in 1206, Buddhist monks, scholars, artists and, most importantly, architects took refuge in the then racially tolerant, multi-cultural, Burmese empire at Pagan. A few years ago, a visit to the great monastery of Nalanda in Bihar state brought home to me the fact that the glory of Pagan, which is its immaculate tile-brick work, comes from there. Indeed, Burmese brick monasteries at Pagan are still known as *kala-kyaung*, Indian monasteries. Is this because the monk was Indian, or the builder? Perhaps both. To this day many of the villagers around Pagan are darker and have slightly hooked noses, betraying sub-continental ancestry, as some of its villages would have been entirely made up of Indian craftsmen. The British were certainly not the first to bring the Indians in.

The architects and craftsmen that had come over from India rapidly grasped the spiritual aspiration of the Pagan kings and donor class. The English scholar who deciphered early Burmese epigraphy in its architectural context, G.H. Luce, was to describe the sentiment as one of aspiration of the spirit expressed in an architecture that reached to the heavens with soaring spires supported by complex systems of gothic-style arches, vaults and buttressing. This was not unlike what was happening during the same period in Europe with the emergence of high gothic architecture. A temple like the Dhamma-yan-gyi, built in around 1170 but never finished, is said to contain a billion bricks, whilst the lofty That-byin-nyu rises 66 metres, 10 metres higher than the Hagia Sophia, and about the same height as the contemporary Cluny Abbey, then the largest basilica in the world.

The moated and walled palace city was tucked in the north-west side of the site, taking advantage of a bend in the river. It is a small area, just a couple of square miles, and it would have been here that the king, court and main offices of the state resided. Beyond the gates, across about 30 square miles of plain, were scattered 10,000 or so brick monuments, great and small, not to mention myriad long-lost teak monasteries, halls and other religious structures built of wood. What is interesting is that most of the working population at Pagan were engaged in temple construction and decoration. In addition to the monastic communities, there were armies of pagoda slaves, usually people captured in time of war and relocated either to the temple or to its glebe lands. Thus, pagoda slaves might be based at Pagan to work in a sanctuary as sweepers, gardeners or whatever, or on often distant landed estates whose revenues would be used to maintain the foundation. In either case these slaves were bonded in perpetuity, and the institution of pagoda slavery was only abolished by the British in the 1920s.

Out of the multicultural commingling that was Pagan emerged a clearly defined Burmese culture, not just in terms of architecture but in language, literature, social organisation and hierarchy, legal systems, kingship and a bureaucratic state. This was to change little till the institutional disruption brought by the British in the late 19th century. Perhaps Pagan's greatest legacy to Burma was a religious one: the dominance of Theravada Buddhism. Before 1100, all types of Buddhism (Theravada, Mahayana, Tantra) had coexisted alongside various Hindu cults, not to mention the animism of the Tibeto-Burmese peoples who had migrated into the Irrawaddy from south-west China in the early centuries CE. It was a similar situation throughout the Buddhist world: in Cambodia at Angkor, Hinduism and Mahayana Buddhism merged into slightly sinister kingship cults producing its spectacular monuments. In Buddhist Indonesia the preference was for the Mahayana, the supreme expression of which was the great monument at Borobudur. Indeed in India itself, religious life had become a cocktail of cults, with a resurgence of militant Hinduism in response to the Muslim conquests, and a corresponding decline in the less martial Buddhist movement. Even in Ceylon, home of Theravada Buddhism, there was a little bit of everything. But then in 11th-century Pagan, King Kyansittha took it upon himself to 'purify' the religion, purging all cults and sects that were not mainstream Theravada, leading to the principal role of a Burmese king becoming that of the purifier of the religion,

What was left after Kyansittha's purification was an austere, some would say puritanical, religion, with little in the way of ritual, ceremony, music or costume, based around the endless recitation of the *tipitaka*, three baskets of scriptures, and the begging for and consumption of a mid-morning meal. This was quite boring for most Burmese and not very helpful when begging favours from the celestial world, so the cult of the nats resurged. The Burmese chronicles describe how Kyansittha had these gods rounded up and imprisoned in a shrine at the Shwezigon pagoda, where they can be seen to this day – though, alas, not the originals. But they did not stay in prison long, and nat shrines may be found everywhere in Burma.

Hindu gods and Mahayana deities were given new roles as protectors of the Buddha, and were no longer objects of worship in themselves. The exquisite Nan-hpaya temple with its stone carvings of Brahma was often cited as being a Hindu temple, but the Brahma figures were carved on columns around the central shrine that would have contained a Buddha image. The nats, who we met just downstream at their Olympian hideout at Mount Popa, became a side religion, co-existing with the official Theravada and providing all the ritual and magic, music and dance to give people some colour in their lives, and a number of gods who would be slightly more responsive than the Lord Buddha, long ago ascended to the ultimate extinction of *parinibbana*.

Thus in around 1100 a reformed Buddhism developed that has changed little to this day, the only disruption being in 1885 with the collapse of the monarchy, whose function was primarily religious. This continued up till the British interregnum, and even they had to set up a civil department office to regulate the order. Post-independence Burma's khaki kings have continued in this role.

Just a couple of hours' sail upstream, we arrive at Pakokku, once home to the Pakokku Thistle football team in the IFC football league. The river was bridged in 2012 with the longest bridge in Burma, and somewhat quaintly cars pay a toll based on their weight, resulting in much mirth when overweight passengers are gently turfed out of their vehicles as the weighbridge is approached. The Pakokku river port was a movable feast depending on water levels and the time of year. In high water a channel runs right by the town and the port is close to the centre. This channel will close and recede as waters fall and the port gets further and further away, much to the profit of the side-car and horse cart owners and the annoyance of ship owners, who must take a long route round. What joy and excitement the arrival of the Pandaw ship gives these side-car sayas. Parked in a long rank they would have been dozing in the passenger chairs, puffing on their cheroots or chewing a cud of betel nut, then our horn would blast and they would leap into a frenzy of excitement. We would place our passengers one to each side-car, and off they would go in a race, the locals running a sweepstake on who would win, larger passengers being given poorer odds. This was great fun, but one year a battle broke out between rival side-car gangs and we had to calm them by using horse carts for a time instead.

Pakokku superseded the ancient regional capital of Pakhangyi under the British in 1888 when the population was under 2,000. By the 1902 census it had risen to just under 20,000 and according to the 2014 census it has over 320,000 inhabitants. The rapid expansion of the town in late 19th century is attributable to the town's development as a port. Beyond Pakokku, the area between the Irrawaddy and Chindwin had been a wild, unpopulated scrub jungle prior to the arrival of the British, but it was soon transformed into the rich farmland found there today, in which groundnuts could be profitably grown. This transformation was a Burmese endeavour, the British providing a means of shipping in bulk and a ready export market, together with a cadastral system giving security of land tenure and a reasonably fair judicial system to settle disputes. There was little of the chicanery that went on in the delta lands with their Indian and Chinese moneylenders; most of the brokers and buyers based in burgeoning towns like Pakokku were Burmese merchants who amassed terrific wealth.

And what wealth! Take a trishaw around Pakokku and you will find a city of palace monasteries, great complexes of Burmese baroque mixed with Anglo-Indian classicism. Just like in Pagan in the 11th and 12th centuries, the donor class lavished their wealth on architectural treasures glorifying their faith rather than on the vanity of a home. At first glance, these treasures may be difficult to discern. The traffic is bad now with everyone buzzing about on mopeds, and it's terribly noisy. Worse still, some truly nasty modern buildings have sprung up around the main market, and there is so much dust it can be hard to see anything. But step back from the throng into the quieter monastic areas and you will find great treasure.

Not to be missed is the wood carved *te-ge*, reredos, at the Shwe-gu-gyi Pagoda. Do not be put off by the fairy lights and usual pagoda tat – look beyond this, through the grubby glass protective screen. Carved in three dimensions, in around 1900, this is one of three surviving works found across the country from a now nameless atelier, presumably in Mandalay. Its master had clearly reached the apogee of the wood carvers' art in Burma, or indeed anywhere. I can only think of two other examples of this master's art surviving, but each work must have taken several years to execute. Another high point of Pakokku's artistic heritage was the paintings by Saya Hsaing, the former court artist, in various *zayats*, pilgrim's rest houses, at Shwe-tan-tit, a village just upriver. Tragically these have been demolished, and all I have to show for his work are some rather poor photos of the Buddha on an IFC paddle-steamer.

Pakokku had been a great centre of Buddhist scholarship and its larger foundations, akin to colleges or universities. Copywriting for a travel brochure in the 1990s, I described the city, with its many splendid colleges about the town, as 'the Oxford of Burma'. The label stuck, and I now see it used in all sorts of literature.

The former regional capital of Pakhangyi is now less than an hour away on the much-improved Monywa road. It is situated strategically on high ground in the centre of the hinterland between the two rivers, and you can still see the moat and walls. This would have been the seat of a *myo-wun*, governor, and judging by the splendid teak monastery that has miraculously survived and was sensibly restored by the Archaeology Department, it was a place of some importance.

Back on board, with much-needed refreshments in hand as we lounge in our steamer chairs, we look forward to our next excitement: the great confluence between the Irrawaddy and Chindwin rivers. Here in the monsoon you can be literally lost at sea in an ocean, losing sight of the banks some 20 miles apart. In the hot season, though, it is more like a desert, and from a distance you will see great line ships seemingly gliding across the white shimmering sands when in fact they are navigating tight channels, weaving their way through the dunes. There are two main shipping channels through the confluence with the Chindwin. One was actually an ancient canal that had long silted up and in 1824 re-emerged during a particularly potent flood.

Tempting though the Chindwin is, we keep straight on, and continue up the Irrawaddy. On the east bank opposite the confluence is the important town of Myingyan, which was the counterpart to Pakokku on the west bank. Myingyan can sometimes be accessed by a tributary, the Myingyan river, but no one has ever been able to keep it open due to rapid silting. The IFC attempted to deploy groynes on the main river to redirect the current back up the tributary, but without much success. When I was there in the 1980s, goods had to be transported from the town's markets to the port by bullock cart down a couple of miles of pitted track that no motor vehicle could attempt. Given these difficulties in access, we will sail past Myingyan, and as the river narrows – and in fact becomes a river again – we pass long, fertile islands with farms and villages, and approach Sameikkon.

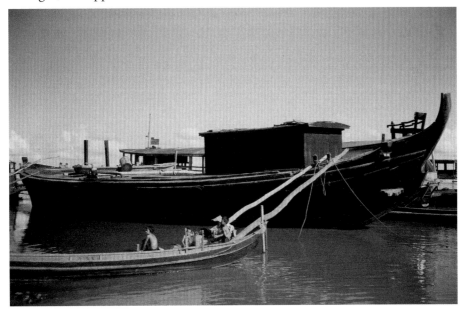

A traditional rice barge constructed entirely of teak.

Sameikkon, like Pakhangyi or Sale, is another of the river villages full of surprises. As you climb the riverbank and cross the adjacent fields you think it's just going to be another of those villages of bamboo and clapboard houses. Suddenly, though, you find yourself in a sort of stage-set of neoclassical houses with arched loggias, pedimented windows and pilastered walls, a tropical Verona. Everywhere the lion and unicorn emblazon entablatures. What are all these mansions doing here? It turns out that, again, during the golden age of Burmese farming even the lesser ports such as Sameikkon, a one-time riverine trading post, could produce a prosperous merchant class able to live in such style. Beyond the town, a wonderful ceremonial walkway crosses a riverbed that lies dry but for the occasional monsoon flash-flood. With teak piers capped with whitewashed stone copings the shape of lotus buds, this long bridge would enable the monks to collect alms from the rich townsfolk and return to their inland monasteries without the risk of muddying their feet. The hinterland beyond Sameikkon is a centre of brick-making; they are mud bricks dried in the sun and then shipped off on brick boats. We know from markings on the bricks of Pagan that many of the brick kilns were at sites far up- or downriver from the city. A favourite stop on any Sameikkon walk is the condensed milk factory where the mix of milk and sugar is heated in old British cast-iron bathtubs with little charcoal furnaces set beneath. Paddles are used to stir the gooey mixture in a sweet steamy cloud. Condensed milk is an essential component in syrupy Burmese tea.

The bridge at Sameikkon that links the village with the monastic area.

But things are changing for Sameikkon. A new industrial zone has been created in the rolling semi-desert to its east and south of Mandalay. Enormous factories have been built in this prickly, inhospitable landscape. Chinese entrepreneurs can now out-source their production to Burma, where workers are paid just $10 per day and live in the most appalling shanties close to these zones. A massive new river port has been built just below Sameikkon, to service this zone with containerised traffic. The singing stevedores are now silent, working on assembly lines.

On the east bank, we pass the village of Yandabo where the Yandabo Treaty was signed in 1826 between the British and Burmese after the First Anglo-Burmese War. This is also the site of our first Pandaw school, back in 1999 – but is not worth stopping at now, as multiple tour boats followed us there and the village is less virginal than it once was. On the west bank we pass Myinmu, famed for its bananas, with pretty waterfront houses, and then on to Sagaing, the second of our former capitals; it rose in the political vacuum of the 14th century following the political collapse of the Pagan empire and the occupation of the Irrawaddy valley by Shan tribes. It is generally recognised now that Kublai Khan did not sack Pagan so much as tax it following his incursion of 1278. The Mongols had moved on from the genocidal policy of Genghis Khan, whose plan had been to eliminate all agrarian civilisation and revert the land to steppe through the elimination of population; instead, Kublai was more interested in exacting tribute. However, the arrival here of the Mongols resulted in a political destabilisation; the king fled, and was known ever after as *tayok-pye*, 'the one who ran from the Chinese'.

The riverside at Sagaing, with the hills beyond.

China may have been ruled by the Mongols, but at the same time the Mongols had become sinicised. It would seem that with the political disorder the Pagan economic system based on temple construction and management had collapsed, and the

Water pots at Yandabo.

great estates endowed to maintain these sanctuaries had ceased producing revenue. Into this void the Shan poured in, most likely from south-west China in the wake of the Mongols and along the very route which the Burmese must have trodden a millennium earlier. It was the Shans, not yet converted to Buddhism, who would have sacked Pagan and ransacked the temples, and various Shan chieftains set up mini-kingdoms, one of which was at Sagaing in 1315 and lasted for 50 years.

Sagaing under the British became the administrative capital of a vast area covering most of the Chindwin valley, stretching from the Irrawaddy to the frontier with India.

It was probably more out of laziness than anything that they sited their capital here at the edge of the district rather than at its natural centre at Monywa. Maurice Collis was a magistrate here in the 1920s and spent his afternoons walking out from his bungalow shooting jungle fowl in the surrounding countryside. Sagaing had clearly changed little from Collis's time when I used to visit in the 1980s, collecting the permits necessary to enable my first Chindwin journey in 1986; it was just a string of wooden administrative buildings dating from around 1900 and not much else. I would sit in creaky offices, surrounded by tower blocks of pink-ribboned files half-eaten by termites, and discuss Kierkegaard with a scholar-mandarin.

The main Sagaing town today sits on the west bank where the bridges make landfall. The original Ava bridge, with a single-track railway running down its middle flanked by car roads, was rebuilt after its demolition in the war, and the new bridge is adjacent. The town is not very interesting, but the Sagaing hills that run from the edge of the town for several miles along the river side northwards are full of wonder. Ignore the advice of guides and guidebooks, and head off into the hills away from the tourist traps. Many a pleasant morning can be spent wandering in these pagoda-tipped hills. There are several hundred active monasteries and nunneries clinging to the steep slopes below or straddling the ravines in groves of magnolia trees. The best time to visit is when the magnolia trees are in bloom in the dry season, between February and April. Sagaing is a particular centre of the women's Buddhist movement dating from the late 19th century when the female order of nuns was revived. The nuns, who range from child novices to venerable abbesses, wear pink robes and, like the monks, have shaven heads. It's a sight to see them forming their alms-gathering processions about the town, sometimes in their hundreds. Most of the whitewashed sanctuaries and religious houses date from the beginning of the 20th century, built in the Indo-Burmese style in which colonial classical meets with Burmese rococo to form something very pleasing. This abundance of dedication reflects the newfound wealth of the Mandalay merchant class; every successful family would have built its own *kyaung*, temple, at Sagaing in the latest style to visit on holy days, to feast first the sacred incumbents and then themselves – a sort of holiday villa on the banks of the Irrawaddy filled with pet monks or nuns for edification and accumulation of merit.

Many of the river cruise ships now moor along the Sagaing riverbank, as Mandalay has become too noisy. Prior to this, ships moored in the bay below the Shwe-kyey-yet pagoda on the opposite bank, a half-mile or so across. Since the 2010s, as trade has grown across the country the entire riverbank between Ava and Mandalay, 10 miles upriver, has been taken over by cargo vessels loading and unloading, the beaches stacked with oil drums, sacks of cement, and mountains of sand dredged up from the riverbed to be used for construction in building-boom Mandalay. Where once we tied up and took pleasant walks along riverbanks filled with bird song and scenes of bucolic farming, a vast squatter camp several miles long now snakes up the river with shacks made from fertiliser sacks and old bits of cardboard, a far cry from the pristine all-bamboo hut of the Burmese cultivator. You will see ships, mainly cargo barges, being built everywhere. Indeed, we too have built several ships along this stretch, for to build a ship all you need is a bit of bank and lots of people. The lofting of the plates is done on the road, and once the order is given, machine and carpentry shops spring up overnight in a makeshift colony about the newly laid keel. Speed is of the essence, as come the monsoon rise the hull will float off, and it must of course be watertight before outfitting.

A fisherman midstream off Mandalay.

The main port for Mandalay was at Gawein, which is latitudinally level with central Mandalay. Even at an important transport hub like Mandalay there were no jetties – just one IWT pontoon for their line ships, which sadly run no more. Most ships would just run up onto the riverbank or raft up alongside each other. An army of stevedores chant and sing against a background roar of diesel generators; the dust is terrible and sun beats down remorselessly, but apart from the diesel the scene today will not have changed much over the past 100 years; perhaps in British times there was a little more order, the ships parking more neatly, and the nearby marshalling yards operating more smoothly.

It was to Gawein that Thibaw and Supayalat were taken to embark in exile. In his father's time, king and court would have observed the steamboat races from riverside pavilions, wagering on swift Italian paddlers. Viceroys and royals would have come ashore to the sounds of bugles and brass bands, with guards of honour presenting arms, and white-gloved, topee-sheltered dignitaries awaiting them. Nowadays the dirty bund is the domain of betel nut sellers and rough sleepers, itinerant pedlars and gangs of slightly menacing idle porters.

Off the Strand Road the IFC had its main compound, with offices and bungalows for the assistants. We found Alister McCrae's house, shown here as it was in the 1930s – and indeed when we visited in the

Boats under construction or repair on the islands off Mandalay.

1990s – and, as you will see if you visit, little has changed. It was then occupied by a Kachin gentleman who was the government ship surveyor. Nearly all the IFC houses were kept in good condition and were lived in by officials of the IWT. Just down the road was the old Yadanabon shipyard, founded by King Mindon to service his fleet of Italian paddle-steamers. After the annexation it was taken over by the IFC and is today run by IWT.

Apart from the IFC compound, the area along Strand Road is somewhat insalubrious, prone to flooding in the monsoon and not considered a fashionable area. Like in Rangoon, the city riversides are smelly, dirty places, where poverty and desperation coexist beside commerce and industry. The real Mandalay lies inland, down long thoroughfares unimaginatively called by British A, B and C roads. These traverse a giant grid-plan of streets laid out by the British to the south and west of the square mile of the moated palace city.

Despite its romantic-sounding name, which conjures up images of tinkling temple bells, swishing silks and orchid blossom, Mandalay must be the ugliest city in Asia. It was not always so, and in 1986 I spent a very happy year there exploring its nooks and crannies, filled with architectural treasures.

What went wrong?

In one word: China. After the SLORC coup in 1988, when General Ne Win went into retirement and General Saw Maung took the reins, Burma entered a very dark period of martial law with a re-energised military whose generals desperately wanted to modernise their country. Apart from building roads and bridges everywhere so they could deploy troops more quickly in case of trouble, they decided that 'modernising' meant demolishing anything old or, in the case of Pagan, rebuilding all the temples. In Mandalay, first up was the gorgeous colonial rail terminus that looked as if it was a stage set from *The Jewel in the Crown*. It was demolished and replaced by a weird concrete edifice with flyovers all around. Then there was the old Zay Cho market, with its neoclassical loggias and splendid cast-iron lattice

Mandalay assistant's house at Gawein, Mandalay.

work from Falkirk – bulldozed to create probably one of the most hideous buildings in the world – a giant concrete box several storeys high. This, the new Zay Cho, was the beginning of the end for Mandalay.

General Saw Maung then went mad and apparently was planning an invasion of Thailand, believing himself to be a reincarnation of King Bayinnaung, the original conqueror of Thailand. That would have been Burma's umpteenth conquest of its neighbour. He was stopped in time by a palace coup and placed under house arrest in his mansion in Rangoon's Inya Road, where he quietly passed from a state of delusion to one of dementia. Thereafter General Khin Nyunt came to dominate the political scene; known as Secretary One, he was keen to reopen the country to investors and tourism, but the West completely misread him and, following the demands of Daw Aung San Suu Kyi, imposed sanctions on Burma. Any overture that Khin Nyunt attempted was rebuffed by the Clinton administration and in the UK, we had something called the 'ethical foreign policy' under Robin Cook and Tony Blair. Khin Nyunt, with his background in the military intelligence, was seen as a Putin figure.

Ironically Khin Nyunt was a progressive, but was under considerable pressure from the dinosaur-like reactionaries in the Tatmadaw, who disliked any foreign contacts whatsoever. Between a rock and a hard place, Khin Nyunt turned to China, and the floodgates were open. An alliance with China took several forms. At an intergovernmental level, there were deals for reequipping the military and investment in new infrastructure such as passenger ships for the rivers and coasts, all paid for with loans from Beijing. The Chinese got a foot in the door strategically to enable a military presence on the Arakan coast, looking across the Bay of Bengal towards India. They had big plans for oil pipelines, railways and deep seaports linking the Indian Ocean to south-west China. This was long before the term 'Belt and Road' had been coined, but Burma was an early example of how China could economically and then militarily dominate a region using the power of money rather than the force of arms. You have only to look at Sri Lanka in July 2022 to see what can happen to a country that, thus entrapped, doesn't kowtow.

Whilst the big deals between Rangoon and Beijing were going on in the background, Khin Nyunt allowed the border with China to open, and in poured Chinese business opportunists in the hundreds of thousands (some say as many as a million Han Chinese crossed over). To them, Burma was an eldorado with its rich resources, and after a quarter-century of socialist autarky few industries or commercial ventures had survived. I was working there at the time, and it seemed to me that almost overnight Mandalay was colonised by this army of busy-bee Chinese. They conquered all not with guns and tanks but wads of cash. Every shop-house in the city centre was bought by Chinese. Entire streets and neighbourhoods, once housing the poets, musicians and scholars who had maintained this, the great heart of Burmese courtly culture, were bought up. Gullible, and often not very commercially minded Burmese, thought they had won the lottery as house prices shot up – only to find that having sold out, and sitting on a bag of cash, they could no longer afford to buy anywhere else to live in their own city. Mandalay, which had contained the essence of Burmeseness, ceased to be Burmese.

Chinese migrants were able to buy Burmese ID cards so could own property, something no Westerner could. Many of those Chinese were single males of the one child policy generation, hence unable to find a wife at home – but in Burma (where according to the census of July 2021 there were 10 per cent – that is, just over 5 million! – more women than men) marriages were easy to arrange. It was easy for the new arrivals to learn the language, take a Burmese name, wear a longyi, have a Burmese family and pay respects in a Buddhist temple. The next generation will be half-and-half, and a new ethnic group is born, like the Anglo-Burmese of colonial times or the Portuguese Bayingyi of earlier times. This is exactly what happened 100 years ago in Bangkok, where today, as a result of intermarriage, the majority of the urban population are mixed Sino-Thai.

Mandalay rapidly transformed, and the charming wooden shop-houses were quickly replaced with concrete boxes and the first shopping malls and condominiums. Buildings started to get higher, too, and just as Rodway Swinhoe was to ask of 1920s Rangoon 'where is the Burman stowed away?' so the same question could have been asked of 1990s Mandalay – and more so now, in the 2020s. I noticed, when going with crew to buy things, that they would no longer ask for a shop owner as the *tha-tay*, rich man, as normal in Burmese usage, but now for the Tayoke, Chinese. Any significant business in Mandalay is nowadays run by a Chinese and it is amazing to think that in the early 1960s General Ne Win confiscated nearly all Chinese-owned properties and businesses. Meanwhile, the Chinese-owned malls and condos are getting bigger and bigger, and the new development areas to the south and east of the city resemble those of outer Bangkok. You may ask where all this money comes from. The answer is that Mandalay had always, even in Ne Win times, been an important trading hub with trade routes converging on the city from China, India and a huge agricultural area around. As I described in my book *Mandalay*, back in the days of the 'Burmese Road to Socialism' there was plenty of quiet money, and a well-established merchant class sat on great wealth. What the Chinese did, then, was take over these networks and markets and, with plenty of seed capital, scale them up.

Underlying all this commercial activity was Burma's most lucrative natural resource – opium. It was to Mandalay that the great drugs barons from the China–Burma borderlands came to invest their profits and live freely, undisturbed by prying governments. Closely guarded mansions have been built in the countryside south of Mandalay looking more like five-star hotel complexes than private homes. They outdo anything Pablo Escobar could have boasted in Colombia. At the time of writing nearly all large Burmese businesses, generally heavily diversified conglomerates, are owned by cronies of the military. Whilst they are headed up by such Burmese figureheads, the investment and expertise will be Chinese and the money comes from the white gold. You cannot escape this anywhere in Burma. Every shopping mall, fancy hotel and state-of-the-art factory is so financed. First under socialism, and then under the sanctions, Burma became economically drug-dependent, and this continues today. The big money now, however, is in methamphetamine factories, which have replaced the heroin refineries as the main source of income.

In the countryside and villages south of Mandalay, we can breathe again after the claustrophobic atmosphere of the city centre. The people here are ethnically pure Burmese, and engaged in traditional industries like silk weaving, bronze casting, sculpting and wood carving, still living in their occupation-defined communities, continuing the social organisation of old Pagan. The two other capitals that adorn our river road are Ava and Amarapura, and though their palaces are long gone – dismantled and reassembled at the new capital of Mandalay in 1857 – the two towns are still worth visiting for their temples, monasteries and glimpses of a lush countryside crossed by rivers and dotted with lakes. King Bodawpaya shifted the capital from Ava to Amarapura in 1783, his grandson Bagyidaw took it back to Ava in 1823, and then in 1841 Tharawaddy moved it back to Amarapura again. Finally in 1857, Mindon, apparently for astrological reasons, moved the capital to Mandalay, though some said it was because the sound of the IFC steamers' whistles annoyed him so much.

Ava's story is the story of Burma. As Scott O'Connor was to write in 1907, 'of all the ruined capitals of Burma which make their appeal on the transitoriness of life … Ava is the most gracious'. Established by King Thalun in 1637, when he shifted capital from Toungoo to this, the heart of the country, it was sacked and fell in the Mon resurgence of 1752 to be re-established by King Alaunghpaya in 1756 who founded a new dynasty, the Konbaung. Whilst there is little to see of the original palace other than the outlines of moats and walls, there are two surviving royal monasteries that are well worth the horse-cart ride to get there. One is the Menu-ok Kyaung, a flamboyant monastery built in brick to the plan and form of a wooden monastery built by Menu, one of Bagyidaw's queens, for her teacher in 1819. The other is the Bagaya-kyaung-taik, built in the mid-19th century of teak, with 267 teak columns. This is one of the finest and best-preserved wood-carved monasteries in the Mandalay area.

At Amarapura there is the still wonderful U Bein Bridge leading to the Thandaman Kyauk-taw-gyi temple of 1847, with its well-preserved Konbaung period paintings depicting King Pagan's works of merit. But it has become very touristy, and is irresistible to child touts speaking all manner of European languages – one minute Italian, the next German and some even try you in Hebrew; Burma has always been popular with Israeli backpackers.

Returning to Mandalay from these once-royal places we cannot help but stop at the great Mahamuni Pagoda, better known to the locals as the Yakhine *hpaya*, Arakan Pagoda. It is the spiritual heart of Mandalay, and indeed one of the great shrines of Burma, and its Buddha image was brought from Arakan, the Land of the Great Image as it was known on account of this monumental figure. In 1784, the same Bodaw-paya who had founded Amarapura conquered the Arakan, adding it to his expanding empire, and transported the Great Image back over the mountains to its present site in south Mandalay. In addition, he brought back Arakanese prisoners as pagoda slaves; this accounts for the fact that many of the market-stall holders around the pagoda are of darker complexion than most Mandalay folk. Bodawpaya also brought back many other treasures, including the Khmer bronze figures to be found in a side chapel dating from the Angkor period, which the Arakanese had captured from the Mon at Pegu, who in turn had raided them from Siam. The Burmese ruled over the Arakan for only about 40 years before the British took it from them, which makes the Arakanese case for independence from Burma quite plausible. It is a curious example of the Burmese psychology that the single most revered image in Burma should be a captive one, its shrine in Mandalay a prison-house, its enforced carers the enslaved nobility of its homeland. The Mahamuni was and still is a celebration of Burmese imperialism, symbol of Burmese suzerainty over subjected peoples and their lands.

The site of Yadanabon, the City of Jewels, as Mandalay was officially named by Mindon in 1857, was carefully selected by the *ponna*, court Brahmins, who would use astrological calculations to determine the most auspicious locations and timings for all the court rituals and festivals that filled the royal calendar. You can still find the descendants of these ponna in stalls around the Mahamuni temple, casting horoscopes inscribed beautifully on plaques of palm leaf. The shifting of the capital was carried out to a prescribed formula dating back to the Pagan dynasty, if not earlier, including the interment of live humans beneath the main gateposts, two to each of the four main gates, the idea being that their imprisoned spirits would guard the city.

The entire compound is over 400 hectares, with each of its four sides 2 kilometres long; it is surrounded by a high crenellated wall and moat with bridges at the cardinal points, and a fifth on the south-west side for inauspicious traffic, such as the removal of dead bodies. Within were not just the royal apartments and audience halls but all the main offices of state, the military barracks and the residences for courtiers. There was the *hluttaw*, parliament, plus a mint, royal baths and gardens filled with Italianate pavilions and loggias. Mandalay was Italy's moment in Burma: Italian architects produced belle époque structures flamboyantly decorated with Burmese motifs; Italian steamers raced on the river (apparently, when they had sailed out from Italy they had been loaded up with Murano chandeliers and other furnishings for the palace); Count Andrieno, who we met in Chapter 4, was first consul and then agent for the Irrawaddy Flotilla; and in the city's watering holes you would meet any number of aristocratic Italian adventurers with grand schemes.

Despite this southern European influence, the main structures were strictly traditional and laid out according to long-established precedent, with the Great Audience Hall as centrepiece, and various secondary halls, and a further 11 throne rooms, about it, connecting eventually to the royal apartments. Much of this was reconstructed from the Amarapura palace, which had been dismantled and transported there by elephant.

After annexation in 1886 it was made the British headquarters, then in 1942 it became the Japanese headquarters – so the Allies bombed it to smithereens. The only original building to survive was the Shwekyaung, which had been relocated outside the palace to the south-east. A visit to this charming monastery, with its richly carved panels, gives an impression of what the palace must have been like. Moreover, as so much of it was reconstructed from the original Amarapura palace, when it was re-erected much of its decorative wood carving would have been mid-18th century rather than mid-19th, though considerably embellished by artists of that period.

Remember that kingship in Burma was largely a spiritual role – a king was there to promote the faith through various acts of merit and the periodic purification of the order of monks to ensure homogeneity of belief. So the nation's peace and prosperity hinged on the king's symbolic fulfilment of this role. Matters of civil governance, economic policy and foreign affairs, entirely secondary to this role, were relegated to the *wungyi*, ministers. The king, surrounded by his queens and many concubines, sycophants and favourites, rarely left the palace city, and would have little inkling of what was occurring in the country beyond the high walls of his gilded cage.

The three Anglo-Burmese wars, and indeed the annexation of all Burma, was very much the result of cultural misunderstandings and sheer ignorance on both sides. Nothing bears this out more than the issue of wearing shoes when in the royal presence. The British, obsessed with their sense of prestige, were intransigent in their refusal to understand the importance of the removal of shoes in Burmese culture, and the Burmese were equally intransigent, making no allowances for ignorant foreigners.

After the British occupation the palace was renamed Fort Dufferin, and an officer's club was set up in one of the halls. The royal apartments were extensively looted by the British, and an auction was held on the palace steps selling off prizes. The main items of royal regalia – heavy gold ritual objects studded with rubies and other precious gems – were shipped off to the Victoria and Albert Museum in London. It was Lord Curzon, visiting as viceroy of India in 1901, who realised the palace's importance and declared it a protected monument under the care of the Archaeological Survey of India; subsequently an Archaeological Survey of Burma was formed. A later viceroy, Lord Mountbatten, arranged for the return of the regalia from London on independence in 1948, and it can be seen today in the national museum in Rangoon.

In the palace grounds a cantonment for the military, together with civil lines, were established. The civil lines were the residential area for members of the Indian Civil Service, which later became the Burma Civil Service. There was even a nine-hole golf course, and so the ruling British were to live in the same gilded cage as the king and his court. Alister McCrae told of how he was under pressure to move into the palace and build an IFC agent's house there, as with increasing civil unrest through the 1930s the river area was considered unsafe; even so, this was something that he resisted doing.

We have touched on the importance of the Irrawaddy commanders in the 1880s, in the final days of Royal Mandalay, when shops would hang a sign declaring themselves as being 'By Appointment to … Irrawaddy Steamer Captains'. As has been shown, the Irrawaddy captains knew their way around the royal apartments and were able to guide the British military delegation through the palace to deliver its ultimatum to the king. The palace had always been a labyrinth filled with gossip and intrigue, where courtiers vied for power and Brahmins conducted a ritualised daily life, where plots piled on plots and coups on counter-coups. Was the British incursion not just another political machination? The British walked into the palace unopposed, not a shot fired. No one for a moment thought their monarch would be deposed and exiled to distant India. When that happened it was such a shock that nobody reacted, as if winded after a sudden blow, and then followed an explosion of anger and energy that resulted in ten years of insurgency. The Third Anglo-Burmese war did not end with the fall of Mandalay; it began then. Up till then, Thibaw had been a remote, disregarded figure, but suddenly he became a popular rallying point. The deposing of this symbolic king was an attack on the faith that he was protector of, it was an attack on all things Buddhist and Burmese. If you look at all of Burma's problems since independence, they begin with the king's one-mile walk from his palace to the IFC steamer *Thoreah*, to take him off to exile.

10

The Upper Irrawaddy

Exhausted by our explorations of the five former capitals, at last we are off upriver again, heading for Bhamo, which for larger ships is the Irrawaddy's most northerly navigable point, 1,000 river miles from the sea. Once again, after the narrows between Ava and Sagaing, the river sprawls across the plain and in low water there are tricky sections, with all ships subject to frequent groundings. Off Mandalay, thousands of boats are moored, some waiting to load or unload, some waiting to be sent off to collect cargos up- or downriver. Everything from ginormous motorised barges to wooden country boats, and moored mid-stream are numerous noisy barges pumping up sand for the city's construction boom. Sadly, now that there is a new bridge and roads connecting either side, the boatmen who would take you across the river in their jolly painted sampans have disappeared. The river scene at Mandalay went from the bucolic to the industrial overnight.

A mile or so across and away from the bustle and noise, we stop on the west bank at the great unfinished pagoda of Mingun, built by Bodawpaya in 1790, said to be the largest pile of bricks in the world. We have met Bodawpaya already, conquering the Arakan and shifting his capital to Amarapura; clearly, he was a busy man. The Pahtodawgyi was his greatest legacy, a monument to a self-aggrandisement of Pharaonic proportions. This temple was to be his great work of merit, and would outshine any Buddhist monument anywhere in the world. There is a model of the temple standing close by that in itself is big. If the temple itself had been completed it would have been 150 metres high. Bodawpaya deployed hundreds of thousands of prisoners of war, rounded up and brought back to Burma from the Arakan, Mon country and Siam, to work on the construction, and as they became depleted by disease, hunger and exhaustion the Burmese population were forcibly mobilised, abusing the ancient *corvée* system in which peasants would provide their labour in lieu of paying taxes. The entire economy of the land became focused on the temple's construction, all revenue and resources diverted into this national cause, and it led to widespread famine and social disintegration. Various prophecies arose, including one that on the temple's completion the king would be cursed – which, it is said, is why he deferred its completion. More likely, though, the country was bankrupted, and they just could not finish it. Such megalomania was not untypical of Burmese kings, seeing the people as a resource to be expended on such flights of egomaniacal fantasy. We shall hear of this again on our journey upriver.

Situated close by is the Mingun bell, the second-largest in the world and largest working one, weighing in at about 90,000 kilograms. Like all Burmese bells, it is rung by being struck on its lip from the outside. The British had found it abandoned, its housing having collapsed during the 1839 earthquake responsible for the great crack down the side of the temple block. So they called in the engineers of the IFC dockyard at Mandalay to rehang the bell in a pavilion still standing.

We continue through a maze of channels as the river scatters across the plain before narrowing at the Third Defile,

The Mingun Bell, at 90,000 kg the largest working bell in the world, was cast for King Bodawhpaya in 1810. It was knocked off its supports by an earthquake in 1839 and rehung by the IFC Mandalay engineers in 1896.

where the flow is fast and deep through scrubby hills. The sheer volume of water that pours down from Himalayan heights makes this an impressive sight. At the entrance to the Third Defile, there are the potteries around Kyauk-myaung; these are one of the marvels of the Irrawaddy valley, and well worth an excursion ashore to explore. Here you will see 20-gallon pots being turned by hand and fired in great kilns the size of churches, whose fires burn for days on end. The pots, which are used for water storage – and every hut in Burma has at least one – are shipped downriver in ingenious rafts whose flotation is provided by the pots themselves, strapped into a bamboo framework. The rafts, like the log rafts, would have a steersman's hut and he would drift downstream, with his family, pets and chickens, to wherever there would be a market for them. Those giant pots would be sold at village pagoda festivals, and farmers would carry them back home in their bullock carts.

The wood to fire the kilns was gathered from driftwood coming down the river, and country boats have been adapted, by using outriggers with nets suspended below the waterline, to collect this wood. Indeed, all the materials required to make a pot, including of course the clay, come free from the river, and it is the river that ships the pots off to market. It doesn't get much more sustainable than that. Tragically, though, this is a declining industry, as cheaper plastic containers flood the market from China. On recent visits we have seen the number of potteries decline. Many of the pottery-owning families have left their villages, their big houses shuttered up, and I was told that most had moved to the bright lights of Mandalay. This is a shame, as when the rich people leave the poor get poorer.

On the east bank are quarries producing a fine white marble, and in 1999 a single block weighing over 600 tonnes, measuring nearly 12 metres high and just over 7 metres wide, was extracted. It was claimed at the time that this was the largest single block of marble in the world. The then Secretary One, General Khin Nyunt, got involved, and decided that it should be taken to Rangoon and carved into a single monolithic Buddha. The issue was how to get it there in a country where at that time a bicycle conferred considerable status on its owner, and was the main form of transport nationally. It was decided to construct a special wide-gauge railway line from the quarry to the riverside, engineering a bogey big enough to accommodate the block, and from there on the bogey would continue on rails onto a specially built barge donated by a leading crony company. Three IWT steamers were deployed to bring the barge downriver, not so much towing it as acting as the brakes, followed by dozens of ceremonial boats. Once in Rangoon the bogey was wheeled off onto another specially constructed railway line, using three lavishly decorated locomotives, to take the block to its final resting place, to be sculpted *in situ* by master craftsmen using power-hammers and chisels. The procession of locomotives was met at the site by Senior General Than Shwe and his wife. This story was front page news nearly every day through 1999 and General Khin Nyunt was often pictured inspecting and 'giving necessary instructions' throughout the transport and carving processes.

Unfortunately the image itself, like the era it personifies, is very ugly, and not very imaginatively named Kyauk-taw-gyi, Great Sacred Rock. It may be visited in its own special shrine in the Rangoon suburbs. This was a project of Pharaonic proportions, not unlike King Bodawpaya's grand designs, and a good example of how the Burmese, when motivated by religious enthusiasm, are capable of extraordinary feats.

At Thabeikkyin a new bridge spans the Irrawaddy. During its construction in the 2000s, one of our ships sailed under it and a couple of minutes later an earthquake caused the central span to collapse into the river. In true Burmese fashion, the crew simply beamed with delight, jubilantly declaring that luck was on our side. Our passengers then joined the earthquake relief effort, taking food and blankets from the ship to distressed villagers.

We are now in the Third Defile where for 20 miles the river narrows to a couple of hundred yards across, and deepens too. There are few villages along this section; the banks are covered in scrub, and the sharp hills dropping down into the river are thickly wooded. Although a captain's dominant fear on the Irrawaddy is that of grounding, here a more sinister fear takes over, that of sinking. If there were to be a collision in the defile and you were taking in water there would be no nice soft sandbank to drift onto; the river is very deep, and the banks are too steep to run up onto.

The only island in the Third Defile is a rare one with a pagoda and monastery clinging to it. Nearly all of the colonial literature on the river makes much of this island monastery, where the monks had trained giant catfish to answer their call and swim in to be hand-fed. Sadly, however, I have seen no evidence of this tradition continuing on my visits. There were tales of these fish being poached by IFC sailors (who were generally Muslim) and being served up as a particularly tasty delicacy at the captain's table. Let us hope that the IFC cannot be blamed for the demise of these domesticated fish.

Out of the slightly spooky defile we emerge into a further great plain, and again the river fragments. In the monsoon season, we chug along on a seemingly infinite ocean of muddy blue waters, fighting the current and hardly getting anywhere, being overtaken by pedestrians along the banks. In the dry season, we bob through silver channels, and frequently become grounded. There is always a laugh in the wheelhouse when we pass Pandaw Island where, on her maiden voyage in 2001, *Pandaw II* spent a worrying five days grounded, but the passengers refused to be evacuated as they were having so much fun on board. No cruise would be complete without a good grounding, which can last anything from a few minutes to a few hours. Our skippers usually manage to wriggle us free, but occasionally a passing tug must be commandeered.

On the way to Katha, we stop always at Kha Nyat on the east bank, which retains its rural charm and is home to my late friend Saya U Tin Win, with his fascinating private museum of local artefacts unearthed during a lifetime of archaeological excavations in this area. Here you will find the grave of Captain Vaughan, killed in the pacification. Our cooks love the market here, and load up with fresh fruit and vegetables. If lucky, they will find for our lunch baskets of river prawn, the most delicious in the world, so sweet they could be served as a dessert.

We also stop for a while at Tagaung, in ancient times Burma's northern capital, with still traceable city walls and a splendid shrine to the nat Bo Gyi, who casts a protective eye over passing ships – as long as he is buttered up with appropriate offerings.

Another favourite stop is Hti-chaing, now a bustling port with roads leading into the interior. A splendid hilltop pagoda offers a wonderful view up and down the vast sprawling river. In 1951, Norman Lewis overnighted at Hti-chaing on a heavily armed steamer coming down from Bhamo. The town was in rebel hands, but in one of those very flexible Burmese arrangements the government steamer was allowed to moor and trade. It is well worth a walk up the pagoda hill here for the view up and down the river, and Hti-chaing being a road point has always had bustling markets and big monasteries (they tend to go together in Burma!) so it always provides an enjoyable stroll ashore.

On the east bank, the Shweli river joins the Irrawaddy. There are sinister-looking Chinese mines in the hills that run along it, and new port facilities with enormous barges alongside. If you ask what the Chinese are doing you will get a mixed bag of replies. The Chinese have many designs on the Irrawaddy, as detailed in Chapter 5.

Between Khan Nyat and Hti-chaing are dolphin grounds, and sightings of these social creatures have always been frequent. But tragically, the Irrawaddy dolphin is now threatened by electric fishing, the most odious of practices where a long pole with an electric conductor on the end attached to big batteries is used to kill any form of marine life within a certain radius. In the past, fishermen would thump an oar on the bottom of their boats and the dolphins would answer the call and help herd fish into their nets, but now they are threatened with extinction by the very fishermen they used to serve. Burma seems to have leapt from the 19th century to the 21st, missing out the 20th. Within a few months of very rapid change, people's needs and expectations have changed, too; whereas a fisherman used to have little in the way of outgoings, he now has to find money for a smartphone, a satellite TV and a thirsty outboard motor.

Until just a few years ago, nearly all the boats had lugsails (often a jolly patchwork of old longyis) or, in the absence of a breeze, were pulled with oars. There were the gorgeous hand-carved Irrawaddy boats with a throne for the helmsman high above the transom. Sadly, they are gone now, broken up for the value of their old teak. In the 1990s at Inywa, just below the Shweli con-fluence, we found what I think was the oldest village in Burma, with narrow,

Fisherman's hut from the 1990s; today they sport a solar panel in order to charge a smartphone.

winding alleys and houses built close together with great teak pillars and floorboards 6 inches thick, quite unlike the usual Burmese villages of bamboo frames covered by rattan panelling. Inywa had the feeling of a medieval village in central Europe. Most likely dating from the 18th century or even earlier, the houses had miraculously survived the twin perils of war and fire. But when we went back in 2001 they were all gone, again sold for their seasoned teak to buy smart phones and mopeds, and replaced by clapboard and corrugated iron.

U Nu, prime minister of Burma, visits the Yarrow shipyard in Glasgow in 1948 to inspect progress on the P-class ships ordered by the newly independent government. On U Nu's right is Sir Eric Yarrow.

To replace the flotilla sunk in 1942, the newly independent Burmese government ordered a new fleet of shallow-draft steamers from Yarrow's of Glasgow in 1947. The then prime minister, U Nu, even visited the Yarrow's yard in Govan to inspect progress (my grandfather George, a naval architect, worked there then, and may have met him). Six sternwheelers were sent out under their own steam from the Clyde, all boarded up for the ocean voyage. One of these was the original Pandaw ship that we refitted in 1998, and Sir Eric and Lady Yarrow came out for the commissioning and maiden voyage. These vessels were all running until just a couple of years ago, but I think our old Pandaw ship is the only one still operational, now in the hands of a Chinese businessman. After 70-plus years, their redundancy was not due to any form of decay, but rather the fact that a road infrastructure has replaced the river. People now bomb up the new highways on overnight buses, and fatal crashes are not infrequent as manic drivers race against the clock, awarded bonuses for arriving early. Before, on a line steamer, they would have spent a few days relaxing on the decks chatting, eating endless snacks, and puffing on their cheroots as the world sedately floated by. But now, with the Mandalay–Bhamo highway running parallel to the river on the east bank, the busy Burmese take night buses to be entertained all night with pop videos and Korean movies. The line steamers are no more. Gone is that scene described so well by Scott O'Connor in 1905 of the steamer's arrival and the excitement it caused, which continued happily till about 2015, when the road was completed.

The river, once pulsating with shipping as vessels of every shape and size traded between ports and every conceivable cargo was carried on the water, has now become eerily quiet. Whilst sailing on a *Pandaw*, nothing was more fun than passing a P-class line steamer packed to the gunwales with merry folk waving, whistling and calling as we passed.

Katha is, and has always been, an important trading post. In 1835 Inverness-born Captain Simon Hannay was perhaps one of the first-ever British visitors, travelling upstream on an exploratory mission on one of the King of Burma's Italian-built steamers. He was amazed to find – long before Upper Burma was annexed by the British – a selection of British-made goods on sale in the market. I first visited Katha in 1986, when Burma had banned exports and imports during its disastrous attempt at self-sufficiency. During the Ne Win years Bhamo, about 85 miles upstream of Katha, was a great smuggling hub, with

Chinese-made goods coming downriver to be redistributed, so the markets were booming. Like all these Irrawaddy ports, thanks to its river trade Katha remained prosperous throughout those hermit years.

In the 1980s Katha was well fortified as a front-line position against the KIA. There were gunboats in the port, and the riverbanks were stacked with munitions. It was not unlike a scene from the film *Apocalypse Now*. Even in recent times, in the early 21st century, whilst the town has remained in Burmese hands, just across the border in Kachin state the KIA are very much in

Housing along the river bank at Hti-jaing.
In the monsoon, water will lap at their doors.

control, though perhaps by mutual agreement the river route remains open. Following my arrest there in 1985 as a foreign spy and my subsequent release a couple of hours later, I was royally entertained by the local commander, who told me that I was the first foreigner to visit their town since the war. I am not sure that that was quite true, but anywhere north of Mandalay had been off limits since the 1962 revolution; and back in 1951, as civil war and armed insurgencies raged through post-war Burma, Norman Lewis was not allowed to dock there, either.

Katha was in fact the setting for George Orwell's *Burmese Days,* published in 1934. Given his scathing treatment of local society, his publishers insisted on changing all names and places, and Katha became Kyauktada. The main features of the map included with the book were reversed, so everything is in the wrong place. Whilst *Burmese Days* is probably the most famous English language book written about Burma, it is in my opinion a book that tells you little about Burma and an awful lot about Orwell. Serving as a colonial policeman, Orwell had been posted in 1926 to Katha, where a simmering disgust at colonialism was later to form the basis of his book. Everybody in it is unpleasant: Flory, the main character, is a depressing figure; his cronies at the club vile racists; the Burmese corrupt and lethargic. The book paints colonial life as mean, small-minded and oppressive. But all the other books about Burma from this period that I know of (and the literature is considerable) present a vastly different picture, with an emphasis that life was not like that in India, being less hierarchic and not at all snobbish. The picture the writers portray is one of open and friendly people stationed in these remote outposts of the empire, who made any visitor or new face in town instantly feel at home. There was a mutual admiration between the British and the Burmese, perhaps each admiring what the other was lacking; the British colonials were, if anything, infected by the natural Burmese openness. When I first became interested in Burma in the early 1980s, I joined the British Burma Society in London, then mainly made up of former colonials long retired to England. How their eyes would light up and positively sparkle on remembering old places and Burmese friends; they may have been retired to places like Tunbridge Wells, but their hearts were still in Burma with the Burmese people. Despite many frustrations and difficulties, there is a real joy to living in Burma that comes from living amongst and working with the Burmese – something I discovered for myself in my 30 years of working there. But I do not think George Orwell experienced that at all, and sadly it's not clear why.

I made the same journey back up the Irrawaddy ten years later, in 1995, with a bunch of fellow Burma buffs on a rickety hulk called *Irrawaddy Princess* we had chartered from a rich Chinese in Rangoon. Burma was then opening up, and the entire town turned out to welcome us. Even the streets leading to the strand road were packed, with people staring in amazed wonder at this bunch of strange foreigners. Today the

A dak bungalow that would have housed a colonial officer like George Orwell.

The racecourse at Katha, today used for athletics.

welcome is less effusive, as they are now used to the sight of a regular Pandaw vessel disgorging its cargo of camera-toting foreigners – but the friendliness and sense of welcome is still there.

In the dry season the ghauts are steep and high, but in the monsoon season when you moor up against the road you can just step out onto it. There is always a bustle of speedboats coming in and out of the chaotic port, taking people and their goods off to their villages. Looming above the ghauts is a great blaze of golden spires – the town's main pagoda sprawling along the top of the river-bank – and next door is an equally romantic-looking mosque. The town itself has not changed too much over the past 35 years that I have been visiting. Streets of charming wooden shop-houses, apparently unchanged from the early 20th century, lead up from the port. They are beginning, however, to be replaced by the ubiq-uitous ugly tiled buildings with mir-ror-glass windows owned by Chinese businessmen intent on hoovering up local real estate. But at the time of writing, the old Katha houses are still in the majority. The shopping streets lead from the port to the heart of the old town, and just to the north of it was once the racecourse. But horse racing was banned by General Ne Win during his puritanisation of Burma in the 1960s, so where jockeys used to gallop around as part of Burma's popular racing circuit, there is today a sports ground with a running track; the grounds were also used for the pageantry of the Burma Socialist Programme Youth Party with lots of parades and waving of coloured flags

To the south lies St Paul's Catholic Church, a pretty wooden structure with a belfry, and the jail, both unchanged from Orwell's day. To the north of the old racecourse, the civil lines remain as they would have been 100 years ago; there are great dak bungalows with galleries of verandas running all around at all levels. Some, like the district commissioner's, are vast, designed for entertaining on a grand scale. It was here, on the civil lines, that Orwell would have had his house, but some guides will direct you to the home of the current police chief on the assumption that Orwell, as police superintendent, would have lived there.

St Paul's Catholic Church, Katha.

After much hunting during many a visit to Katha, I finally found the Club,[37] by following a sign in Burmese for the Tennis Club. It is a nondescript and rather sad structure on a bank overlooking the flood plain. Now a local government archive, it had been a Burma Socialist Programme Party office after the 1962 revolution. If you go in, you can see the hatch through which Indian bearers would pass the chota pegs[38] from a servery. It is not very impressive, a low-key drinking den with a token tennis court out front. No wonder that after the introduction of the dyarchy in 1923, and the handing over of government to an elected Burmese administration that led to the admission of Burmese to the Clubs, few Burmese could face going into them.

This rather sad building was identified by the author as The Club at Katha, where much of the action in George Orwell's Burmese Days *takes place.*

A must when visiting Katha is a stop at the fire station to see the fire bells. Only they're not fire bells – they're ship's bells,

---

37   the British-only retreat, as found in almost any colonial settlement
38   whisky and sodas

The bell of the Japan *salvaged from her wreck and now hanging in the Katha fire station.*

taken from IFC steamers scuttled here at Katha in 1942. The bells of the *Japan*, *Taping* and *Siam* came off the greatest steamers the IFC ever built.

When in 1942 the British evacuated Rangoon and scuttled many of the flotilla ships here in Katha, an enterprising fire chief managed to save the bells. Some years ago I made an offer for them, but without success. Norman Lewis, in *Golden Earth: Travels in Burma*, describes great jungle-covered hulks sticking out of the river when he passed here in 1951 – but as I have mentioned earlier, by the 1980s when I first visited Katha, the ships seemed to have long rotted away and all I could see was sandbanks. Then in the mid-1990s, when Burma seemed to be waking up after 30 years of self-imposed isolation and the country was abuzz with enterprise and industry, entrepreneurs started salvaging hulls. The great sand island off Katha turned out to be a graveyard of ships – dozens of them. Using enormous pumps, the sand was shifted, and these hulls were laid bare. There were the *Japan*, *Siam* and *Taping*!

I can proudly say that I have walked their decks. Divers, attached to what looked like garden hoses, swam deep into the holds bringing up all manner of artefacts; I purchased from them various bits of cutlery and crockery embossed with the company livery, and at long last a ship's bell of my own. I souvenired four Bren gun cartridge-cases lying on the decks, and even pocketed a rivet or two. My best find was an actual cardboard ticket, found in the ship's safe in the purser's office that somehow had survived 50 years under water (see page 65). I showed it to an elderly Burmese friend, who instantly remembered these tickets, with the names of the stops printed along the sides in Burmese on one side and English on the other – they would be clipped at the name of the port you had bought your ticket for. The enormous Siam class ships had all broken their backs, but the crafty salvagers cut them in two and welded on new bows or sterns. These great ships sail again!

Perhaps one of the most enjoyable events on any visit to Katha over the years was a trip into the jungle to visit an elephant camp. This was something we could never guarantee, as sometimes the camp could not be found, even after driving around on bumpy rutted jungle tracks for hours, usually with our guests swaying in the back of an old lorry or pickup truck. After all, working elephant camps do tend move around depending on where the work is. If and when we found one, it was important for us to get the timing right as elephants have very strict working times and very precise body clocks; they do not take kindly to being pulled away from their afternoon foraging break or having their evening bath delayed by the arrival of a bunch of camera-clicking tourists. If we got it right, then it was a thrill to see the elephants stacking logs in perfect order and working in harmony with their *oo-si*, mahout, some of them teenage boys riding an elephant of the same age, who they would have grown up with.

As mentioned earlier – and I make no apology for repeating it – one of Burma's most important stories during its 30-year isolation was the continued good management and conservation of its forests. Using a German system adopted by the British, mature trees were selectively felled and extracted using elephants, causing minimum disruption to the biostructure. For every tree felled, several saplings were planted and thus there was a policy of renewable forestry that had existed for over 100 years. Then came the sanctions called for by Aung San Suu Kyi, responsible for so much of what went wrong with Burma: the West's 20-year denial of basic humanitarian aid, coupled with Chinese exploitation of all resources, including human resources. The heavily sanctioned military junta was unable to trade with the wider world, and ceded vast tracks of forest to its cronies. In went the big machines, clear-felling vast tracts and resulting in environmental devastation. For 20 years we would see log raft after log raft go down that river – it was hard to believe there were so many trees in Burma. Today there are very few rafts of teak; now we pass the odd cargo of jungle wood stacked on a barge, but gone are the great one-acre rafts with whole villages camped out on them in

pretty little huts. The phenomenal amounts of money earned from the teak went to the Russians for T54 tanks and MIG 29 fighters, and to the Chinese for gunboats.

Back to the elephants. With mechanised logging they were out of job, and their handlers came up with the idea of setting up an elephant camp for tourists – mainly domestic tourists but aimed also at foreign tourists – not that Katha gets many. How tragic it is to see these splendid beasts, who I feel sure would have taken pride in a useful day's work, being put through their paces to do tricks for tourists. It is a difficult question for us in operating Pandaw, as we are pres-

A young oo-si works his elephant.

149

sured by animal rights groups to not support these elephant camps – but if we do not, how will the animals and their handlers eat? A number of 'woke' tour operators have even threatened to boycott us if we do not boycott the elephant camps. They have also stopped us from visiting schools, once a popular feature of any Pandaw expedition, for equally perverse reasons.

Barge loaded with teak today; in earlier times these logs would
have been rafted downriver to the waiting sawmills.

Katha also boasts a golf course which, unsurprisingly for Burma, is situated within the army cantonment area in the lush and lovely countryside inland. Despite its being in the middle of an army base there is no issue going in, and the club secretary is happy to take your green fees. They seem to add a new hole each year, and on my last visit were up to 14. Rather oddly, some holes cross each other and on one occasion my son Toni, who is ethnically Burmese, strolled across an intersecting fairway, scruffy teenager that he was, dressed in flipflops and ragged T-shirt. A Burmese group playing across the other way stood astonished, then a very angry man started roaring with rage. I was informed by my caddy that this was the military commandant of the Katha region, and he was going to have Toni shot. We played on nevertheless, and then after the game in the clubhouse the colonel, as he turned out to be, proved very charming and apologised, having not realised that Toni was with us, and we all had drinks together. Learning that I was in the travel trade, the colonel was keen to promote Katha as a golf tourism destination, and I obligingly promised to spread the word, which I am doing now.

Despite such forays into tourism, Katha has really changed very little over the 30-something years I have been going there. If less innocent and exuberantly generous, people during the democracy years of the 2010s became freer and more relaxed than they were under socialism, and with greater prosperity, buzzing about on mopeds and scooters as they went about their business. The friendliness is still there, as are all the pretty wooden shop-houses and the colonial dak bungalows, which extraordinarily linger on despite their 100-plus years and perishable materials. Like its architecture, Katha's charm would seem to be eminently perishable, but like the big old bungalows it lingers on.

Back on board we cast off in the early morning as the river is abuzz with country boats coming in for the market, and express boats – fast and ugly, with people crammed in and so unlike the steamers of old – shoot by in a hurry to reach outlying villages or bomb down to Mandalay in a day. We go a few miles, then the mist comes down and all traffic stops and waits an hour for it to lift. Morning mists are the norm in the winter, and it would be foolish to try and navigate through them. Though Bhamo seems close, it is still 84 miles distant, a full day's sail away.

Crossing the state line, we enter Kachin and reach Shwegu, another pot-making village. Shwegu specialises in the smaller drinking pot that you will see roadside throughout the country, each placed in its own little house as an act of merit, to quench the thirst of travellers with water cooled in the unglazed terracotta pot. We might stop for a walk on the island opposite Shwegu, with its many stupas and monasteries before continuing to the great Second Defile. This is the most spectacular of the three Irrawaddy defiles. It was the objective of any colonial traveller and one of the great sites of Burma, but since the 1940s few people have managed to visit it due to the war with the KIA. During the years of peace in the 2000s we were able to run ships up to Bhamo, but then the situation deteriorated, and on my last trip in 2016 we learnt that the KIA controlled nearly all the surrounding countryside and the Burmese army could only keep the roads and river open in daylight hours.

In the Second Defile the river is deeper than

The Irrawaddy's second defile; here, the water runs very fast and very deep.

151

the cliffs towering above, and Captain Chubb describes one ship which put down all its anchor chain only to lose its anchor. The defile runs for several miles and at its narrowest point is just a couple of hundred feet across. In the monsoon the water level here will rise 300 feet. There are no villages, and little evidence of human activity along this section other than the occasional intrepid fisher. Once we are out of the defile and heading on the last stretch to Bhamo, away from that nagging worry of 'what happens if the engines fail and we lose control?' the river sprawls and we are back to worrying about groundings again. In IFC days during the low water season ships did not always make it all the way, and cargos would be discharged on the bank 20 miles below.

Bhamo is the northernmost port for larger ships on the Irrawaddy and, sitting on the east bank, is almost exactly 1,000 river miles from Rangoon. From the earliest times, Bhamo has been a place of unfulfilled expectations. Dubbed by the late Victorian press as a Chicago of the East, Bhamo had the potential to be a great inland port that would dominate a vast Chinese hinterland. It was partly to prevent the French from accessing these alluring Chinese markets and in order to access them itself that Britain went to war in 1886 and annexed Upper Burma. However, under British rule between 1886 and 1942 this ambition was never realised, and a projected railway was never built. Stability in China collapsed under the fragmented rule of warlords during the final days of the Qing in 1911 and the Sino-Japanese wars that began in 1931. Joseph Conrad was to write in 1922 of the city he never visited:

[In] Bhamo, a town on the very frontier of the Chinese enigma … caravans incessantly come and go through mysterious valleys and … rumours live from day to day.

Now in the 21st century there is once again a lot of talk of railways as China implements its Belt and Road policy. In January 2019, Aung San Suu Kyi signed an agreement with President Xi Jinping for the construction of a Rangoon to Kunming high-speed railway. From Momein (Teng-yueh) on the China border to Bhamo there is now a truck highway, so the town once again has prospects, being seen as a great entrepôt for cargoes and trade through the Irrawaddy corridor and the world beyond. Yet, much of the countryside around Bhamo being in the hands of the KIA, plus the fact that anywhere north or east of Bhamo is effectively a war zone, serves to dampen such Chinese ambitions, just as after the 1875 Second Bhamo Expedition and the Margary Affair (of which, more below) the Kachin caterans[39] and Shan-Tayok bandits scuppered the British plans for a railway there.

---

39   bandits

Bhamo at low water, 1904.

Back in the 13th century when Marco Polo visited – if indeed he did – Bhamo, or Pot Village in Shan, was probably of little consequence. It was Sampenago, a few miles upstream at the confluence of the Taiping and Irrawaddy rivers, that was the capital of this one-time Shan state, and its outline can still be traced. Sampenago long commanded the trade route, the Road of the Ambassadors, from Burma and its seaports to Yunnan and Imperial China beyond. Yet even at the end of the 13th century, the prospects for trade may have been limited, with Pagan's fall in 1278 following Kublai Khan's incursion and the overrunning of Upper Burma by Shan hordes, as yet uncivilised by the tenets of Buddhism. Then by the mid-19th century the Shan cultivator had been displaced by the Kachin cateran.

We do not hear much about Bhamo till Alexander Dalrymple, writing in 1796, claimed that the East India Company had a factory with Englishmen based there in the early 17th century, though this remains unproven. We know that King Bodawpaya settled Assami soldiers nearby, at the village of Wethali, following his conquest of Assam. Otherwise, life in the area seems to have continued peaceably, with a steady trade handled by Chinese merchants sending goods up the Road of the Ambassadors. The outgoing trade from Upper Burma to China was cotton, and silks were brought back. There are rumours of a Portuguese settlement, and indeed many Portuguese veterans of the king's armies were settled throughout Burma and given wives and land. Portuguese trading settlements dotted the Burma coasts, shipping fine Chinese porcelain back to Lisbon, so perhaps these fragile cargos were carried by caravan to Bhamo, then shipped downriver to the Portuguese ports in the delta and onward to Europe.

In 1835, Inverness-born Captain Simon Hannay was permitted to travel upriver with the Mogaung governor's party of 34 country boats, towed with ropes from the riverbank. Again, British interest lay in trade with China, but like today the Kachins were in a state of rebellion and the opening of a trade route was unlikely. Hannay never reached Bhamo, instead going to Mogaung, on a tributary of the Irrawaddy, and travelling on foot from there to India.

R. Talbot Kelly 'Bhamo from the fort', 1905, from his book.

In 1863, Dr Clement Williams, the British resident in Mandalay favoured by King Mindon, gained permission to travel upstream. The journey, rowing him up to Bhamo, took 20 days, during which time he effectively surveyed the river. In 1868, he returned to Bhamo with the new resident, Colonel Sladen (Clement Williams now being the IFC agent for Mandalay), travelling on the king's new Italian-built steamer, the *Yeinan Seika*, which made the 450-mile journey in just eight days and established the river's navigability up to almost exactly 1,000 miles from the sea. Sladen was then able to join a mule caravan as far as Teng-yueh,[40] in Yunnan, 135 miles from Bhamo, and thus establish the possibility of a trade route to China. King Mindon, keen to increase trade even if this meant teaming up with the agency of the British and their flotilla company, had signed a treat in 1867 enabling

'The Joss House at Bhamo' by W. Burn Murdoch, 1908.

40   now Tengchong

the British to set up a residency in Bhamo and allowing a steamer service to operate.

Captain G.A. Strover, now appointed the resident, sailed upstream in 1868 on *Colonel Fytch*, the first IFC steamer to reach Bhamo. He travelled with a trade mission of Rangoon merchants, mostly Scots, keen to see the possibilities for themselves. In 1871 J. Talboys Wheeler made a similar journey, to visit Strover, and describes the lonely captain, bereft of bread, tea, cheroots and the company of English people for seven months. Talboys Wheeler was, though, extremely optimistic towards the commercial prospects, and on his return to Mandalay was interviewed by the king. Soon after the 1868 First Bhamo Expedition, the IFC inaugurated a monthly service from Mandalay to Bhamo, and the ships and their flats were soon laden with the entire Upper Burma cotton crop to be transhipped by mule across the mountains to Yunnan. By the 1870s, Chinese merchants were sending 1,000 mules a month to China, such was the increase in trade volumes.

The inner courtyard of the Joss House, or Chinese temple, at Bhamo.

R. Talbot Kelly, 'The Bhamo Bazaar', 1905. from his book.

From 1860 to 1874 Yunnan was in the hands of the Moslem Panthays, who had rebelled against Beijing. In fact, the British contacts in Yunnan were aligned with the Panthay rather than the Chinese imperial administration, and the Panthays themselves were keen to trade with the British. So in 1872 the Panthay Crown Prince Hassan travelled from his capital, Talifu, via Burma to London in the hope of kindling support (which he failed to gain). On his return journey whilst at Constantinople, he learnt of the fall of Talifu and the death of his father, ending the rebellion.

Yunnan being in Panthay hands meant that British trade had not yet penetrated properly into China. So, following the fall of Talifu in 1874, a second Bhamo expedition was organised, but this time in conjunction with the Beijing government: the so-called Shanghai Party under a diplomat, Augustus Margary, would set out from the Chinese side to meet up with Colonel Horace Browne from the Burma side. Margary reached Teng-yeuh early and decided to reconnoitre the route, but without sufficient escort. He and all his party were murdered by Shan-Tayok tribesmen, who correctly believed that the party was there to survey for a railway, which was against the tribesmen's interests. Browne and his party were similarly ambushed coming up from the Bhamo side, but escaped back to Bhamo with the remnants of the Shanghai Party, all returning to Mandalay by steamer. This debacle became known as the Margary Affair, and it escalated into an international incident, enabling the British to enforce an indemnity to be paid to Margary's relatives and the concession of treaty ports from the Chinese under the Chefoo Convention of 1876.

Kachins on the 'Road of the Ambassadors'.

Even so, the Margary Affair set British plans back considerably, as black reports came in from the follow-up expedition sent to investigate the murder. The enthusiasm for a railway waned. Prior to this, no one had considered the lawless nature of the country, with its uncontrolled dacoity and the vested interests of the tribespeople, whether they were the wild Kachin permanently engaged in vendettas, or Shan-Tayok bandits exacting tolls and protection payments – really, much the same as today!

Throughout the 1870s there had been a considerable lobby in England to open a Burma–China railway, mainly at the instigation of Captain Richard Spyre, a retired India Army officer. The Manchester Chamber of Commerce and various other chambers across Britain took up the call, lobbying the government incessantly to progress this project. In 1860, *The Times* concluded 'by confining our trade to the southern and eastern seaboard of China, we are but scratching the rind of that mighty realm. The best Chinese products, and customers for our products all lie inland towards the west.' However, the Margary Affair dampened enthusiasm. In many respects, the lobbying of the chambers of commerce for a railway was a forerunner to their lobbying for final annexation – an annexation which, when finally achieved in 1886, was intended to deliver to them not the markets of Upper Burma but those of China. Interestingly the British never gave up on the railway idea, and there were various surveys up until the First World War.

By the late 1930s, as all China's seaports were in Japanese hands it was decided to supply inland China with materiel through a Burma corridor, which became known as the Burma Road, completed in 1938. This was exactly what the colonial planners had been considering back in the 1880s. Today, under China's Belt and Road policy, the same route is intended to strategically circumvent the Malacca Strait, a significant maritime chokepoint, and to include oil and gas pipelines, truck superhighways, high-speed railways and super-barges bound for Bhamo on an Irrawaddy tamed with dams and locks.

The Fort, Bhamo, 1897.

Clement Williams described Bhamo in 1863 as a sad sort of place. As a result of Kachin raids, many of the Shan villages with their orchards of orange trees had been abandoned. The town itself had recently suffered a fire – apparently it was a tradition that the *myo-sa*, town-eater (the Mandalay-appointed governor), would burn the town down at the end of his tenure to despoil it for his successor. Although there were lead and silver mines, they were no longer worked due the depredations of Burmese officials, making the mining not worthwhile. The Chinese merchants, with their godowns filled with bales of cotton, sat idle in their shop-houses waiting for Yunnan caravans that never arrived, disrupted by Kachin raids and the Panthay rising.

Early sketches of the town show it as more Chinese than Burmese in appearance, and nearly all early accounts describe the temples (which seemed to double as casinos), and splendid merchant's houses with their inner courtyards. Sadly these are now all gone, and modern temples have been constructed on the sites of the ancient joss houses.

By the 1890s, following the annexation of Upper Burma, there was a sizable European community in Bhamo. The IFC agent was the centre of intelligence gathering and business activity; everything and everyone passed through his hands. IFC agents were the unofficial consuls of empire, and a Bourbon exile by the name of d'Avera, formerly a minister in the service of King Mindon, took up the post. In 1911, Hugh Fisher mentioned d'Avera as being himself something of a tourist attraction to American globetrotters, who gathered around him. (Interestingly, the main tourists to Burma in this period seem to have been Americans on imperial tours; a cruise up the Irrawaddy ranked with the Taj Mahal and Benares as a must-see.)

Around the turn of the 19th–20th centuries, several travel writers passed through Bhamo on their way either to or from China or as part of a Burma tour. R.F. Johnston quotes a Dr Morrison of 1894:

> There is a wonderful mixture of types in Bhamo. Nowhere in the world … is there a greater intermingling of the races. Here live in cheerful promiscuity Britishers and Chinese, Shans and Kachins, Sikhs and Madrasis, Punjabis, Arabs, German Jews and French adventurers, American missionaries and Japanese ladies.

Johnston found Bhamo much the same when he visited in 1908, except that 'the French adventurers and Japanese ladies had fled to other pastures'.

In 1904, Scott O'Connor wrote 'Bhamo, like the river on which it is built, leads a double life.' When you arrive today by boat, you'll see that the strand road remains much as it was when Scott O'Connor visited, with teak bungalows along the riverbank shaded by great rain trees. You can still find the IFC agency building, now the office of the IWT. Inside the town, however, little of what Scott O'Connor describes remains. Back then it was a typical old Chinese town of wooden shop-houses and splendid merchant houses. Now it is a typical modern Chinese town of ugly concrete-frame blocks, often clad with blue mirror glass. The Indian Street, once filled with Indian tailors, has gone, though there are still plenty of Indians around, not to mention Gurkhas and various others left behind from the empire. Armenians are there too, long pre-dating the British in Burma as bankers to the Burmese crown. (I was to meet remnants of these communities in the countryside outside Katha in the 1980s – their house shrines, where in any Burmese home the family Buddha would be kept, filled instead with glimmering icons.) The Bhamo billiard saloon was kept by a Jew, and the fort was garrisoned by Sikhs in splendid red turbans. A German called Kohn ran a sort of department store where you could buy just about anything. American Baptist missionaries were arriving in force, their sights set on the unruly Kachins, and no doubt the Japanese ladies had been replaced by ladies drawn from less distant lands. Scott O'Connor, as always, says it all:

> A Sikh sentry, with bayonet gleaming in the sun, walks to and fro before the treasury; in the litigant's shed the witnesses are assembled; on the grass of the courtyard the harnessed mare of the Deputy Commissioner feeds complacently, aware of her privileges. Burmans in silken kilts and flaming headgear, Shan in loose trousers and big straw hats, come and go in an incessant leisurely stream. And out on the white high road a British soldier swings by, his shoulders square, his boots creaking, the silver head of his regimental cane glinting in the sun.

Until the late 1890s the IFC ran an occasional steamer service for the final 220 miles to Myitkyina, which must have been quite an adventure, navigating in the First Defile through boulders the size of apartment blocks. George Bird made this passage in 1897, and his account in his *Wanderings in Burma* remains the best description of the route. At Sinbo, where the river is just 300 feet across, there were records of 90-foot rises at the onset of the monsoon. Scott O'Connor mentions a rise of 50 feet overnight, and during the rainy season a country boat would take three weeks to travel upstream to Myitkyina – and six hours to travel back down! In 1896, the Mu Valley State Railway, which had run as far as Naba with a branch line to Katha, was extended to Myitkyina, and thereafter there was little need for a steamer service to run in such risky waters.

D'Avera's successor as IFC agent was Captain Medd, who had served with the flotilla since 1892 and was appointed Bhamo agent in 1911, where he remained until his death in 1930. Writing in 1973, Captain Chubb recalls meeting him in the early days of his service: 'he was a gentleman of the old school'. Medd's office must have been something of a museum, and Chubb recalls seeing early IFC house flags hanging on the walls. Major Enriquez describes Medd in his wonderful book about the Kachins, *A Burmese Arcady* (1923):

> The ghosts of Kublai Khan's generals, the foundations of British and Portuguese factories, fill the countryside with a romance which in his kind, patient way he imparts to those of the slightest aptitude. Medd is the guide of tourists in their pathetic ignorance; the mainstay of Chinese traders; the friend of Burmese and Kachins. The charm that Bhamo holds for me is very largely Medd.

IFC House flag.

Medd was the source of the Conrad quote above. Conrad never visited Bhamo, but wrote the preface to his friend and literary agent Richard Curle's travel book on Burma and Malaya, and picked up on the mystery of the place. Curle tells of his encounter with Medd:

> I found awaiting me there in Bhamo the agent of the IFC; a man replete with knowledge, who illumined for me later in one sentence something about Bhamo I had instinctively felt since the first moment. 'On the frontier,' said he, 'we live on rumours.'

In 1904, Scott O'Connor visited Sinulum Kaba, a hill station 6,000 feet up in the mountains above Bhamo, established by N.G. Cholmeley of the Indian Civil Service, which had gardens with peach and cherry trees from England. Sinulum Kaba, rather than Bhamo, became a centre for justice for the Kachin, far from thieving lawyers and the inflexibility of a district court. Kachins would come in and have their cases heard in a humane and sympathetic way. Under a sense of fair play projected by British administrators and with no fear of them striking a fatal blow with a *dah*, a peace settled over these hills that had never before been known.

Walter G. Scott, an assistant superintendent at Sinulum Kaba, promoted the idea of Kachin levies serving with the Burma Rifles during the First World War, and he seems to have introduced the bagpipes to this highland people. Enriquez believed that the experience of the Kachin levies in the First World War was far more effective than 50 years of administration. Duwa[41] Scott died of dysentery at Sinulum, but was remembered by Kachins for generations to come, and the Kachin regimental pipes still bear the Scott tartan in his honour.

Enriquez had recruited and trained Kachin troops in the First World War, travelling with them from Bhamo to distant Mesopotamia, where they served with the Burma Rifles with great distinction. On the soldiers' return from the war with their years of pay saved up, they emptied the bazaars of Bhamo of gongs, the ambition of every Kachin being to own one. Never before had there been such an influx of cash into the Kachin economy.

Enriquez had a vision of the possibilities of taming the wild Kachin and sending them off around the world to serve the empire, rather like the Nepali Gurkhas. In recognition of their bravery and discipline, and with this idea in mind, the Kachin Rifles was formed shortly after the First World War. At the same time the Kachins were being tamed by other means; American Baptist missionaries (though there were Roman Catholic missionaries too) were extraordinarily successful in subduing the Kachin where Burmese kings and British military expeditions had failed.

And here we are 100 years on, and the Kachins are at war once again with the Burmese, after an all-too-brief 60-year Pax Britannica and an even briefer honeymoon with the newly independent Burma of the 1950s. In 1960 the Burmese leader U Nu declared Buddhism to be the state religion: this antagonised the predominantly Christian Kachin and drove them into open rebellion. As a large number of the Burmese army were Kachin, they split off, and formed the KIA – which, heir to the Kachin Rifles, is modelled on the British Army; it is well funded, and the men well disciplined and well trained. There is even a military academy, modelled on Sandhurst. Fighting between the KIA and the Burmese army continued until 1994, when there was a 17-year truce. This was broken by the Burmese in 2011, and war continues to this day.

Kachin state is rich in resources, the most famous of which is jade – but also the increasingly valuable water, with the headwaters of Burma's great rivers rising there

---

41   an honorific: Chief

– which, as we know, the Chinese are keen to get their hands on. Given the area's rich resources, it is not beyond the bounds of possibility that it might one day become an autonomous protectorate of China.

During the colonial period, Bhamo attracted 'sportsmen', and it was agreed that sport in Burma was as good as in Africa. Nearly all colonial accounts describe duck shooting along the river's sandbanks, fowling in the jungle or big game hunting for tiger deep in the forest. W.G. Burn Murdoch *in From Edinburgh to India and Burmah* describes pistol-shooting otters on the riverbank – this perhaps helps explain why there are no otters to be found in these parts. As mentioned earlier, dolphins have survived to date, and on one occasion, sailing up towards Bhamo on the *Kalaw Pandaw*, we were escorted for many miles by a pod swimming just to the fore of the bow. When the unthinking captain took a wrong turn and landed us on a submerged bank, the dolphins swam around as if in admonishment. If only we had followed their lead – they are the surest pilots on the river. Yet our best friend, the dolphin, is under threat by humans ourselves, intent on electric fishing.

If you strike lucky when cruising up the river, you might see a leaping golden mahseer. This migratory fish is known as the Himalayan salmon, but is much larger, growing as big as 50 kg and up to 2.75 metres long. In colonial times, anglers travelled to Bhamo specially to fish for these monsters in the First Defile, and even built a club house nearby.

I finally made it to Bhamo in the early 2000s after being thwarted first in the 1980s by military engagements and then in the 1990s by underpowered ships. But in 2001 the then brand-new *Pandaw II* with her powerful Caterpillar engines made it up there in high water without too much difficulty, and we were able to go up to the spectacular First Defile by country boat. When we went back again in 2010 and set out again for the First Defile we discovered that the KIA had machine-gun nests guarding the river at the entrance to the gorge. On one occasion we were late returning to town following a boat trip upriver to see the Taiping confluence. Due to low water, we had moored our ship 10 miles downstream and continued overland, but then as dusk fell we were told that we could not return to it as the roads were unsafe, being under the control of the KIA. After much negotiation we persuaded the police to let us go back downriver by boat with an armed escort. This brought home to me the fact that Bhamo has become a Burmese island in midst of a KIA sea, with little or no control over surrounding roads or countryside.

11

The Chindwin

The Chindwin, at about 750 miles, is the Irrawaddy's greatest tributary and Burma's third-longest river after the Irrawaddy and Salween. It is navigable in small ships for 440 miles up from its confluence with the Irrawaddy. Its source is high in Kachin state's Hukawng valley, draining the waters of the Patkai hills across the border in India. The average flow rate is 170,000 cubic feet per second, compared to the Irrawaddy's just over 500,000 cubic feet per second. If the Irrawaddy's waters can be sapphire blue, then the Chindwin's are jade green. As a river, it is even more extreme in the variation of seasonal depths than the Irrawaddy, with a faster flow in the monsoon and almost no flow in the dry season. I have seen large and powerful vessels thrown back downstream by a rapid, and their progress upstream, even when hugging the banks to get out of the main stream, can be slower than that of a bullock cart. I have travelled down in a day what it took a week to get up. Here as well, in the dry season I have seen ships grounded for several months, the consequence of a momentary lapse in concentration on the part of the pilot.

Tree roots.

Fishermen, Fisherman's Shelter.

Fisherman on the Chindwin.

The Chindwin with its enchanting scenery may be the prettiest of rivers, but it is also one of the most violent. Its valley, and those of its main tributaries such as the Mu, Myittha and Uyu, are amongst the most fertile areas of an otherwise fertile land. A consequence of this wealth was that its villages were rich with fine wood-carved monasteries, often in the latest court styles, created by craftsmen sent from the capital. I have sailed the Chindwin several times, from my first voyage in a cargo boat in 1986 to taking various *Pandaws*, large and small, up and down. It is a river which never ceases to overwhelm with its sheer picturesqueness, as range upon range of delicate wooded hills drop down to the river forming bluffs and racing narrows. Then there are the islands of whispering elephant grass; the glistening white beaches; the great rain trees mounted on the banks.

The Chindwin is the heart and soul of Burma, the people by virtue of their isolation continuing a way of life that is the quintessence of Burmeseness, with few outside influences and little change till recent times. Even the changes that came with the opening up of the 2010s were benign ones, mobile phones and motorbikes making everyone's lives a little bit easier. When I travelled here in the 1980s, sleeping in monasteries, I was amazed by the respect enjoyed by the Buddhist clergy. When I walked with a monk friend through villages, any passer-by or bystander would slip out of his shoes as we passed.

Most people think of the Irrawaddy valley as the core of Burmese culture and life, yet the reality is that it was the Chindwin that was the heart of Burmese agricultural life, trade, culture and religion. As we have seen, until the arrival of the British much of the Irrawaddy valley, from the delta to middle Burma, was depopulated and uncultivated. Even today, much of the Dry Zone is a barely inhabited desert, and north of Mandalay jungle and forest take over, and human habitation is along the few flat strips of riverbank or in the valleys of tributaries or in flat pockets of countryside, islands in the midst of barren scrub. Before the British came it was in the rich lush Chindwin valley that the majority of Burmese lived, farmed and prospered.

Whilst the river between its main port, Monywa, and the confluence is not without interest, there are some important villages with splendid monastic complexes, such as Hsalingyi or Yimabin. But most travellers would join a ship at Monywa. A wander down the river bund at Monywa brings one back into a world of the 1920s or 1930s, as nearly all the colonial buildings are still intact. In addition to the offices of the agent of the IFC were all the main offices of government and commercial firms and further up the splendid dak bungalows of their officers. Somewhere along here was the Monywa Club where the Chindwin commanders would congregate before and after voyages exchanging titbits of navigational information, not to men-

Fields on the sandbanks.

Rafting.

tion steamy gossip from the villages they called at. We can picture Stanley 'Chindwin' White, the famous superintendent of pilots, holding forth here, and the institution was a must for any traveller seeking local colour. Monywa is today the capital of the Sagaing Division, which was the 1990s was sensibly moved to this more central position from Sagaing itself, on the furthest edge of the state.

High on the bank today you will see the carcasses of the last few IWT Chindwin vessels built in Scotland in the late 1940s and early 1950s, now used as accommodation for IWT crewmen's families. These were running until relatively recently, but are again the victim of new roads and bridges. Despite this there remains a healthy traffic of motorboats carrying produce down from the villages and goods back up, and water bus services which operate on privately owned super-fast boats. Yet it is nothing like the volume of traffic previously enjoyed, and the loss of the line ships means of the loss of a whole way of life on the river, as we have seen on the Irrawaddy.

There are now two bridges over the Lower Chindwin: one below Monywa, connecting the Irrawaddy's rail and road corridor between Bassein and Mandalay; and one upstream, which links to Pakokku and the fertile agricultural hinterland between. An improved road follows the Chindwin, connecting Monywa to the India border and right up the valley to Homalin.

Even back in the 1980s, Monywa was a busy, prosperous town, both because of its trade with India and because it was the hub of a huge agricultural area into which commodities would be carried by river and stored in the great godowns of its merchant who lived in palatial apartments above. On my first trip upstream, in 1986, the 'moto' boat laboriously towed barges of pulses destined for India. Today Monywa boasts a huge Ocean supermarket and shopping mall, and past prosperity very much continues into present times.

The countryside inland from Monywa is idyllic, and there is nothing more pleasant than driving down the rain tree-shaded roads to visit the Buddhist sanctuaries at places like Budalin with their many artistic treasures. For those who enjoy contemporary kitsch there is the Disneyland religious complex at Maha-bodhi-taung, but once is enough. The best excursion of all out of Monywa is to the caves at Hpowindaung across the river. These really are important, with schemes of mural paintings dating from the late 18th century and through to the late 19th, narrating Buddhist scriptures, cosmography and the various past lives and final life of Gotama Buddha. There are still plenty of hermits, wizards and other such types found in off-beat Buddhist places, vying for your attention along with troops of monkeys.

Casting off to the tooting of horns and blast of sirens and many a wave from the numerous riverside audience that attends the departure of any Pandaw ship, we are out in the mainstream and hard to starboard, pointing upriver and to another world beyond. The gateway to that world is the first narrowing of the river at Shwe-say-yar, where there is a year-round whirlpool between the rocky outcrops of each facing bank. In high, fast water the whirlpool can be something of a concern, and when the whirlpool rises 30 feet, to the level of the bluffs on either side, masters know not to attempt it. In times of old, the local boatmen made a good living as pilots guiding boats through.

Narrows on the Chindwin at Shwe-say-yar.

Kani village on the west bank was always our first stop, with a pleasant walk or mountain bike ride into the interior. When we used to stop here in the 1990s you could hear a pin drop; nothing seemed to move. Then during the democracy years it was all abuzz as the locals enjoyed their newfound freedoms to trade and interact without the interference of the Ne Win socialist party and more recently the military. Such new-found freedoms the people of Kani – and indeed much of Burma, once so repressed – will never give up lightly, and at time of writing Kani is a battlefield between the military and the people's defence forces. On the approach to Kani is a rocky bluff, and it is from here that Myin Byu Shin, one of the pantheon of 37 nats who died heroically in defence of freedom, leapt to his death on his white horse and is thus known as Lord of the White Horse. Let us hope that Myin Byu Shin protects the people of Kani in these terrible times and casts his benevolent spell on the Chindwin.

These lower Chindwin townships are oases of agriculture amid hills and jungle, all linked to the river. As the newly cut roads can be undependable in the monsoon months, the river remains the main link between these towns and the outside world, and the conduit of prosperity. The river winds dramatically, looping round in great circles as we negotiate eddies and white waters from town to town. It would be good to stop and explore them all, but time presses and we must reach Mingkin by nightfall.

Mingkin, on the west bank, is a place of great fascination. Before the age of steam and Scott O'Connor's 'fire boats' of the Irrawaddy Flotilla, which opened this valley to the world, a small town like Mingkin, even though it was at least a couple of weeks' paddle from Mandalay, was a centre of splendid monastery-building in the latest court styles.

In 1986 I spent a week exploring this area, staying in monasteries which I described in my book *Mandalay*. For example, at Gyi Taung Oo village, just upriver from Mingkin, is the oldest working monastery in Burma, founded in 1728 by U Thya. Quite unlike the classic monasteries from the Konbaung period, centred as it is on a block rather than a longitudinal succession of halls and chambers, it is decorated within with red lacquer and gold leaf decoration like the monasteries of Luang Prabang in Laos, and gives a good idea of what monasteries were like prior to the rise of the Konbaung dynasty – and, indeed, what the palace apartments would have been like in the original pre-Konbaung palace at Ava. Even so, we get a feel of what the 13th-century monasteries of Pagan were like prior to stylistic revolution that occurred under the Konbaung, reaching their culmination in the Yadanabon or Mandalay style from the mid-19th century and continuing into colonial times. Known as the Ni Kyaung Daw Gyi, or Great Sacred Red Temple, it continued in the 1980s as a centre of meditation and spirituality, with the surrounding villagers talking in whispers so as not to disturb the lords in their practices. Other archaic practices continued here, including the wearing of lacquered parasol hats.

A mile or so further up the river on the same west bank is Kan village, where I have enjoyed a friendship with the *sayardaw*, village abbot, for over 30 years. Thanks to his guiding hand Kan has always been the best kept village in Burma, and you will find no litter here. Even back in the 1980s he had rubbish bins made from old cans positioned down the main street. He then fought a running battle with the officials of the socialist party, who would descend on the village in droves to extort money from the near-penniless peasants and impose innumerable restrictions. One farmer, who had planted a row of banana trees, was told to cut them down as they were not in the five-year plan. Another was told to take down a cowshed as he did not have the right permit. The sayardaw battled on their behalf, using the power of his robe and natural spiritual aura to keep the socialist parasites at bay. Then came SLORC, and his battles continued, this time with soldiers and the local juntas formed of army officers who, like the myosa

Temple guard at Kan.

of old royal Burma, were there to pillage these villages for their own enrichment. The sayardaw kept them all at bay. As a result of this protective role, the Kan sayardaw enjoys an adoration and respect over and above that you would normally find in any Burmese village. On my last visit, in 2018, following the great relaxation, first under General Thein Sein and with an elected NLD government, the village was booming, and everyone seemed to be rebuilding their house bigger and better. As they were free to plant what they wanted, agriculture was booming, as was river trade.

The Kan monastery itself was a reconstruction, as the original one dedicated by U San Shin in 1874 had apparently collapsed, but the sayardaw had saved the wood carvings, which are richly fashioned in the same three-dimensional style as the ones we met at Salay, and the work of a late 19th-century atelier that achieved a high point in wood carving. (There is another monastery near Minbu which I would presume to be also the work of this atelier – just three sites surviving and not even the name of the master.) What were these lavishly endowed monasteries doing here in so remote a place? Most likely U Thya in the 18th century and U San Shin 100 years later were courtiers who had originated from these villages. The Burmese administration followed the Chinese meritocracy system of exams, usually monastic, for entry and ascent through the civil service. Poets and authors of philosophical treaties were promoted above all. With high position and wealth, it was customary to dedicate a monastery back in their home village, and they would spare no expense to ensure that these were made of the finest materials, employing the most celebrated artists and artisans in the latest court styles. Thus although there is little remaining at Ava, Amarapura and Mandalay themselves, there is much of Ava, Amarapura and Mandalay in the remoter villages of Burma.

Alister McCrae, in his tale of a Chindwin journey taken in 1935, tells a good story about Mingkin that deserves to be quoted in full here:

> The Captain told me he had a small party of American tourists for a round trip in the previous cold weather. Arriving at Mingkin … the party went ashore to see the fine carvings in an old *hpoongyi-kyaung* in the village. They were somewhat taken aback to be shown there a tin coffin full of honey, in which the body of a Sayadaw was lying embalmed. It was explained that he was being kept thus until sufficient money was collected for a *hpoongyi-byan*, when the body would be cremated in the traditional Buddhist manner.
>
> The steamer got under way the next morning early and at breakfast it was observed that a jar of honey had been added to the usual marmalades, etc. A lady of the American party called the butler. 'Where did you get the honey from butler?' she asked. 'The honey, Missee,' replied the Madrassi butler,

obviously proud of his acquisition, 'is from the hpoongyi-kyaung at Mingkin.' After a stunned silence he was told it would not be required.

Just below Kalewa at Shwegyin there is a bay in the river and a bowl in the hills around it, and before the construction of the new bridge at Kalewa this was the ferry crossing point. This was where General Bill Slim's 14th army crossed the river in retreat from the Japanese in April 1942, using six of the IFC's smaller S-class steamers under the command of John MacNaughtan, a IFC assistant commissioned as a lieutenant in the naval reserve, who worked tirelessly day and night to ferry 500 men per trip in vessels designed for half that number. Around 30,000 men were shipped across the river by the flotilla. A boom had been positioned across the river to prevent Japanese vessels advancing further, but eventually in early May they crossed it and penetrated the Bowl, as it was known. So it was necessary to move the crossing point further up, where Chief Engineer Hutcheon, taking command of a vessel, managed to ferry 2,400 men across a creek. His fellow engineer John Murie was awarded a military cross in the field by General Alexander for his part in rescuing cut-off forces. We visited Shwegyin in 2018, and were disappointed to find few vestiges of the crossing, any abandoned vehicles long since picked over for scrap. However, on enquiry one villager produced a British army bayonet, which he used as a poker for his fire.

Kalewa, situated on the confluence of the Myittha river and the Chindwin, is a very different sort of town from Mingkin with its ancient monasteries. Kalewa is the river port for Kalemyo, the main town situated further up the Myittha, which flows down from the Chin Hills. The Myittha is navigable between Kalewa and Kalemyo by *loned-win*, paddy boats, which bring the crop down from the fertile hills to be transhipped down the Chindwin. Above Kalewa the Upper Chindwin truly begins, and if Monywa is the capital of the lower Chindwin then Kalewa is the capital of the upper river. The town has extensive markets, as you would expect from so important a hub, but otherwise is not so attractive, being given over to commerce rather than art. It is a good place to provision before setting forth into the upper river.

From here the character of the river changes markedly. For one thing, it is narrower, and it has less of the broad sweep of the lower river. Navigation becomes easier, too, with an increase in depth, though on sharp bends as buffs meet river there can be rapids. There will be less traffic here, and the countryside along the banks is richly cultivated with paddy fields about picturesque villages – such a surprise after the great swathes of groundnut farming in the Dry Zone. Running down the ridges of the intermittent ranges of hills that meet the river are the inevitable covered walkways leading to summit pagodas, shimmering white and gold against the lush forest foliage. It is Burma at its most beautiful and pristine best.

Fishing in the lee of rocks.

Mawlaik was the British administrative centre, and its location provides a fascinating insight into the British colonial mentality. The obvious place to site this centre would seem to have been at the junction of Kalewa or indeed Kalemyo, but instead the centre was founded in a clearing of jungle in the middle of nowhere. At the time it was declared that this would attract commercial activity and traders, and markets would be based there – but no Burmese merchant was going to be bothered to relocate a day's sail upriver, away from the action. The main residences and public buildings at Mawlaik are arranged around a very quaint golf course, and I believe that this is, in fact, the real reason why the town was sited here; Kalewa and its surroundings are far too hilly for golf. However, McCrae reckoned that it was the duck shooting in the surrounding jungle ponds that attracted the decision makers. Perhaps it was both.

Many of the grand residences are now ghost houses, others lived in by Burmese officials. Built in a sort of Arts and Crafts meets Anglo-Indian style, they are extremely attractive. We managed to get into the largest one, then unoccupied. It must have originally housed the deputy commissioner, and we found spacious reception rooms designed for entertaining imperial visitors and the local society, consisting of other colonial officials and company men. There were tennis courts in the garden, and what would once have been manicured English lawns. What a wonderful posting! To be sent to Mawlaik and follow a round of golf or tennis with tea on the lawn, then dress for pre-dinner cocktails before a roaring fire, followed by a feast of game shot in the surrounding hills.

Continuing upriver from Mawlaik, we reach Pantha. Deep in the hills above, some 27 miles inland from here, were oilfields and a pipeline that ran down through the jungle to Pantha, where there was a small oil refinery. Once refined, petroleum was pumped onto a river tanker, called appropriately *Chintank,* which, with twin screws and a deeper draft of 3 feet, could only work in the higher water seasons. The expatriate workers in these fields had natural gas piped straight from the wells into their bungalows for cooking and heating. In the monsoon the only transport up there was by elephants, who carried everything, including people, in and out. At times even the elephant trail was impassable, and the undoubtedly well supplied employees of the Indo-Burma Petroleum Company lived in companionable isolation. Apparently, the phone line was made of barbed wire to stop monkeys from swinging on it.

Dak bungalow.

Petroleum apart, the main economic activity for the British in this remote region was logging, and the largest of the timber companies there was the Bombay Burmah, founded by William Wallace of Edinburgh in 1863. By the 1920s, it was one of the City's largest colonial companies.

District Commissioner's house.

The officers of the company in Burma were usually former naval officers, and would disappear into the jungle for months on end living in camps or occasionally housed on station in places like Mawlaik. These could be eccentric characters, used to rough living. A bottle of whisky a day was not considered excessive. Gordon Hunt, who worked for the 'Bombai', wrote a marvellous book on his life in the forests, *Forgotten Burma*, which itself has been sadly forgotten, but remains in my opinion the most outstanding memoir of life in the jungle, or indeed colonial Burma. Their lifeline was the IFC steamers bringing mail, provisions and no doubt cases of whisky to get them through the long, lonely jungle nights. The steamers also acted as floating ATMs, and any company officer could sign a chit to draw cash from a steamer captain in order to pay his men and local costs. These chits would be reconciled between the head offices back in Rangoon.

The most famous of the timber men was of course the Cornishman J.H. Williams, author of *Elephant Bill*, which has become a classic on elephant management and husbandry. After the First World War, when he served in the Camel Corps, Williams joined the Bombay Burmah and managed an area of 400 square miles with ten camps, and 70 elephants and oo-si. What comes over in *Elephant Bill* is the way in which man and beast lived in total harmony, with – just as it is now – an oo-si of the same age as his elephant, growing up together through childhood, training together in adolescence and then starting work together, for a lifelong partnership. We still see elephants on the Chindwin waving their trunks from the bank in response to a blast from our ship's horn, and if you are particularly lucky you will see one of the forest department's elephant boats transporting the great beasts from station to station on the river.

Elephants crossing the Chindwin.

There is a marvellous story of a drinking session by the campfire with Elephant Bill and the ubiquitous Chindwin White, who keeps popping up, as he would have on his voyages up and down the river, supervising pilot stations and buoy boats. Surrounded by their bearers and camp followers and talking in a drunken sort of Burmese, one of the two men suddenly insulted the other, and there was a horrified silence all round, apart from the other of the two, who responded in the vilest of terms. Obscenity was heaped on obscenity, and any self-respecting Burman would by this point have reached for his *dah*. On they went, now standing and shaking fists at each other as they cursed each other in impeccably foul Burmese. The Burmese followers in a circle around the fire watched, horrified yet spellbound. Then simultaneously, both White and Williams burst together into fits of giggles, much to the delight of the Burmese who realised they had been completely duped.

Back in 1752, when Sieur de Bruno had been killed and his men resettled, some of those men served Alaungpaya under the Chevalier Milard in a French corps within the royal army, and on retirement were given lands in the Shwebo area. This resettlement of prisoners and absorption of defeated foreign forces into the army had been standard Burmese policy for a thousand years. Godfrey Harvey, in his *History of Burma* says the French who settled here had their hamstrings cut so they could not run away. But who would want to run away from matrimonial bliss in so delightful a place? When I visited one of the French villages, I was disappointed to note that any resemblance to the French had long faded, and unlike in the Portuguese communities the people were no longer Catholic, though it is said that there is a residue of Catholicism in the French villages around Shwebo. On meeting the French ambassador and telling him of my visit, his eyes opened wide to the Francophone opportunities. Alas for these remote communities, however, neither a lycée nor an Alliance Française materialised.

Thoungdoot is a Shan enclave, and until independence a Shan *sawbwa*, prince, reigned autonomously with little interference from the British. The Shans, who are a Tai people, can be found as far west as Assam and to the north in Yunnan, where they are called Dai; and groups of them may be found as far east as Vietnam. Despite this geographical range their cultures are remarkably homogenous: they are all Theravada Buddhist; they wear similar clothes; and they have similar traditions of handicrafts, cuisine and folklore. The main concentration of Tai is of course in Thailand and on the huge Shan plateau, which – worse luck for these Shans, thanks to the British protectorate policy – now forms part of Burma, whereas they were previously under the more benign suzerainty of Siam. The Thoungdoot *sawbwa*, ruler, lived in some state in his *haw*, palace, and all the rituals of kingship were observed, with white and gold umbrellas, sacred regalia and strict sumptuary laws regulating an extensive royal family. The British were only ever called in to settle disputes over succession, or feuds between the offspring of multitudinous wives and other such domestic issues. Otherwise, the *sawbwa* ruled with little interference.

We pass Sittaung, always a sad spot for me, as it was here that the Chindwin fleet was scuppered in 1942 to deprive the advancing Japanese of their use. From here there was a road of sorts to the Indian border post at Tamu. As with the abandoned fleet at Katha, the ships' commanders were last off and last out. There is no sign of the ships now. Today with the border open, the rebuilt Tamu road is abuzz with trucks coming to and from India, and a healthy trade has been established. Sadly, the trucks rattle down to Monywa by road rather than transhipping by river, the most economical form of transport though also the slowest.

Homalin is as far as most ships get, and to reach it we need the high water of the monsoon, or at least the tail-end of the monsoon. Homalin has an airfield, so when we ran ships in that area we could fly our passengers in and out. The town has a mixed ethnicity of Burmese, Shans, Kuki and Nagas. The Nagas have a colourful new year festival that has become something of a tourist attraction, with people flying in specially for it. In addition, the Nagas, who span both sides of the Burma–India border, are famed as head-hunters; by secret techniques they shrink the skulls down to a miniature size. When Alister McCrae travelled up to Homalin in 1935 the government was still having to deal with occasional head-hunting raids by Naga warriors coming down from the hills. There is no single Naga tribe, but rather numerous tribes with a common culture spread over a vast area in remote and often cut-off valleys; there are at least 89 different Naga languages and dialects. The one thing they all seem to have in common is wonderful handwoven shawls and magnificent talismanic jewellery, not to mention a splendid martial culture with war dances, beating drums and the like. Indeed, there can be no finer sight than a dancing Naga warrior in full fig.

Homalin attained some notoriety when an army-owned heroin factory was located here in the 1990s. Today the talk is about hydropower, and agreements have been signed with India to harness the flow of the river – but mercifully these have yet to materialise. The nearby Uyu tributary has considerable panning activity, not just for gold dust but also solid nuggets, sometimes huge. The river remains navigable for another 100 miles or so as far as Hkamti, but only in high water during the monsoon. This part of Burma gets 88 inches of rain a year, so it would be a wet voyage. I have yet to get that far on this most wonderful of rivers.

Naga dancers at Homalin.

12

The Salween

Moulmein sits on the estuaries of three rivers: the Salween, the Gyaing and the Ataran, which spread out like a great map when viewed from the Kyaik-tha-lun hilltop pagoda.

Kipling only spent a day in Moulmein; he disembarked for a tour of the town on his way to Japan in 1889 and was inspired to write his great poem 'Mandalay'. Moulmein is of course nowhere near Mandalay and the Irrawaddy, which he never visited either. Kipling later wrote that that day he fell in love with a Burmese maiden whilst visiting the town's main pagoda: 'Only the fact of the steamer departing at noon prevented me from staying at Moulmein forever.' We must thank the nameless belle who was an inspiration for one of the greatest poems in the English language. Ironically, the words 'Kipling' and 'Burma' became synonymous, yet despite the brevity of his visit, no European, whether in the 1890s or today, has ever captured the magical essence of Burma better than Kipling.

The Salween, Thanlwin in Burmese, is at 2,044 miles long almost the same length as the Irrawaddy, but is a far narrower river, with an average discharge of 230,000 cubic feet per second compared with the Irrawaddy's 500,000 plus. The greater part of the Salween is actually in China, where it is called the Nu, and it passes through an area of Yunnan settled by the Nu people. Its source is a glacier in Tibet, and from there it flows through Yunnan in gorges as deep as 14,800 feet, known as the Grand Canyon of the East, with an outstanding biodiversity, so rich that even the Chinese have managed to restrain themselves from damming it; this section of the river is now a world heritage site. However, the Chinese have hydro-electric dams on several of its tributaries, and MOUs have been signed between the Burmese and Thais for enormous schemes in the Shan states section of the river, to create huge reservoirs that would significantly alter the geography of the area. The Salween basin is home to several peoples: the Tibetans at its source; the aforementioned Nu; various tribal peoples in the hills of Yunnan and the Shan states; the Shans themselves; further down, the Kayah and Karens; finally, the Mon, occupying the area around its mouth. Noticeably absent are the Burmese, other than in the garrisons they hold in their 70-year civil war with nearly all of these ethnic groups. The Salween has in many ways been a several-hundred-mile riverine battle-ground between the Burmese and their subject peoples, traversed by armies advancing and retreating. Where the river forms a border with Thailand, refugees have crossed to take sanctuary in Thailand, and have happily traded teak and opium in exchange for arms.

On the Salween.

Despite these troubles the basin is agriculturally very rich, and the river, its trib-utaries and the lakes it feeds offer fisheries that provide the main source of protein for the human population who dwell there. In the lower valley, which is tropical in climate, wet rice cultivation is the staple, and in the more temperate climate of the Shan hills there are orchards of fruits, tea gardens and even coffee plantations. The British introduced rubber to the coastal areas, and the rubber estates along this strip were more part of a Malayan world than a Burmese one, with planters downing their *stenghas*, whisky and sodas, at sundown. In Burma proper, few British were cultivators or planters, being traders, but here on the southern coast it was a different world. Likewise in Burma proper, few expatriates went to live there for the enjoyment of it, but rather to make money. However, contemporary accounts of the southern coastal ports describe a bohemian expatriate life of beachcombers and remittance men long gone native and happily intermarried, their main form of dress the singlet and longyi.

The river is only navigable on larger vessels for about 50 miles, as far up as the Karen capital of Hpa-an, and thereafter transport is by country boat and long tail. The IFC ran launch services out of a hub at Moulmein, a launch in that case being a small steamer of anything up to 150 feet. There was an IFC dockyard at Moulmein with a

Dumbarton superintendent, and the company absorbed several competitors such as Dawson's Fleet, which came with the aforementioned Dawson's Railway. (There was also a Dawson's Bank operating in the delta areas; it would be interesting to learn more about Dawson.) The most famous merger was of course the fleet of the Mon entrepreneur U Nat Auk, who dared to take on the IFC and whose story has gone down in Burmese history as the supreme example of imperial unfairness.

The IFC also ran services on the Ataran river, which went far deeper into the interior than was navigably possible on the Salween, and the Gyaing. The Ataran leads up into the teak forests, an area the British were to open and exploit to great profit, and Moulmein's development as a town was linked to the successful navigation of the Ataran.

The Salween at Hpa-an.

Moulmein was a British creation following the First Anglo-Burmese War of 1824, when the territories of Tenasserim and the Arakan were ceded to the British. Opposite was the Burmese town of Martaban, which had been an important provincial capital for centuries, sitting at the mouth of the great Salween, the longest river in Burma, so Moulmein's northern point, in a strategic location with rivers on two sides, was called Battery Point, its guns pointing across the river at Burmese territory.

The East India Company had absorbed this new territory with some degree of reluctance, as its Board of Directors in Calcutta had felt it would be costly to garrison and administer, with little potential for profit. The EIC's board were soon proved wrong, however, and Moulmein developed into an important economic hub: initially teak extraction; then ship building, taking advantage of the abundant timber; later, rubber planting and tin mining. Colonel Bogle, the first civil commissioner, built himself a palatial mansion, Salween House, in a spacious park on one of the hills. Later this was considered too grand for a civil servant's residence and it was turned into the court house and town offices.

Many of Moulmein merchants were Scots, including of course T.D. Findlay, who had come to Moulmein in 1840 by way of Penang. John Crawfurd, a native of Islay who had been an army doctor and former resident at the Court of Ava, and Dr Wallick, the superintendent of the Botanical Gardens in Calcutta, had travelled on the *Diana*, the first steam paddler in Burma, which had been brought over from Bengal in 1824 for the Anglo-Burmese War. Despatched to Moulmein it made an expedition up the Ataran River with Crawfurd and Wallick to inspect the forests and logistics of its shipping. What they found surpassed all expectation, so even after political power had shifted to Rangoon Moulmein remained a teak town, by the 1910s shipping 60,000 tons of teak a year, about one-fifth of the country's total production.

William Darwood, the *Diana's* chief engineer, realising the possibilities, stayed on in Moulmein, where he married the daughter of the ship owner Captain Snowball, who had also just settled there. Snowball was famous in all the Indian Ocean ports, and it was significant that he chose to settle in Moulmein. In 1825 this was the place to be. An Englishman, Darwood had served in the Bengal Marine and lost a leg in the *Diana's* assault on Martaban in 1824, for which he had been awarded a pension. He set up as ship builder, and between 1833 and 1841 launched 11 vessels. Darwood was one of over 20 ship builders established in Moulmein by the 1840s. As wooden hulls gave way to steel by the 1850s, ship building declined in Moulmein, and after the Second Anglo-Burmese War the larger vessels were to be built on the Rangoon River at Dalla. The riverbanks at Moulmein, however, still abound with boat builders constructing trawlers and river launches.

Moulmein was important for only 30 years, as after the Second Anglo-Burmese War it was Rangoon that became the capital of all Lower Burma. Thereafter Moulmein became a somewhat sleepy provincial town, of economic rather than political importance. It was regarded as a very pleasant and comfortable town, and a place of retirement for Europeans who chose not to go 'home'. This was the Bournemouth of Burma, with quiet shady streets, dak bungalows and huge gardens.

If you climb the Kyaik-tha-lun pagoda hill to stand where Kipling stood (mistaking the Salween for Irrawaddy and becoming besotted with that pretty girl) you can see the original town laid out between the corniche and the small range of hills which the pagoda dominates. It originally consisted of three thoroughfares, the Strand, Main Road and Upper Road, running parallel to the river, along which the merchants' godowns and counting houses stood, with their occupants looking out across the Strand at their ships at anchor. You can see now that the town has spread inland to the eastern side of the hills. Ranged along the town hills are diverse pagodas and monasteries, nearly all dating from colonial times and in a hotchpotch of colonial classical and Burmese rococo styles. The largest and most splendid Hindu temple in Burma sits brilliantly amongst this architectural melee. Gazing across the town, you will see that all religions are represented, and I would hazard that there are as many mosques as pagodas, for under the British this was very much an Indian town. Not to be outdone by mosque or pagoda, church towers and steeples soar skywards in a mix of Gothic and Romanesque. Just beneath on the west side you will see a huge prison radiating out from its main block like a fan. Moulmein Jail, once a model prison, memorialises the legacy of the British as much as the churches and godowns. For the British were to pacify a territory where dacoits terrorised villages, and pirates preyed on coastal traders. (Looking through my zoom lens I could see a very active prison population playing football and *chinlone*, caneball, cheered on by the guards.) To the north the great Salween graciously curves its way on the journey to distant Tibetan peaks. Closer, you will see the jagged Zwekabin range of hills, the most prominent of which was known as the Duke of York's nose (though which Duke of York remains a mystery). From the east, the Salween is joined by the Ataran and Gyaing Rivers, which used to bring rafted teak down from the great forests that abutted Siam. Three enormous rivers thus meet in the estuary between Moulmein and Martaban, so it is no surprise that Moulmein became such an important port and trading post.

From Moulmein you can travel easily to Hpa-an, capital of Karen state, by car in a couple of hours but better is a day trip by boat up the Salween. I was lucky enough to do this in the late 1990s when IWT was still running line ships between Moulmein and Hpa-an, and on the other rivers too. This surely is the only way to go, with magnificent scenery as we follow the Zwekabin range, which runs parallel to the river on its east bank. At times you could think you were in Guilin in China, so wonderfully mystical is the karst landscape, particularly in the early morning mists.

Hpa-an is now a lively, prosperous city and a centre of education with several universities and colleges. The Karens here are predominantly Buddhist. Worth a stop is the Mahar-sadan cave. You can walk through several great Buddha-filled caverns (take your shoes with you, as you will need them later) and you pop out of the other side to be rowed back round the mountain across a lake, through further grottos and then along a mini-canal which the industrious Karen dug out all in the name of local tourism, which they seem to benefit from.

Moulmein was once home to the young colonial policeman, Eric Blair, who was later to adopt the nom de plume George Orwell. His essay 'The Shooting of an Elephant' was set in Moulmein and begins with the wonderful sentence: 'In Moulmein, in Lower Burma, I was hated by large numbers of people – the only time in my life that I have been important enough for this to happen to me.' Orwell had strong Moulmein connections as his mother's family, the Limouzins, were from here. His great-grandfather, a Frenchman, was a ship builder from Bordeaux and founded Limouzin & Co. in 1826. Orwell arrived exactly 100 years later; in the previous year his grandmother had died in Moulmein. In downtown Moulmein there is still a Limouzin Street.

In 'The Shooting of the Elephant' Orwell shows an early disillusionment with the colonial system of which he, as the town's police superintendent, was a pillar. He describes how he was pressured by a crowd into shooting an elephant in musth even though it had ceased rampaging and was no longer a danger. Somehow the prestige of the British required him to act in an unnecessarily cruel way, causing immense suffering to the beast as it died a long, slow death. The shooting was a symbol of colonial rule. In *Burmese Days*, which is set on the river in Katha, which we visited on our voyage on the Upper Irrawaddy, Orwell went on to ridicule the tedium of provincial colonial life. His record of life in Burma was deeply cynical, at variance with nearly all other contemporary accounts from this time.

The fact that the poor elephant was a Moulmein elephant is relevant, for Moulmein was Elephant City: teak rafts were floated down the three rivers to be gathered at their mouths and brought ashore by elephants; the logs were transported by elephants, even stacked in neat piles by elephants. Working elephants were everywhere in Moulmein, a feature of daily life. I wish there were statistics on this, but even so there must have been several thousand stabled here. Elephants have identical lifespans to humans, so most beasts were good for 40 years of service. They were thus very valuable items. I once met a member of the Wallace family of the Bombay Burmah Trading Corporation who returned to Burma in the 1990s and encountered elephants branded BBTC before the Second World War still working away.

When I first visited Moulmein in 1986. I was going to visit Professor Hla Pe, who had been emeritus professor of Burmese at London University before my time there, and had retired to Moulmein. I had heard many stories of Saya Hla Pe's erudition and eloquence and had longed to meet him. Back then, under the Ne Win dictatorship, foreigners were only allowed to travel to the usual tourist spots and I had to get special permission to go down to Moulmein. As the roads were so bad the train was the best way to get there. The terminus was at Martaban from where a ferry took me across the mile-wide Salween to Moulmein.

As I crossed from the railway platform to the jetty I was confronted by a beaming police officer. 'You are going to visit Saya U Hla Pe' – a statement rather than a question, for the only foreigners ever to arrive in Moulmein were Saya's guests. The police were very kind and insisted on taking me across the river in a police launch, and on the other side a police jeep was waiting to take me to Saya's house.

This was the first of several visits to Saya over the years; the professor was one of the most erudite men in Burma and a fount of information on Burmese literature, language and culture. After a dram or two he would hint that life in the Burmese Bournemouth could at times be dullish and thus he was all the more delighted to receive overseas guests. His wife was from Moulmein, and had insisted that they live there after his retirement from London University, but at least an index-linked UK pension went quite a long way in Burma back then, so Saya lived in fine style and was something of a local celebrity receiving the obeisance of the town's great and good. On one occasion, not long after Roser and I had been married, we were sitting having dinner and the lights went out. Saya rushed to the phone and I heard him berate the manager of the local power station: 'Didn't you hear that I have VIP foreigners staying?'

Saya is no longer with us, and Moulmein, as with so many Burmese towns, has seen some change. When we returned in the early 1990s, after the SLORC putsch and a scramble to develop the country, which collapsed into sanctions and the clasp of the Chinese, the old wooden godowns and counting houses were being demolished along the Strand in favour of the most architecturally miserable apartment blocks imaginable. Yet there are still many architectural gems to be found in the residential areas.

It is best to start with the churches. My favourite is St Matthew's, which is C of E, and so quintessentially English that for a moment you might think you have been transported back to the Home Counties. Consecrated in 1890 by Bishop John Miller Strachan (my adopted ancestor!) who was the first bishop of Rangoon, it was designed by the fashionable London firm of St Aubin & Wadling, and said to be identical to the English church in Dresden. The construction was funded by a single donor, A.W. Kenny, of whom I wish we knew more. The tower was added by the Bombay Burmah Trading Corporation, in memory of their young men who lost their lives in the First World War. Nearly all the memorials that would have covered the walls were desecrated by the occupying Japanese forces in the Second World War, except for one plaque in memory of those of Moulmein who fell in the First. Burma buffs will recognise one or two old Burma names there, including two Foucar boys, their family firm of Foucar & Company a leading timber merchant. Moulmein and its colonial families go back further than anywhere else in Burma except perhaps Akyab in the Arakan. People like the Foucars stayed on and on. They may have sent their children back to be educated in England at absurdly early ages, but those kids came back, generation upon generation. E.C.V. Foucar, a Rangoon lawyer and the fourth generation of his family in Burma, was author of *I lived in Burma*, one of the best anecdotal descriptions of colonial life between the 1920s and 1940s – far more true to life, in my opinion, than Orwell's diatribes.

St Matthew's dedication stone.

St Matthew's dedication stone may be seen on the front of the church, and was laid by Sir Charles Crosthwaite, Chief Commissioner of Burma and author of *The Pacification of Burma*, a classic work on insurgency that the Americans – and the British – ought to have read before heading into Afghanistan in 2001.

The choir stalls and ceiling bosses are said to be made from English oak, and if you climb the belfry you will see the bell cast in the foundry at Madras. There was a complex clock, with four clock panels working off its single mechanism. It was explained that the one man in Moulmein who knew how it worked, and could repair it, had died – and alas, the clock died with him.

The church was used by the Japanese to store salt during the war, and the salt has caused erosion in the brickwork. One Pandaw passenger in the 1990s was kind enough to donate a considerable sum towards the church's restoration; some pointing work has been done, but there is still much to do. When I was there previously the priest had shown me a collection of Christian headstones he had rescued when SLORC appropriated the Christian cemetery for redevelopment. I did not see them on this visit, though; I wonder what happened to them?

The Roman Catholic Cathedral, with its broad nave and lack of aisles, is more French in feel, and was reroofed following war damage. The presbytery adjacent is a fine brick colonial house and typical of nearly all the colonial residences of Moulmein, with its shaded loggias running around and crisscross-leaded fenestration. I love the anchored crosses found on the doors – something I have seen on only the churches

of Burma – emphasising a strong nautical element within colonial Christianity. An elderly nun showed us the tombs of French priests set within the north transept, including that of Père Chirac of the Mission Étrangers de Paris.

Across the road is the American Baptist Church. This was the first church in Moulmein, and its first incumbent was Adoniram Judson (1788–1850) of Middlesex, Massachusetts, who had been in Burma since 1813. An indefatigable character, he travelled throughout Burma with personal bibles in English, Latin and Hebrew. Judson was the first person to translate the entire scriptures into Burmese, and his bible is

St Matthew's, Moulmein.

still used in most Burmese Christian churches, whatever their denomination. He is the King James of Burma. Judson also produced the first Burmese–English dictionary, a well-thumbed copy of which sits on my desk as I write.

In fact, his success amongst the Burmese was minimal, but amongst the animistic Karen in the jungles of Tenasserim, just upriver from Moulmein, Judson was viewed as a messianic figure. His legacy is huge: not just in Burma, where there are Judson memorial churches everywhere, but also across in America, where there are Judson colleges, universities and libraries; there is even a town called Judsonia in Arkansas. In fact, far away from the USA in torpid Moulmein it was Judson who theologically defined the American Baptist Church – some would say invented it – and his legacy lives on not just in Karen villages but in the panhandle of Texas.

Of the religious edifices around Moulmein, whether cathedral, masjid or joss house, my favourite remains the Buddhist monastery of Sein Don Mipaya, situated on the town hills just to the south of the Kyaik-tha-lun pagoda, and connected to its south stairway. Sein Don had been one of King Mindon's queens who had fled to British territory following the palace coup of Thibaw in 1859 and the subsequent cull of his rival claimants. Given a house and pension, she lived with her court in some style in a Moulmein suburban house and decided, as her act of merit, to build this most sumptuous of monasteries. Despite its appalling condition, it remains one of the finest in Burma. The queen summoned artists and craftsmen from across Burma to work, and you can see they were the crème de la crème when it came to wood carving. The bracket

The doors of the Roman Catholic cathedral, Moulmein.

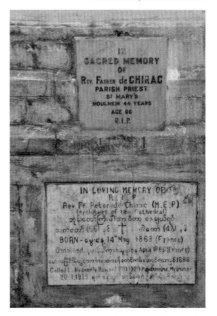

Memorials at the cathedral, Moulmein.

*Fenestration in the Roman
Catholic cathedral, Moulmein.*

*Wood carving in Sein
Don Mipaya monastery.*

figures supporting the column capitals are dynamically carved and full of vigour. The figures carved on the doors are full of wit and humour. When I first visited, in the early 1990s, the monk showed me gaps where figures had been stolen in a nocturnal break-in; at that time, when Burma was so poor, there was much thieving from religious sanctuaries, the loot going onto the international art market. Today Moulmein is a rich town once again, and you can see that wealth being showered in ambitious new shrines throughout Mon state, it is a shame some of that money does not go into restoration of the existing ones.

It is well worth pottering around the monasteries dotted along the town hills. There are several fine examples of colonial Burmese religious buildings, and do not miss the monumental bamboo image. You can see that it was not just the dour Scottish merchants who prospered during these times. These splendid monasteries, prayer halls and shrines are the work of merit of a very prosperous Buddhist community, both Mon and Burmese.

Along the Strand, despite the depredations of the SLORC military planners in the 1990s, there is still a good feel. There is a lively night bazaar where you can gorge yourself on barbecued seafood, and a couple of very good restaurants. Moulmein today is the cleanest city in modern Myanmar, and when I was last there I was amazed to see plastic-recycling stations; it would seem the Mon are far more houseproud than their neighbouring Bama. There is a good museum of Mon culture that is worth a visit, too. It is great to see the Mon going around in their traditional costumes with very jolly-coloured checked taipon jackets.

Sein Don Mipaya monastery, Moulmein.

Over a river bridge to the west of Moulmein is Bilu Kyun, Devil Island. Guide books will tell you of artisanal villages: there is one that specialises in making slate tablets for schools and another for smokers' pipes. We visited the pipe village and bought quite a nice pipe for Roser's brother. The shopkeeper explained that

Loggia of Sein Don Mipaya monastery.

although the trade for pipes had been good, nowadays few people smoke, so the wood carvers have branched out into other heavily carved products, more suited to the local market.

An essential excursion out of Moulmein is to Than-byu-zayat, about one hour south of Moulmein. Situated close to it is the Death Railway built by the Japanese in the Second World War, where they brutally expended prisoner of war labour, not to mention local slave labour. Here the Commonwealth War Graves Commission maintains the war cemetery as immaculately as if it were in the English counties. A visit is deeply moving and it would be a hard-hearted person not to feel the tug of tears coming on. Look at the ages of the fallen: many the same as my own son, in his early twenties. Alongside British servicemen are laid to rest young Australians, Dutchmen, Gurkhas and Indians. The Muslims' graves point to Mecca and Christians' to the East. Their sacrifice was huge and their name really does live forever more.

We went down to Amherst Point, now called Kyaik-ka-me, partly in the hope of finding some good beaches and partly to look at possible mooring positions and road access points for the *Andaman Explorer* when she was to call here as part of her one-time Burma Coastal Voyage. Unfortunately there were no nice beaches (they are further south), and the pagoda complex on the point was tacky and of little interest. Along the way, you will see endless rubber plantations, and judging by the number of trucks we saw bearing mats of raw rubber, the industry must be booming. More fun is a stop at the Wan-sein-toya complex on the road back from Than-byu-zayat. Here you will find the largest reclining Buddha in the world that the fit can climb up, through a system of internal staircases. This was the work of the late Wan-sein-toya Sayadaw, whose tomb you can visit close to the car park. He is enshrined within a very symbolic gilded sampan.

Memorial at the Than-byu-zayat war graves.

Moulmein is visibly prosperous today, just as it was 200 years ago; although the estuarial port is too shallow for modern shipping, the town's connections now go the other way, the Pan-Asian Highway connecting it to Thailand and beyond. Although it was of political significance for only 27 years its legacy remains strong, whether from its literary connections or its architectural remnants. It is now the heart of a resurgent Mon regionalism, where after 50 years of Myanmar suppression the Mons can emerge again, proud of their identity, language and culture. The Mons were the first of the South-East Asian peoples to be enriched by Buddhism, producing emotive sculpture and an enduring interpretation of Buddhist texts. It was thanks to the Mon-Khmer that we have the temples of Angkor Wat; and in 11th century Pagan the captions on the mural paintings are in Mon, not Burmese. It was through the Mon that Buddhist literature, art and iconography disseminated throughout the region. The town at the confluence of the three rivers may not be very ancient, and it may not have been important for very long, but it represents today a long, rich and deep culture.

Coffin of the Wan-sein-toya abbott.

Reclining Buddha at Wan-sein-toya.

Bibliography

Andrus, J.R. *Burmese Economic Life*. Stanford, 1947.

Bird, George W. *Wanderings in Burma*. London 1897.

Burn Murdoch, W.G. *From Edinburgh to India and Burmah*. London, 1908.

Cady, J.F. *A History of Modern Burma*. Ithaca, 1960.

Chubb, H.J. and C.L.D. Duckworth. *Irrawaddy Flotilla Company Limited 1865–1950*. London, 1953.

Collis, Maurice. *Trials in Burma*. London, 1937.

The Grand Peregrination: The Life and Times of Fernão Mendes Pinto. London, 1949.

The Journey Outward: An Autobiography. London, 1952.

Into hidden Burma. London, 1953.

Crosthwaite, Sir Charles. *The Pacification of Burma*. London, 1912.

Curle, Richard. *Into the East: Notes on Burma and Malaya*. London, 1923.

Dalrymple, Alexander. *Oriental Repertory*. London, 1791–97.

Enriquez, Major C.M. *A Burmese Arcady*. London, 1923.

Fisher, A. Hugh. *Through India and Burmah with Pen and Brush*. London, 1911.

Foucar, E.C.V. *I lived in Burma*. London, 1956.

Furnivall, J.S. *An Introduction to the Political Economy of Burma*. Rangoon, 1931.

Harris, Walter B. *East for Pleasure*. London, 1929.

Harvey, G.E. *History of Burma from the Earliest Times to 10th March 1824 and the Beginning of the English Conquest*. London, 1925.

Hunt, Gordon. *Forgotten Burma*. London, 1967.

Johnston, R.F. *From Peking to Mandalay*. New York, 1908.

Laird, Dorothy. *The Story of Paddy Henderson and Company*. London 1961.

Langham-Carter, R.R. *Old Moulmein*. Moulmein, 1947.

Larkin, Emma. *Finding George Orwell in Burma*. New York, 2005.

Lewis, Norman. *Golden Earth: Travels in Burma*. London, 1951

McLynn, Frank. *The Burma Campaign: Disaster into Triumph 1942–45*. London 2011.

McCrae, Alister. *Scots in Burma: Golden Times in the Golden Land*. Gartmore 1990.

Tales of Burma. Paisley 1981

McCrae, Alister, and Alan Prentice. *Irrawaddy Flotilla*. Paisley, 1978.

Orwell, George. *Burmese Days*. New York, 1934

The Shooting of an Elephant. New Writing, 1936.

Pollok, Colonel, and W.S. Thom. *Wild Sports of Burma and Assam.* London, 1900.

Powell-Brown, Mrs E.M. *A Year on the Irrawaddy.* Rangoon, 1911.

Raven-Hart, R. *Canoe to Mandalay.* London, 1939.

Scott O'Connor, V.C. *The Silken East: A Record of Life and Travel in Burma.* London, 1904.

Shalimar (F.C. Hendry). *Down to the Sea.* London, 1937.

Singer, Noel F. *Burmah: A Photographic Journey, 1855–1925.* Gartmore, 1993.

Old Rangoon: City of the Shwedagon. Gartmore, 1995.

Slim, William. *Defeat into Victory: Battling Japan in Burma and India, 1942–1945.* London, 1956.

Stewart, A.T.Q. *The Pagoda War: Lord Dufferin and the fall of the Kingdom of Ava 1885–6.* London 1972.

Strachan, Paul. *Mandalay: Travels from the Golden City.* Gartmore, 1994

Pagan: Art and Architecture of Old Burma. Arran, 1989.

Talboys Wheeler, J. *Journey of a Voyage up the Irrawaddy.* Rangoon, 1871.

Williams, Clement. *Through Burmah to Western China.* London, 1863.

Williams, J.H. *Elephant Bill.* London, 1950.

Yule, Sir Henry. *A Narrative of the Mission to the Court of Ava in 1855.* London, 1858